Signs from the Ancestors

"Dedicated Early Artist," drawn in charcoal pencil by Alex Seowtewa, Zuni artist and muralist. Artist's caption: "Ancient native artists had the patience to express the 'SYMBOLS' of the universe, nature, and humans in their rock art. We of the present Indian generation appreciate their art where it still exists."

SIGNS
FROM THE
ANCESTORS

ZUNI CULTURAL SYMBOLISM AND
PERCEPTIONS OF ROCK ART

M. JANE YOUNG

Publications of the American Folklore Society
New Series
General Editor, Larry Danielson

University of New Mexico Press
Albuquerque

Illustration Credits

Contemporary photographs taken by Nancy L. Bartman, Robert H. Leibman, and M. Jane Young. Fieldwork conducted and photographs taken with permission of Zuni Tribal Council.

Historic photographs used with permission of National Anthropological Archives, Smithsonian Institution, Museum of New Mexico, and School of American Research, as designated in figure captions.

Drawings by Murray Callahan, Snowden Hodges, and Alex Seowtewa.

Library of Congress Cataloging-in-Publication Data

Young, M. Jane, 1950–
  Signs from the ancestors.

  (Publications of the American Folklore Society)
  Bibliography: p.
  Includes index.
  1. Zuñi Indians—Art. 2. Zuñi Indians—Religion and mythology.
3. Rock paintings—New Mexico. 4. Petroglyphs—New Mexico.
5. Indians of North America—New Mexico—Art. 6. Indians of
North America—New Mexico—Religion and mythology.
I. Title. II. Series
E99.Z9Y68   1988   709'.01'1309789   87-30242
ISBN 0-8263-1039-7

To the Zuni people

Elahkwa, A:shiwi

Contents

Foreword

Dell Hymes
University of Virginia

This book is about meaning, but it could be written because the people of Zuni and the author share a concern for preservation. Let me stress that by way of beginning.

Symbols inscribed on rock have fascinated many and become the object of speculation and collection to some. Too often such symbols have been treated as if they were flowers by the wayside, available to anyone who came upon them or went to where they were. I have been horrified to see on public television a program designed to teach viewers how to take rubbings and where to go to get them. That was in the Pacific Northwest, but even the basalt of the Columbia River basin is not immune to abrasion, and in the territory of the Zuni, as Jane Young points out in this valuable book, the sandstone on which rock art is created is vulnerable indeed. And it is clear that the rock art in the Zuni region is not a lost world to be appropriated by curious outsiders. It is an integral part of a continuing way of life.

By showing this to a general audience, *Signs from the Ancestors* may not only assist the people of Zuni in discouraging vandalism, while documenting and preserving what they have, but assist all of us. The rock art of the country as a whole should be regarded as "signs from all our ancestors," inscribed by those who went before us in this place. If we, like the Zuni, cannot be certain of precise meanings for ancient designs, we yet can preserve and respect and ponder them, and make them part of an understanding of what it means to be where we are.

Some Indian people, indeed, not having the continuity in place and descent of the Zuni, look to whatever has been Indian as a concern and responsibility, and a potential source of meaning in the present. For other places where rock art is present (or indeed, can be created), the Zuni may prove an invaluable example of what such meaningfulness may have been and can be. A known example does not dictate the interpretation of other cases, but it makes speculation responsible, discouraging some conjectures and suggesting others.

Much of what other rock art is taken to mean may be novel, to be sure, but interpretation at Zuni is not static. Indeed, this book shows that it would be misleading to call Zuni tradition "conservative." Where the world is centered, meaningful and whole, expressions of sacramental relationship to it, songs and visual symbols, can joyfully enact a maxim of modern poetry, *Make it new.*

Certainly there is much more to be learned and written about rock art at Zunis, and some of it, one trusts, will be written by Zuni themselves. Those who use the land, traversing different canyons and grazing areas, have varied knowledge of where such art exists. Those of different age, gender, craft, and ritual involvement sometimes assign diverse meanings. The sum of collective Zuni knowledge probably has not yet been assembled, and, given continued vitality of the art, probably never can be. Such art continues to be made. Photographs of it become part of homes and a source of design in other media. New information about astronomy and space is brought to bear upon it. Past ethnology and current archaeology are taken into account, as in the striking remarks made by one Zuni to Von Del Chamberlain (see chapter 4). Much of this book, indeed, shows Zuni to be a model of thoughtful integration of tradition and change.

Young herself integrates what is known and what is new, drawing on other information about Zuni history and culture to provide a context for the rock art itself. In doing so she makes a contribution to the ethnography of communication, understood as a concern with the ways in which diverse modes of communication and expression are employed and related in a community. Rock art, pottery, masking, dance, song, the other genres of verbal art, have each their niche no doubt— some specificity to contribute to the resonant accumulation of meaning portrayed here. Modes may differ in their degree of what Uriel Weinreich called *terminologization*, the elaboration of vocabulary for them, whether from communicative need or aesthetic involution. The focus, nonetheless, is on commonality of pattern.

Young makes a contribution in this regard that she modestly does not call to attention. Her transcriptions of a number of interviews and comments show that Zuni use of pattern numbers extends to discourse in English. In Chapter 4, for example, the account of one man's "breakthrough into performance," stimulated by Von Del Chamberlain's mention of story (see n. 25), shows the whole impromptu statement to be organized in terms of the pattern number four, and, in part, three. Young does not label the parts, but indentations visually identify them. Of such parts, each beginning flush left, there are seventeen. The first four and the last four stress that Zuni legend is based on fact. These two sets of four enclose two sets dealing with what the anthropologist Frank Cushing found. One deals with his first stay, one with his coming back later on. These middle sets employ three-part patterning. The account of the first stay has three pairs of units, the account of the return has just three units.

If letters are used to label the parts visually identified by Young, and lower case roman numerals the major sections, then the discourse has this profile:

i	a	b	c	d
ii	ef	gh	ij	
iii	k	l	m	
iv	n	o	p	q

Verbal repetitions go together with these relationships, as do initial words and phrases frequently used in English to mark parts of discourse.

In **[i]**, (a, b) share "based on fact(s)," and (b) begins with "So." (c,d) share "a lot of," and the two together constitute a verbal exchange.

In **[ii]**, (e) begins with the introduction of an actor in the account (Cushing), and (f) with "and" and a time expression ("And for five years"). (g, h) are linked by the same initial time expression ("And in time"). (i) begins with "But because" and ends with "everything" (cf. the ending of (f) and the discourse as a whole in (q). Verbal exchange (j) ends with the emphasis of *"landmarks"* (cf. (l, m)). (The two last lines of (i) end with something of a parallelism, analogous to the explicit parallelism of the two last lines of (c)).

In **[iii]**, (k) begins with a return and time expression ("he came back later on"), and (l, m) each reiterate "landmarks," and each end with a parallel expression ("where the Zunis said they were," "bearing out the traditions of the Zunis").

In **[iv]**, (n, o) begin with the analogous "And so this," "And a lot of this." (n) ends reiterating the opening theme, "based on facts," while (o) introduces "the archaeologists." (p) begins with "So" and repeats "the archaeologists," while (q) ends with an emphatic "everything."

The last two verses of **[i]**, and the last two verses of **[ii]**, consist of six and three lines, respectively. The central scenes concerned with Cushing **[ii, iii]** consist of six and three verses. The recurrence of such grouping on both levels (lines, verses) indicates that it is part of the rhetorical patterning available to the speaker, along with grouping into fours.

The interweaving of two principles of rhetorical patterning has been found in other American Indian traditions. So far as is known at present, one principle is the general, or unmarked, usual one. A second is employed for emphasis, heightening. Where three and five constitute the usual pattern, as with the Chinookans, Sahaptins, Salish and Kalapuya of the Columbia River and Willamette Valley in the present states of Washington and Oregon, pairing is marked. Where two and four constitute the usual pattern, as among the Tonkawa of Texas, three and six are marked. Perhaps further study of Zuni use of such principles will show a similar relationship. If so, then the two central sections of the discourse above are highlighted with patterning involving three, embedded in opening and closing sections based, so far as groups of verses are concerned, on four, but employing three (including three groups of two) as well for grouping of lines (c, d; q).

All this fits what Young points out about the presence of six- as well as four-part relationships in discourse in the Zuni language and in the culture otherwise. It shows that Zuni discourse in English may make use of English vocabulary and syntax in rhetorical, or ethnopoetic, patterns that are themselves Zuni. Even English itself may be integrated into the continuities of Zuni life.

We can hope that this volume will fulfill the desire of both its author and the people of Zuni that it contribute to the appreciation and preservation of rock art, and that it will take a valued place among other cooperative contributions which demonstrate respect for and understanding of Zuni culture.

Preface

My initial interest in Zuni focused on Zuni linguistics and early Pueblo Indian astronomical practices. During the summer of 1977 I served as a team member of a project sponsored by the National Geographic Society to investigate the astronomical alignments of prehistoric tower structures in the Southwest and to photograph any rock art associated with the tower structures. That experience led to my interest in analyzing the structure and poetic pattern of Zuni linguistic material recorded by Ruth Bunzel in the 1930s. I was able to show that not only were the poems structured by the repetition of initial particles, words, and phrases, but sometimes entire sections were set off by the repetition of words describing astronomical phenomena (such as the apparent movement of the sun along the horizon).

Because of my previous experience recording rock art in the Four Corners area of the Southwest, the Zuni Tribal Council and Zuni Archaeology Program invited me to do fieldwork at Zuni. The Zunis regard pictographs and petroglyphs as an important part of their Zuni cultural heritage, and tribal members and archaeologists wanted it to be documented. They hoped that documenting and displaying the richness of their heritage of rock art would decrease vandalism.

I spent the summers of 1979, 1980, and 1981 directing the Zuni Rock Art Survey team in photographically recording the tribe's rock carvings and paintings. This survey, however, is far from being complete. Most of the sites I did record had been located previously by the Zuni Archaeology Program members during their survey work; they have discovered others since then. I obtained permission from the Tribal Council before recording any site, and, in a few cases, was told not to record sites that had some relationship with Zuni religious practice. During the summer of 1981 I also conducted the research that forms the core of this book: formal and informal discussions with Zunis about rock art, and a card-sorting experiment with which I attempted to elicit contemporary perceptions of the rock art. The men and women with whom I talked (including recognized religious leaders, painters, fetish makers, and potters) ranged in age from sixteen to eighty. They had diverse occupations and varied involvement in, and knowledge of, Zuni religious life. I included women in this study even though rock art production appears to be a predominantly male activity. I did so because women are the principal producers of pottery and, to a lesser extent, of fetishes, both of which use images similar to some of those appearing in the rock art. I conducted all such conversations in English, but occasionally Zunis used words or phrases in the Zuni language for those things that were "hard to say in English."

The card-sorting "experiment," devised in collaboration with John M. Roberts of the University of Pittsburgh, required Zuni colleagues to sort a stack of sixty four-by-six-inch cards, each bearing one rock art image or cluster of images hand-copied from a color slide, into two or more groups such that the images in each group seemed to "go together." I asked each Zuni to perform this task twice, with two different stacks. One stack consisted of images chosen randomly from a collection of what I believed to be representations of humans, and the other consisted of animal and bird images. These are the two largest categories of image types in the rock art of this area. When they finished sorting, I asked Zunis to identify the individual images and discuss why they had put particular images together. These identifications and categories are discussed at the end of Chapter 2. They form part of the data base for Chapters 3 through 6, in which I include rock art depictions in the more general framework of Zuni cosmology and cultural symbolism.

Throughout my fieldwork I found that Zunis, on the whole, felt they had very little to say about the pictographs and petroglyphs. They suggested that it was something the "old people" would know most about. Even those acknowledged experts did not have many direct comments to make about the rock art. Some suggested that I talk to the Hopis, because they are thought to know more about "those designs on the rock." Asking Zunis to sort through drawings and photographs was particularly useful, for it provided a context for "talk about rock art," during which certain images evoked stories and descriptions of ceremonies and events. Generally, with the permission of my Zuni colleagues, I tape-recorded the conversations that occurred as they looked at drawings, photographs, and sometimes, slides projected on a living-room wall. I also was able to visit rock art sites with a number of tribal members. This was particularly fruitful because during such visits Zunis included the entire environmental setting of the rock art in discussions of meaning rather than focusing on the image alone. They not only placed individual images in the context of the whole corpus of rock art figures at that site, but also included other features of the landscape, such as springs, plants, birds, and so on. Rock carvings and paintings are, after all, integral parts of the landscape surrounding the pueblo, and like other features of that landscape, Zunis frequently associated them with events from myth and legend that transpired there.

The Zunis with whom I worked knew that this data would be used initially in my dissertation and later in various academic articles, and perhaps a book. Since it was extremely difficult to approach complete strangers, particularly with a request so unusual as that of sorting through rock art images, ultimately most of those who took the time and had the patience to complete this task were friends and acquaintances made during my previous fieldwork at Zuni. Although most people enjoyed looking at and talking about the figures, it was time-consuming, and most Zunis are busy in the summer because of farming and religious activities. I am, therefore, particularly grateful to the Zunis who so kindly and patiently gave me their time.

I have omitted the names of my Zuni colleagues or, on occasion, given them pseudonyms, largely because opinions within the community towards giving aid to outsiders vary considerably, and no one wants to be known as "the person who said the wrong thing about Zuni." Since my project did not involve documentation of shrine areas, and Zunis generally did not regard rock art as a subject that should not be talked about, I have no reason to suspect that people "told me things they shouldn't." Nevertheless, I have heard strong criticism of those who have offered information to other "Anglos" and, for this reason, wish to maintain the anonymity and privacy of those with whom I talked. In the few cases in which I have used photographs of Zunis in this book, I obtained permission to do so from the individuals involved.

Although I use the words "Zuni colleagues" throughout this book, vastly preferring them to the terms "informants" or "respondents," it would, perhaps, be more accurate to refer to these people as my "Zuni teachers"; certainly they contributed a great deal to my education, not only about Zuni but about life in general. I did not pay for people's time with money, but rather with reciprocal actions when possible, such as driving people to Gallup to buy groceries, giving them photographs, helping with family and tribal activities, and, more recently, exchanging lessons in mathematics for lessons in the Zuni language.

At first my project was regarded with some puzzlement by many Zunis who did not understand why I was so interested in rock art. I was a stranger then. Later my assistant and I were referred to as "those people who help so much with the Tribal Fair every year." We had demonstrated that we were willing to help out, and by then had become more accepted in the community, forming friendships with several families whom we continue to visit as often as possible.

The drawings included in this book have all been made by tracing images from projected slides. For the most part the illustrated motifs have been taken out of context and grouped together as examples of individual design elements. Technique, size (height × width), and site references are listed in the captions. Identifications of images, particularly names of individual kachinas and masks, are generally those provided by Zuni colleagues during my fieldwork.

The orthography I have used is one that was suggested to me by several Zunis with whom I worked closely when I was writing a popular pamphlet on rock art for the Pueblo of Zuni. I cannot say, however, that it is the official orthography of the pueblo. There are differences of opinion about such matters and I can only say that some Zunis who have had experience reading and writing the Zuni language (many Zunis have not, because theirs is a predominantly oral language), suggested that I write the Zuni words in this manner. The following chart shows the way in which the orthography I have used, labelled "Zuni style," differs from Ruth Bunzel's transcriptions as well as the technical and practical orthographies used by Stanley Newman in his *Zuni Grammar:*

Bunzel	Newman (technical)	Newman (practical)	Zuni style
tc	č	ch	ch
h	h	j	h
ł	ł	lh	ł or lh
kw	kʷ	q	kw
c	š	sh	sh
ts	c	z	ts
'	ʔ (glottal stop)	/	'
(V)ˑ	(V)ˑ (long vowel)	(V):	(V):
t	t	t	d
p	p	p	b

I have made an attempt to present Zuni commentary, where possible, in an ethnopoetic style, breaking phrases into lines on the basis of breath pauses. Although I would not describe such commentary as poetic in every respect, it is clear that there is patterning in the everyday speech of Zunis even when they speak in English—a second language for most Zunis. Shorter Zuni sentences, phrases, and words, such as those used in this preface, are set off by quotation marks.

The term "Zuni" is used to refer to the people, the place, and the language. As is clear from my bibliography, early anthropologists at Zuni wrote the word as "Zuñi," but that pronunciation and spelling are no longer used by the tribe; today simply "Zuni" is used. The Zunis generally refer to themselves as *A:shiwi*, which translates into English as "the people." Although the term "Anglo" is not a technically accurate means by which to refer to all Euro-Americans, it is the term used by Zunis to refer to non-Indians, and I have adopted that usage.

Acknowledgments

I am most grateful to the Zuni people for the opportunity to live and work with them for three summers and to return for shorter visits since then. I shall never forget the beauty of that landscape or the hospitality, warmth, and humor of the people who live there; I hope to return often in the years to come. I am particularly grateful to friends who patiently sorted cards with rock art images on them, discussing the meaning of various figures. I am sure it seemed a rather strange way to spend time, but they recognized its importance to me. Special thanks go to Pesancio Lasiloo, Governor Robert E. Lewis, the late Andrew Naptecha, the family of Gus and Lori Panteah, Alex Seowtewa, Roger Tsabetsaye, Frank Vacit, and the family of Margaret Sheyka, particularly Arlen and Virina and their children. I am also grateful to Vance Cheama and Carlton Jamon, who were members of the Zuni Rock Art Survey team during the summer of 1979.

Many tribal agencies were involved directly or indirectly

with my work. I thank, in particular, the members of the Zuni Tribal Council, the Tribal Accounting Department, the Zuni Rangers, the Zuni Archaeology Program, the Zuni Museum Committee, and the Tribal Fair Committee.

Ray Williamson and Polly Schaafsma have given me constant advice and friendship. They both served as advisors for my earliest work at Zuni and joined me for brief periods during my fieldwork there. Both taught me to love the Southwest and sparked my interest in Native American cultures.

Nancy L. Bartman shared the first summer of fieldwork at Zuni with me and, even afterwards, continued to be a source of encouragement. She drew my attention to many books and articles that have helped me to formulate ideas expressed in this book. Michele Albert worked with me for several months in the summer of 1980 and was of great assistance in producing the traveling exhibit of Zuni rock art.

Von Del Chamberlain kindly gave me copies of his tape recorded interviews that were conducted at the Pueblo of Zuni in the summer of 1978. Both William Beeson and Ted Frisbie sent me copies of slides of rock art that they had taken in the Zuni-Cibola region, thereby strengthening my data base. I am particularly grateful that these scholars were so willing to share information that they knew would be of help to me. Ted has continued to read and comment on almost everything I have written that relates to Zuni; his energy and sensitivity provide a most welcome model. I also thank Charles Hoffman for taking the time to guide me to a number of rock art sites in the area of Lyman Lake, Arizona. Elaine and Roger Thomas gave me friendship and guidance, listening patiently to my ideas and sharing their own knowledge acquired from years of living at Zuni Pueblo.

Margaret Hardin offered advice during fieldwork at Zuni and recommended important avenues of inquiry. T. J. Ferguson and Barbara J. Mills, both of the Zuni Archaeology Program at the time, facilitated my fieldwork in many ways, offering me invaluable suggestions, the use of office space and equipment, and access to the Program's library and archaeological records. They encouraged the rock art recording project from the beginning and helped make my introduction to the Pueblo of Zuni a pleasant one.

John M. Roberts of the University of Pittsburgh suggested the initial card-sorting experiment that I used to elicit Zuni commentary on rock art. His articles and personal communications have helped me a great deal in understanding a wide range of expressive behavior.

I am grateful to Murray Callahan for her superb artwork. Although she has never been to Zuni, she has caught the spirit of the rock art and in many cases her drawings do more to show the detail of the imagery than do my photographs. My thanks also go to Alex Seowtewa and Snowden Hodges for permission to use their wonderful drawings.

I wish to thank the Smithsonian Institution for granting me a Visiting Student Research Assistantship for the summer of 1978. With the kind assistance of the archivist, James Glenn, and Elaine Mills, along with the rest of the National Anthropological Archives staff, I was able to research unpublished materials on Zuni, especially those of J. P. Harrington, that have been of importance to this book. Ives Goddard, who supervised my work during that summer, was extremely helpful. I am also grateful to the National Anthropological Archives of the Smithsonian for permission to use some of the photographs from their collections as illustrations in this book.

Ruth M. Christensen, librarian of the Southwest Museum in Los Angeles, facilitated my work with the Zuni materials there in the summer of 1981. The staff of the Anthropology Laboratory of the Museum of New Mexico have been a steady source of help, both during my fieldwork and in my research since that time. I wish especially to acknowledge the help of Marsha Jackson, Marina Ochoa, Stewart Packham, and Curtis Schaafsma. I thank the Museum of New Mexico and School of American Research for permission to photograph selected Zuni pots in their collections and to include some of those photographs in this book.

The rock art recording project, as well as the subsequent production of a traveling exhibit with brochure and a 48-page booklet on rock art written by M. Jane Young and Nancy L. Bartman, was funded in part, under the sponsorship of the Pueblo of Zuni, by grants from the Youthgrants in the Humanities (1979), the Special Programs Division of the National Endowment for the Humanities (1980), and the New Mexico Humanities Council, an affiliate of the National Endowment for the Humanities (1980). I wish to acknowledge the American Association of University Women Vassie James Hill Endowed Fellowship that made fieldwork at Zuni in 1981 possible, as well as providing me with time for research and writing. Further time for writing and funds for photographs were provided by the University Research Institute of the University of Texas, Austin; their Summer Research Award in 1983 made possible the initial draft of Chapters 4 and 5, while their Special Research Award in 1986 paid for some of the artwork included in this book. The findings and conclusions presented here do not necessarily reflect the views of the New Mexico Humanities Council, the National Endowment for the Humanities, the American Association of University Women, or the University Research Institute of the University of Texas, Austin.

Certain parts of this book are based on an article published in the *Journal of American Folklore* in 1985. I am grateful to the American Anthropological Association for permission to present a revised version of that material here. Some of this book is also based on my dissertation, but has been greatly changed since the completion of that preliminary work.

I acknowledge, with thanks, the authors of books and articles that helped me formulate various ideas about Zuni cultural symbolism that are central to this book. These authors include the late Robert Plant Armstrong, Keith H. Basso, Ruth L. Bunzel, Claire Farrer, Dell Hymes, Sally McLendon, Nancy Munn, Polly Schaafsma, Robert J. Smith, Barbara Tedlock, Dennis Tedlock, and the late Victor Turner.

During various stages in the writing of this book I solicited critical comments from colleagues whose help ranged from discussing ideas with me to reading selected chapters or taking the time to read an entire draft of the book. My thanks in this regard go to Richard Bauman, Marilyn Englander, Deborah Fant, Claire Farrer, T. J. Ferguson, James Neely, Polly Schaafsma, Suzanne Seriff, Kay Turner, and Ray Williamson. In addition, discussions with Richard Bauman, Ken Foote, Henry Glassie, Rayna Green, Dell Hymes, Virginia Hymes, and Robert Mugerauer have helped to shape many of the ideas that are central to this book. I am especially indebted to my good friend Leslie Prosterman, who took time out of a busy schedule to read all of the many versions of my manuscript and listened thoughtfully to my ideas via long-distance telephone. She offered many useful suggestions, encouraged me to have faith in my own abilities, and made me laugh when I began to take myself too seriously.

Marta Weigle considerately encouraged me to submit my manuscript first to the University of New Mexico Press, and later, to the Publications of the American Folklore Society editor, Larry Danielson. Larry responded with enthusiasm, read the manuscript carefully, and kindly included it in the PAFS Series.

Beth Hadas, Director of the University of New Mexico Press, has made the entire process, from manuscript submission to final production, go as smoothly as possible. Editor Claire Sanderson has been an accessible and calming influence to an author nervous about her first book. Claire's skills have added greatly to the quality of this book. I also thank Sarah Nestor for her careful copy editing touch.

I am grateful to my mother for her constant encouragement throughout my graduate and later academic career and to my father for teaching me the love of the land that is an important part of his life. I believe he has much in common with the Zuni farmers and would enjoy spending time at Zuni if the circumstances so permit.

My very special thanks go to Robert H. Leibman, who not only shared two summers of my fieldwork at Zuni but also listened patiently to my ideas for various publications based on that research, offering abundant advice. His warm personality at Zuni helped us form lasting friendships, and his caring and support made it possible for me to write this book.

Signs from the Ancestors

Introduction

June 1980

We leave the pueblo just after dawn: this morning's team is composed of my husband (Bob), myself, and Fred, an elderly Zuni religious leader who is very interested in Zuni rock art and befriended us two years ago during our research at Zuni Pueblo. Fred has finished his morning prayer to the Sun Father and is ready for the day's activity. He is taking us to Hanlhi-binkya, an important shrine area west of the pueblo that is also an extensive rock art site. Everywhere people are stirring, beginning the day. Already women wearing traditional Zuni shawls light fires in the beehive-like outdoor baking ovens. We pass the stone and adobe houses of the old village, then the trailers and more modern subdivision homes; we go by one of the village laundromats and are soon driving through Zuni rangelands populated with cattle. The area is dotted with piñon and juniper trees, sagebrush, and, in the eyes of one who grew up in the lush farming area of western Pennsylvania, rather scant grass. To the north, the silhouettes of the Twin Buttes break the flat valley. These mesas, distinctly banded with red and white sandstone, are the sites of abundant rock art; looking at them now reminds us of days spent in the hot sun recording pictographs and petroglyphs and looking for further rock art sites. To the south are the farming villages and fields where many Zunis cultivate vegetable gardens. As we drive west we pass men dressed in white with brightly colored scarves knotted about their heads. They have been planting prayer sticks and performing other religious observances at various shrine areas in the lands surrounding the pueblo and are walking back—some to have breakfast and begin their jobs, others to spend the day in seclusion, fasting and praying.

Although usually loaded down with equipment for recording rock art—cameras, tripods, meter sticks, clip boards, recording forms, compasses—for this trip we have left all but the water canteens behind. We have permission from the Tribal Council to return later and systematically record the site. Today is a chance to see this place through the eyes of the kind man who has helped us in our fieldwork for over two years.

As we drive along we drink coffee from a thermos and talk about other days like this one: early starts so that we can photograph rock art before midday when the gnats become fierce and also so that the oblique rays of the morning sun will bring out the contrasts of the images carved in rock; early starts, too, so that Fred can get to his tribal job before the morning is over. We're in no hurry today, though, because he has the day off. Fred mentions that he hopes to find a rock art representation of the creation of the second pair of Twin War Gods, an event that, according to Zuni mythology, occurred at the site to which we are heading. He adds that other Zunis have told him it is at this place and he is sure he'll know it if he sees it. He doesn't say what the image will look like and, not wishing to pry into religious matters, we don't ask.

Finally we leave the reservation lands behind and exchange the paved road for a gravel and then a dirt track. Our little Honda Civic spins its tires in a muddy spot and I remark for what seems the hundredth time since we began our research that we really should rent a jeep the next time we come to Zuni.

The canyon that contains the rock art comes into view. We park the car in the rather skimpy shade of a juniper tree and start the climb down. Bob and I are wearing heavy hiking boots, jeans, long-sleeved shirts to avoid sunburn, and sunglasses. Bob carries the snakebite kit, which we try never to leave behind, and we each have a canteen (there is a large plastic container of water in the car just in case we get stranded somewhere). Fred wears a pair of battered but serviceable cowboy boots, jeans, a long-sleeved shirt, and a faded cowboy hat. He has spent much of his life as a rancher and often hikes in the land about the pueblo. His movements are agile and assured as he climbs down into the canyon; he chooses to follow a trail marked by a pile of rocks on the canyon rim. We follow him somewhat gingerly, slipping occasionally.

We reach the bottom and stop to look around. Directly in front of us is a rock face covered with hundreds of petroglyphs, many of them carved on top of older, barely visible images. There are animal figures, animal and bird tracks, and geometric designs; their beige color contrasts sharply with the dark reddish brown of the rock surface. We look at the images in silence for a long time. Fred walks up to the rock face for a closer look and gently traces the outlines of some of the figures with his fingertips. He says that "People say this is where the Zuni clans originated. Some of these look like clan symbols."

Fred turns from the rock carvings and walks to a nearby pool of water that has been formed by the recent heavy rain. He prays and scatters sacred cornmeal over the water. He fills a small metal container with water to take back and sprinkle on his cornfield. Nearby are some plants with small white flowers; Fred bends down and scrutinizes them closely. He tells me that they are used by the medicine societies in healing rituals.

Beyond the pool of water a cavelike area opens into a part of the canyon that has no access except through the cave. On the roof of the cave, where sunlight penetrates only dimly and it is almost too dark to see, we notice a number of carved images: mountain sheep, deer tracks, a spiral, a fluteplayer, and a series of humanlike stick figures holding hands as if dancing. In the area beyond the cave a series of very abstract masks or faces catches our eye; perhaps they are quite old, because they are fainter than the other petroglyphs here. We count seventeen of them in this very circumscribed area; they seem to constitute a dominant but place-specific motif since we find no more of them during the rest of the day. This enclosed part of the canyon is striking because the wind has worn deep pockets into the rock. Some of these pockets are large enough to hold a person, and most of the rock art in this area is located on the smooth walls of these curved depressions.

The canyon is covered with rock art—thousands of images, some of them so high on the canyon walls that we can't reach them. Animal figures are abundant, as are animal tracks, human hand- and footprints, sandal tracks, human stick figures, humpbacked fluteplayers, intricate geometrical designs (especially concentric circles and spirals), insect figures, and snake figures. Varicolored lichen has grown in the indentations of some of the more deeply pecked figures so that they appear to be brightly painted in greens, golds, reds, and oranges. We spend the morning going from rock art panel to rock art panel, looking and talking, sometimes laughing; at other times we are silent. Although he is quite serious at times, Fred delights in teasing us about interpretations for some of the images: "That one looks like a table lamp," he says. "This one is an upside-down man." But he is serious about the clan symbols and others that he describes as "clouds, rain, and lightning." Although there are many images that he doesn't even try to interpret, he is obviously interested in all of them.

Once Fred points out a bird nest high overhead on a ledge of rock projecting from the top of the canyon. He says it is a hawk nest and that there are probably baby birds there at this time of year. He is happy to see the nest and says they are good birds to have around. As we walk through the canyon, Fred notices and often comments on everything there—not just the rock art depictions, but pools of water, vegetation, insects, birds, an occasional animal track—he seems to be drinking it all in. This is a special place and everything in it is significant.

We find a shady spot for lunch at noon. Then we walk to the end of the canyon, looking at the rest of the rock art as we go. Here we find petroglyphs that are different in content and technique from everything else we've seen today and during our total fieldwork at Zuni, for that matter. These images have a whimsical quality, evident in the mountain sheep playing a flute, the humanlike figure that has wavy, elongated arms and legs, and the turtle that sports an elaborate headdress. There is a somewhat comical rendition of a duck; human figures seem to be in motion, elaborate geometric designs are everywhere. All of the figures are deeply and solidly pecked on heavily patinated rock surfaces. These images seem to belong to a different cultural tradition than the others in the canyon and make us wonder about the playfulness and imagination that motivated the artist or artists. We come to the last rock art figure and decide to try to climb out here at the end rather than return to the trail we used to climb down. No trail out is marked, however, and we spend over an hour climbing over boulders, trying to find a way up the steep walls. Fred never loses his sense of humor and we all laugh when what looks like an easy climb turns nearly impassable at the next bend. Finally we reach the top.

Before we go to the car, Fred stands for a moment looking over the canyon and its multitude of petroglyphs, easily visible even from this height. Though he never found the particular image that he had been looking for, he is not greatly perturbed. He plans to come back and look again sometime—perhaps when the weather is cooler. We all agree that many of the earlier images (especially those that had been carved low on rock faces close to the ground) have been obscured by the silt that has collected at the bottom of the canyon, so maybe he never will find it. After a few minutes of silence, Fred says: "This is our history." And then, responding to questions I had asked throughout the day about the meaning of the imagery, he adds: "I don't know what it means, but I know it is important."

We get into the car and drive back to the pueblo. Fred falls asleep in the back seat. Bob and I talk quietly on the way home.

My interest in contemporary Zunis' perceptions of the rock art about them arose initially from a desire to explore the meaning and function of that rock art. For many rock art sites throughout the world, the context in which such art was initially produced and in which it continues to exist as an almost permanent part of the landscape is almost impossible to explore except in the most general terms. The rock art at Zuni, however, offers a corpus of material that is located close to a group of people who have lived in that locale for hundreds of years and who have demonstrated a high degree of cultural continuity. Although influences from other, neighboring cultures are in clear evidence, and some images are the products of non-Zunis, most of the rock art in that area probably was produced by ancestors of the Zunis, both recent and distant. Furthermore, it continues to be produced to this day by some tribal members.

In such a context, it seemed reasonable and possible to seek clues to the meanings and functions of these petroglyphs and pictographs in the archaeology of the area, in the extensive ethnographic material collected over the past one hundred years, and in the comments of contemporary Zunis concerning their perceptions of what these figures were and to what they might refer. I also had to recognize and keep in mind the limitations inherent in these various lines of inquiry. Traditional forms of expressive culture certainly have been affected by the widespread social and cultural changes that have occurred since many of these ethnographies were written. Still, despite such changes, the form, meaning, and function of Zuni verbal and visual arts give evidence of striking continuities over that period, and the core of Zuni social organization and religious activity seems to have remained fundamentally constant. Thus, I found that I could use much of this material to supplement and add depth to the data gathered through my work with contemporary Zunis.

The rock art created in prehistoric times was most likely produced for entirely different reasons than those for which it is produced today. Moreover, specific design elements may have changed through time, or, where they haven't, their meanings may have. For these reasons, the identifications of specific rock art images and the explanations of their meanings I elicited from contemporary Zunis probably proved most informative with respect to those more representationally drawn images of relatively recent date (post-A.D. 1325). Many of these depictions are similar to those found in other forms of Zuni visual art, and their symbolic meanings are still known and understood by most Zunis. One cannot assume, however, that contemporary interpretations always reflect ideas that are rooted in Zuni traditional life. In some instances such interpretations reflect the influence of outside sources and cannot, therefore, simply be taken as an index of perceptions of rock art that have persisted through time.

Whatever they reveal about the past, however, such interpretations clearly serve to illuminate the present. On the one hand, contemporary interpretations of the older, more ambiguous carvings and paintings on rock surfaces quite likely have very little to do with the "original" meanings or functions of these images. On the other hand, the manner in which they are related to events described in the Zuni origin myth (or, in the case of some of the most abstract images at least, to the time of the myth) illuminates the process by which Zunis appropriate these images so that they become records and constant reminders of the past.

The Zunis believe that some of the oldest pictographs and petroglyphs in the area were created by their ancestors, frequently for the express purpose of communicating a message to contemporary tribal members. Thus rock art is of special import because it demonstrates the involvement of the ancestors in present-day life, the fluid boundary between the events of the myth time and those of today. Because certain rock art images evoke recitations of traditional narrative, I regard them as a means by which to investigate the relationship between verbal and visual communicative codes. This interrelationship is revealed in the way that the Zunis use these codes to recreate and structure the world of the myth time, making it a vital part of their contemporary existence.

Zuni cosmology is based on an underlying integrating concept or model of the world, a six-directional scheme that is derived from the apparent annual motion of the sun along the horizon plus the zenith and the nadir; these are also the directions from which the rain- and snow-bearing winds emanate. Zunis interpret many rock art figures as relating implicitly or explicitly to this model. Thus, Zuni perceptions and interpretations of rock art reveal much about Zuni world view as well as about their attitudes toward the landscape. The Zunis believe that they have lived where they now reside ever since "the finding of the Center place" back in "the time of the beginning." They do not regard that time as past but as everpresent, constantly informing the here and now. For them, certain features of the landscape, as well as images carved and painted on rock surfaces that are integral to that landscape, encode events that happened in the past. Rock art depictions in particular have the power to evoke that past; they serve as vehicles that bind together past and present, linking the ancestors and the myth time to contemporary Zuni life.

In this book I examine the various levels on which pictographs and petroglyphs operate in Zuni society, explicating the way in which Zunis attribute significance to these images. Chapters 1 and 2 provide an introduction to the ethnography, archaeology, and rock art of the Zuni area. Chapter 3, a discussion of Zuni cosmology and symbolism in general, sets the stage for a more specific focus on interpretations of rock art within that cultural system. Chapters 4 through 6 center on the meaning and function of rock art for contemporary Zunis. This analysis of the meaning of rock art imagery thus serves as a key to understanding Zuni cultural symbolism, illuminating Zuni attitudes toward the landscape and the mythic past and revealing the way in which the Zunis draw all elements in their environment into a vast network of symbolic associations.

1

Continuity and Change: The Ethnographic Perspective

July 1981

In addition to showing us rock art sites, because of both his interests and ours, our closest Zuni friend loves to take my husband and me to archaeological sites—the places on the reservation lands where the ancestors of the contemporary Zunis lived. I remember in particular a visit to the abandoned village, Hawikku, when his whole family came along and we had a picnic. The excavated village was little more than an unimpressive mound, but there were potsherds everywhere— mute evidence of the artistic past. Our archaeological lessons came back to us and we left the sherds where they were, but everyone was excited by having seen pieces that were decorated with distinctive patterns.

Another favorite outing was to the site called the Village of the Great Kivas. During one visit the dirt road was impassable in a small foreign car because of recent heavy rains, and I, to my later regret, suggested that we walk to the site, leaving the car at the side of the nearest paved road. I was sure it was only a little way. In the end, we walked over eight miles there and back. The mud stuck to our shoes, severely impeding our progress, and my feet were sorely blistered by the time we reached the car because I hadn't thought to wear proper hiking shoes. This site has always been compelling, though, because of the carved and painted images on the rocks, the depressions in the ground below that had once been kivas, and the carefully constructed walls of ruins. These walls are made up of tiny stones alternating with larger ones, arranged in intricate patterns that must have satisfied the mason though they were never seen by others because they were plastered over. Today the plaster is gone, but the pattern remains to attest to the skill and patience of the long-gone builders. Walking back we took a shortcut that led past flocks of grazing sheep and old abandoned shacks that were once used by sheepherders, but are now falling apart because the availability of cars and trucks has made it easier to commute from the village. We skirted stands of piñon and juniper and climbed in and out of arroyos muddy with recent rains. Always we looked for birds, butterflies, and animal tracks. Sometimes we found feathers on the ground that could be used for making prayer sticks and decorating the costumes of the kachina dancers.

In any of my walks or more strenuous hikes with Zuni companions through the reservation lands, I was always aware of the great respect that the Zunis accord to their environment and their intimate knowledge of every detail. They are closely linked to this place of incomparable beauty through their stories, their rituals, their everyday life. It is frequently this environment—its denizens, its patterns, its vibrant colors—that is mirrored in various Zuni art forms, a means by which to draw the landscape closer to the fabric of daily existence.

Ecological setting

The Zuni perception of their immediate environment and the value with which they imbue the landscape are important aspects of their socio-cultural life.[1] The banded sandstone mesas (Figure 1), the variegated colors of the sunset, the bright markings on the wings of a butterfly, the brilliance of cactus flowers in full bloom against a desert background—all contribute to

Figure 1. Overview of Kyaki:ma (ZRAS site 2) on Dowa Yalanne, southeast of Zuni Pueblo. Photograph by Nancy L. Bartman, 1979.

a principle of aesthetics in which "the beautiful" is dynamic, distinct, various, and multicolored.[2] There is no subtle shading of colors in this environmental scheme; everything is sharp and clear. Prominent features of the landscape such as mesas provide a striking contrast with flat valleys, forming part of an overall panorama that is breathtakingly beautiful as well as harsh, stark, and demanding. Indeed, the landscape surrounding the Pueblo of Zuni is noted for its distinctiveness and beauty. One cannot easily forget the dramatic purples and reds with which the setting sun dyes Corn Mountain (*Dowa Yalanne*), the canyons and arroyos that carve channels in the lowlands, and the view from the mesas when one has climbed high enough to see the whole pueblo in miniature. Not only is the landscape beautiful, but for the Zunis it is an emotionally charged symbol; incorporated within it are the significant events of Zuni myth and history—the past is made visible by features in the landscape that stand for those events. The signs of the events include natural features such as boulders, lakes, rivers, and mesas, as well as artifacts created by human hands: the numerous images carved and painted on a variety of rock surfaces, the potsherds scattered near old habitation sites, and the stone and adobe ruins that dot the landscape.

The modern Pueblo of Zuni in western New Mexico lies in the southeastern part of the Colorado Plateau just west of the Continental Divide and the Zuni Mountains (Map 1). These mountains, the most prominent topographical feature of the region, rise at their highest point to an elevation of 9,000 feet—2,000 feet above the plateau. Water from the Zuni Mountains and nearby washes, including the Zuni River that runs through the pueblo (often little more than a trickle in the spring and fall), flows into the Little Colorado drainage system. To the south are the Mangas and Gallo mountains, rising a few feet higher than the Zuni Mountains. The two mountain ranges are separated by a wide tableland, overgrown in places with piñon and juniper and, in others, covered with lava. The southern branches of the Zuni River and Carrizo Creek drain these highlands.

The ecological setting displays great diversity.[3] Ponderosa pine, Douglas fir, oak, and aspen flourish in the higher regions. The area of middle elevation is predominantly a piñon and juniper woodland, while sagebrush and grama grass grow in the western lowlands. Cholla and prickly pear are the most common types of cactus in the area. Mountain greenery, much of which thrives in the same areas where springs and streams originate, is an important component of Zuni ritual drama. Summer rain dancers often carry branches of pine, which they gather in the mountains, in their hands and tie them around their ankles and wrists. During one such dance that I observed in the summer of 1980, a group of Zuni clowns distributed the leaves of a small herbaceous plant—described to me as "mountain mint"—to the matrons who sit on the south side of the plaza during these performances. One man told me this was done to bring water, and hence green growth, to the fields

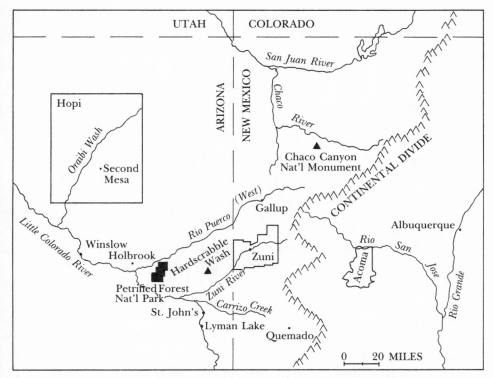

Map 1. Zuni Pueblo and its surroundings. Designed by Murray Callahan and Robert H. Leibman.

where crops are planted. "The mint grows up there where the springs are," he said. It fits with the respect accorded to the older women of the tribe that these special plants were given to them.

The climate is predominantly arid and dry; the little precipitation provided by snow and rain occurs primarily in winter and summer. The yearly precipitation average is about twelve inches—just barely sufficient to support the various crops that the Zunis raise. Yet even this amount of precipitation is unpredictable. Some years widespread droughts leave the fields for miles around dry and parched; in others, rain falls profusely across the border in Arizona, just beyond the western edge of the Zuni reservation lands, while Zuni goes without. But it rains too much at times as well: sudden, violent cloudbursts wash out fields and roads or cover them deep in mud.

The Zuni environs include few springs or permanent streams. Those that do exist have their sources in the areas of highest elevation, but the amount of water they yield is small. It is not surprising, then, that the agriculturalist Zunis venerate springs as shrine areas and regard the Zuni River as the pathway the dead take during their four-day journey to Kachina Village, located in the middle of Kachina Lake. The Zunis consider all bodies of water to be of special importance. Those who traveled to New England with ethnologist Frank H. Cushing in 1882 wanted particularly to see the Atlantic Ocean, the "Ocean of Sunrise," and to bring some of its sacred water back to Zuni.[4]

Zuni Salt Lake, a site of great significance to the Zuni people, is about forty-three miles to the south of the pueblo in the Carrizo Valley. It is a shallow body of water fed by a spring covering a salt deposit that yields unusually fine salt; two black volcanic cinder cones rise from its center. The lake plays an important role in Zuni mythology: when Salt Old Woman fled her home at Black Rock because of the Zunis' lack of respect for her she stopped at this lake, and she remains there still. Today Zunis make pilgrimages to Zuni Salt Lake. There they perform rituals and gather salt for domestic and ceremonial use. Because the Zunis consider this site to be a powerful place, and dangerous to females, women do not join in those pilgrimages.

The Zunis have met the problem of scant rainfall with irrigation. Agriculturalists for hundreds of years, they continue to grow corn, beans, squash, and melons (a post-Spanish introduction), although the economic importance of agriculture has recently decreased. In former times Zunis cultivated "waffle" gardens (consisting of squares of built-up ridges that trap

Figure 2. View of Zuni Pueblo looking southeast, showing waffle gardens in the distance and squash and corn drying on rooftops. Photograph by John K. Hillers, 1879. Courtesy of the Smithsonian Institution, National Anthropological Archives (Neg. No. 2301-B-2).

water, Figure 2); in dry spring seasons they used these waffle gardens as seedbeds for their important crops. Because of the water-trapping capability of the ridges, hand-watering was sufficient to enable the seeds to germinate. Zunis also tended peach orchards in the recent past, but such agricultural practices have largely disappeared today. Most Zunis find that they must resort to wage labor to meet the demands of their growing incorporation into a cash economy.

Cattle, pigs, horses, and domesticated sheep, introduced by the Spanish in the sixteenth century, continue to be raised in modern times, but as with agriculture, the raising of livestock is not as economically viable as it was in the past. The wildlife known to have inhabited the Zuni area in prehistoric times includes bear, bison, bobcat, coyote, deer, prairie dog, prong-horned antelope, otter, rabbit, ground squirrel, turkey, and gray wolf.[5] Some of these animals are pictured in the early rock art of the area, and a number of them form the powerful class of beasts of prey that are the subject of Zuni fetishes (small carved images of animals that the hunter carries for success in the hunt—see Figure 53). Today, deer, rabbits, bears, and coyotes populate the rangeland surrounding the pueblo. In the past hunting was an important supplement to farming, and Zunis conducted the search for game animals in a highly ritualized manner. Success in the hunt is still a frequent request of Zuni ritual prayers; recently this request has come to represent prosperity in general as well as luck in hunting game more specifically.

Zuni interactions with all aspects of the natural world were in the past, and still are, characterized by the principle of reciprocity and an attitude of respect for all living beings. (For the Zunis, the earth, too, is a living being.) They value harmony in all things and consider that disruption of the delicate balance between humans and nature is the result of failure on the part of humans. For instance, if they conduct a rain dance and still no rain falls, they attribute this failure to one who participated in the ceremony "with a bad heart." Furthermore, when a Zuni man kills a deer, he thanks the deer for the gift of its life and performs a ritual so that the spirit of the animal will be at peace. But hunting is more difficult these days, for much of the game was killed off at the beginning of the century, when many Anglos settled the area around Zuni.

Indeed, contemporary Zunis find that even their physical surroundings have undergone considerable change, as is described in a pamphlet on tribal history produced for use in the Zuni schools: ". . . as the white culture began to wash over the Zunis, like huge waves, changing the very contour of the land, the Pueblo began to rely more and more on the outside world for its needs."[6] Yet despite this reliance on the outside world, the most fundamental values of the Zunis remain constant: the gods still dance in the plazas and roam the landscape surrounding the pueblo in the guise of deer, and various features of that landscape continue to evoke the time of the myth.

Archaeological and Historical Setting

Archaeologists have divided the prehistory and history of the people of the Zuni area into time periods that reflect significant changes in the means of subsistence from hunting and gathering to agriculture, as well as in the types of dwellings developed.[7] At present, the cultural antecedents of the Zuni people can only be traced on a broad regional basis because the data and analytic techniques are insufficient to permit a detailed delineation of the movements of particular peoples from site to site in the prehistoric era. Because of the symbolic nature of Zuni origin myths and the lack of archaeological detail, it is impossible to correlate archaeological cultural history with Zuni accounts of their origin and travels in search of the Center. Nevertheless, according to archaeologist T. J. Ferguson and southwestern historian E. Richard Hart:

... the Zuni origin accounts and archaeological culture history share certain basic and major themes, including an economic shift from hunting and gathering to corn agriculture, the prevailing movement of people across the landscape, occasional violence and hostility between groups of people, and the assimilation of two cultural traditions with Zuni culture.[8]

It is noteworthy that these sequences delineating change in cultural traditions bear directly upon the rock art sequences in the Zuni vicinity. Specific archaeological sites can be dated and located within one or more of these time periods on the basis of the architectural remains and artifacts, such as stone tools and pottery, found there. The following is a brief outline of these periods.[9]

Paleo-Indian (prior to 5000 B.C.). Evidence of the earliest human use of the Zuni area—a few large spear points and isolated artifacts—dates to this period. It was characterized by a subsistence economy based on hunting and gathering and a relatively low population density.

Archaic (ca. 5000 B.C.–A.D. 1). During this period there was a gradual increase in population and a mixed hunting-gathering and horticultural economy. Sometime after about 1500 B.C. peoples in highland Mexico introduced the cultivation of corn, and later beans and squash.[10] Some dwellings were situated in natural rock shelters and others were roughly built, circular, shallow semisubterranean and surface houses made of perishable materials. There was very little pottery, but basketry and cord-weaving were sophisticated. Tools were made of stone and bone, and weapons such as atlatls, throwing sticks, and clubs were made of wood.

A.D. 1–650. The people of this time period began to rely more heavily on agriculture, which contributed to the development of sedentary villages, usually comprised of several deep, semisubterranean "pit houses." After the advent of pottery, around A.D. 200, regional cultural traditions developed that can be distinguished from each other on the basis of pottery style and other distinctive forms of material culture. Grayware utility pottery and black-on-white decorated pottery characterized the Anasazi cultural tradition that developed in the northern part of the Zuni area during this time. This was the cultural tradition that also gave rise to circular kivas (specialized, sometimes subterranean, ceremonial structures). The Mogollon tradition, located in the southern part of the Zuni area, developed square kivas and was associated with brownware utility pottery and redware decorated pottery. Buffware pottery was associated with the Hohokam cultural tradition that developed in southern Arizona. All of these cultural traditions were characterized by increasing village sedentism and agriculture.

A.D. 650–900. By the beginning of this period, small Anasazi villages of pit houses were located close to the area that later became Zuni Pueblo. Sometime after A.D. 700, pit houses were associated with above-ground masonry storage bins. Although hunting and gathering were still an important part of the overall subsistence pattern, pit house villages contained granaries and grinding stones—indications of the increase in the storage and processing of agricultural produce. Archaeological evidence, including jewelry made from shell from the Pacific Ocean and the Gulf of California, shows that these early villages were linked to a regional trade network extending throughout the Southwest. Pit house villages in the Zuni area were associated with a series of decorated black-on-white pottery types.

A.D. *900–1150.* Dwellings during this period were small clusters of contiguous-room pueblos built of stone masonry or jacal (wattle and daub) and closely associated with circular underground kivas. The large number of these small sites, both in the Zuni region and the Anasazi area more generally, suggests that people frequently shifted their homes around the landscape, perhaps in response to small changes in the amount of rainfall or some other environmental change. In the Zuni drainage, many of these small Anasazi house sites seem to have been organized into communities oriented around a large ceremonial structure—a great kiva. This kind of community center was exemplified by the Village of the Great Kivas, the ruins of which are on the Zuni reservation today. They are an outpost of the Chaco Canyon civilization.[11] Similarity of pottery type as well as architectural traits support these relationships.[12]

In addition, much of the rock art above the ruins at the Village of the Great Kivas seems to fall within the same time frame and is stylistically similar to that of the Chaco Canyon area. (Figure 23, for example, pictures elements belonging to a rock art style that was common to the northern Anasazi groups at this time. These elements include human stick figures, meandering lines, mountain sheep with nearly rectangular bodies, fluteplayers, spirals, and geometric designs. Most of these figures are solidly pecked.) Archaeologists currently hypothesize that community centers like the Village of the Great Kivas were organized into a large regional trade system with its center at Chaco Canyon to the north of the Zuni area in the San Juan basin. At its peak, the northern Anasazi culture was characterized by skillful production of various forms of arts and crafts and an elaborate ceremonial life linked primarily to agriculture. Furthermore, as is evidenced by the astronomical alignments they incorporated in their ceremonial buildings as well as other structures, these Anasazi peoples had developed a sophisticated knowledge of astronomy, which they used both to determine the planting times for crops and to establish the timing for recurrent ritual activities.[13] During the twelfth century, for reasons not yet completely understood, this system was reorganized and the northern settlements were abandoned. The people from this area moved southward to the Little Colorado and the Rio Grande and its tributaries—areas occupied by the predecessors of the contemporary Puebloan peoples—and, through time, blended with these groups.

A.D. 1150–1540. Sometime after 1150, the people living in the Zuni area began to interact more with peoples living to the south in the Mogollon area. In the early part of this period, small pueblos continued to be the most prevalent type of settlement. After around A.D. 1250, however, intensification of agriculture led to settlements that were largely multiroom, multistory stone masonry pueblos that had many kivas and were oriented around plazas. These settlements were built in open valleys, at canyon heads, or in natural rock shelters. Water management systems were developed at this time. Between 1250 and 1540, these large plaza-oriented pueblos dominated the Zuni area. Zuni Pueblo was probably founded about A.D. 1350 and, like many of the later aggregated pueblos, was located downstream of a river in an area of good soils to provide abundant resources for farming.

In the early fourteenth century (ca. A.D. 1325–1350), an extensive artistic and ceremonial complex originating from Mexico spread from the Jornada Mogollon south of the Little Colorado region to the Rio Grande drainage and then west to Zuni and Hopi. This complex blended with and contributed to earlier extant Anasazi art and ceremonialism, yielding an elaboration particularly in those religious concepts and ceremonial institutions that are based on the kachina cult.[14] Although retaining some elements of the Anasazi tradition and its own distinctive attributes, most forms of Zuni artistic expression, including rock art, show considerable similarity to the Rio Grande style from this time period to the present (see, for example, Figures 34, 36, 69, 71, 74, 80).

The populations living in the Upper Little Colorado Valley gradually consolidated in the late prehistoric period. At the same time, settlements to the south of Zuni in the Mogollon area were abandoned, and some of these peoples probably moved into the Little Colorado River Valley. Most archaeologists agree that this small group of immigrants mingled with the Anasazi population, which had long resided in the Zuni drainage. The prehistoric Zuni Indians emerged from this amalgam.

From the thirteenth to the mid-fourteenth century there was a network of communication and exchange between the Pueblo groups of Zuni and Acoma.[15] A well-traveled path, which included the site of Atsinna (at present-day El Morro), connected the two pueblos. Atsinna and some of the contemporaneous pueblos nearby were abandoned near the end of the fourteenth century. The people who abandoned these sites probably added to the population of the six large villages that constituted the early historic settlements of the Zuni.

The Historic Period

Two of the prehistoric villages in the Zuni area, *Hawikku* and *Halona:wa*, continued to be occupied in historic times. The four additional towns inhabited at the beginning of the historic period were *Kyaki:ma*, *Mats'a:kya*, *Kwa'kin'a*, and *Kechiba:wa*. Due to the persistence of Apache and Navajo raids, along with the population decimation caused by diseases introduced by Europeans, the Zunis abandoned five of these towns by the end of the seventeenth century and settled in Halona:wa. This village became present-day Zuni. Legends the

Spaniards had heard of the large and rich "Seven Cities of Cibola" may have been based on the existence of these six villages. Such legends spurred Coronado to explore the area in 1540 and marked the beginning of extensive Spanish influence on the Zunis as well as on the other Puebloan groups. Coronado's initial introduction to the Zuni villages was a great disappointment to him, however; instead of legendary riches he found a rather poor people whose main subsistence base was agriculture supplemented by hunting. Spanish chroniclers who arrived after Coronado's exploring party were impressed with the multistoried stone and adobe buildings and made brief notes about Zuni culture and religion, reporting that "what they worship most is water."[16]

During the early 1600s the Spaniards established missions throughout the Pueblo area, using native labor to build massive churches and extensive outbuildings. The first Spanish churches at Zuni were completed by 1632, but they and other missions in New Mexico were destroyed during the Pueblo Revolt of 1680 when the Pueblo groups joined in attempting to overthrow Spanish rule. At that time, to avoid Spanish reprisals the Zunis fled to "refuge villages" on top of *Dowa Yalanne*, which offered a more defensible position than the pueblo in the valley.[17] Some of the Zunis remained in those villages to escape the raids of neighboring hostile tribes. When the Spaniards re-established control at Zuni in 1692, Diego de Vargas discovered that the Zunis had carefully preserved the Catholic ritual objects (altars, candles, vestments, books) taken from the churches.[18] De Vargas decided that this behavior was a sign of the respect the Zunis had for Christianity. It is likely that the Zunis regarded these images as having a potency similar to that inherent in their own religious icons—the carved wooden images of the Twin War Gods, for example. They may have preserved them either to avoid the disastrous consequences that the destruction of such powerful objects might entail or in order to acquire some of that power.

By the mid-1820s, the Franciscans had discontinued their missionary efforts at Zuni because of continued Zuni resistance to conversion and the increasing number of raids by Apaches and Navajos. Nearly three centuries of Spanish contact had contributed the use of metal tools; important agricultural crops, particularly wheat, oats, and peaches; sheep and burros; and a variety of ideas and practices that Zunis incorporated into their sacred and secular life.[19]

For the next thirty years, Mexican traders as well as Anglo travelers motivated by the discovery of gold in California, passed through Zuni frequently. Navajos continued their raids on Zuni until the establishment of Fort Wingate by the U.S. government in the early 1870s. Gallup, a town forty miles to the north of Zuni, was established when the Atlantic and Pacific Railroad reached this part of the Southwest in 1881. The railroad opened the way for considerable numbers of traders, missionaries, and settlers to the area. Gallup continues to be a center of commerce for Zunis and Navajos today.

The first anthropological expedition to study the Zuni, organized under the aegis of the Smithsonian Institution, arrived in 1879. This group included James and Matilda Stevenson and Frank H. Cushing, all of whom later made important contributions to the knowledge of Zuni life. Cushing remained in Zuni for nearly five years and became an adopted member of the tribe (Figure 3). In 1883 he took six Zunis back with him to visit Washington, D.C. and other cities on the East Coast, a trip undertaken in part to acquaint his Zuni friends with Anglo civilization. The Zunis who went on this trip formed the nucleus of a progressive movement when they returned to the pueblo. After the initial efforts of Cushing and the Stevensons, Zuni became a very popular area of study for anthropologists, archaeologists, folklorists, linguists, and others; it is still frequently visited by scholars with diverse research interests. By the 1890s there were quite a few resident Anglos in Zuni: teachers, missionaries, traders, and U.S. government officials. They exerted considerable influence on the affairs of the pueblo, especially promoting Zuni dependence on traders and the federal government.[20]

In the eighteenth century, Zuni expanded when its people

Figure 3. Ethnologist Frank H. Cushing posing as Zuni Mudhead (Koyemshi). Photograph courtesy of the Smithsonian Institution, National Anthropological Archives (Neg. No. 23-A-1).

established summer villages near farmlands fifteen to twenty-five miles distant from Zuni. All of these farmlands existed near springs that provided much-needed water. In the early nineteenth century there were three of these seasonally inhabited farming villages: Ojo Caliente, Nutria, and Pescado. In the early twentieth century the Zunis established a fourth such village, Tekapo. At that time, all four villages had year-round residents.

In summary, the many interactions among prehistoric and historic groups in the Zuni-Cibola region contributed to the modern culture with its complex social and religious organization and its clear cultural ties to neighboring Pueblo groups. Obvious stylistic influences from the surrounding areas on the rock art at Zuni help to define the communication networks of the Zuni-Cibola region, although this rock art retains certain distinctive attributes as well.

Socio-Cultural Setting

In his major work on Zuni history, historian Gregory Crampton aptly described the pueblo as a place where "history becomes real" and "the ancient past lives."[21] As one Zuni has said: "Today we live in the present ways of our people, we live also within the realm of our ancestors, for we are sustained through the rituals and beliefs of long ago. We live in accordance to the ways of our people, which bring life, blessings, and happiness."[22] Over the past one hundred years or so, a number of anthropologists have described the "ways" of the Zuni people, their rituals and beliefs.[23] Although not all of them wrote thorough or even reasonably objective ethnographies, they did agree on many points—a testimony not only to the accuracy of their reports but also to the stability and continuity of the *facts* they describe.[24] This ethnographic record shows that despite much contact with Anglo- or Euro-American culture during the recent past, Zuni demonstrates considerable continuity from its past to its present. The pueblo today has a population of over 7,000, most of whom describe

themselves as full-blooded Zuni Indians. Though many are
fluent in English, particularly those of middle age or younger,
the Zuni language remains the language of social discourse.

Zuni social, religious, economic, and political systems are
all closely intertwined.[25] The mother's household was in the
past and is today the basic social, religious, and economic unit.
It is still common at Zuni for married couples to live with
the wife's mother, although this pattern is changing. At birth
a child belongs to her or his mother's household and clan. This
lineage determines, to some extent, the child's subsequent
role in the religious system, especially because certain religious offices can be filled only by members of certain clans.
Edmund Ladd, a Zuni man who is a highly respected anthropologist, describes the complex interrelationships as follows:

The Zuni socioreligious system is composed of four interlocking
systems, each operating independently yet synchronically to provide
for the physical and psychological needs of the users. Superimposed
one upon the other are the clans, the kiva groups (which together
make up the "Kachina Society"), the curing societies . . . and the
priesthoods.[26]

The child's clan and, to a lesser extent, the child's father's
clan also determine specific duties and networks of support,
especially in times of need and crisis.

According to anthropologist Fred Eggan, the "outstanding
feature of social life" for all of the Western Pueblo groups,
Zuni included, is the division into matrilineal clans, each
named or given a totem "after some object or aspect of nature."[27] Clan membership continues to be extremely important at Zuni right up to the present.[28] The clan is a lineage
group and its members are considered to be genealogically
related. They refer to one another in kin terms and are expected to behave in a manner that is appropriate to such relationships. In the past, certain lands may have been reserved
for the use of particular clans—an exchange for services rendered to the village. Several Zunis have suggested that the
older rock art images that seem to depict clan symbols might

have served to mark some of those clan lands.

The clan can also be described as the basic ritual unit: the control of ceremonies and ritual paraphernalia is in the keeping of certain clans. Such paraphernalia is stored in the "clan house," both an actual and a symbolic construct that is under the care of a brother and sister pair, the clan uncle and clan aunt. The clan is further defined as a social group, made up of one or more matrilineal lineages that claim descent from a common ancestor.[29] A child belongs to her or his mother's clan and should marry outside this clan and also outside the father's clan—a practice that appears to be changing somewhat in modern times at Zuni. Stating that the Zuni clan system is "in a continual state of flux," with some clans dying out while others are inactive for a period of time, Ladd lists fifteen clans for contemporary Zunis, giving the following English translations:

Dogwood (with Twig Dogwood, Macaw and Crow divisions), Eagle (with Golden Eagle and Bald Eagle divisions), Sun, Badger, Turkey (with White Turkey and Black Turkey divisions), Corn (with White Corn and Black Corn divisions), Frog, Crane, Coyote, Bear, Tobacco, Tansy Mustard, Deer, Chaparral Cock (Roadrunner), and Yellow-wood.[30]

In former times these clans were associated in ritual activities with the six directions (depending on the ceremonial context, either the cardinal or semicardinal directions, plus the zenith and nadir). According to Cushing, for instance, there were at one time nineteen clans, all but one grouped in threes to correspond to the Zuni six-directional scheme. The one clan not so associated represented the sum total of all of them, the "midmost" or "all-containing clan of the entire tribe." Furthermore, this directional association of the clans related to the physical attributes of the species represented. Thus, the Crane clan, for example, was associated with the north because cranes are able to endure the cold and fly northward in their yearly migration, and so on for all the clan groups.[31]

Despite considerable changes in the pueblo economy during

the recent past, women still retain their traditional dominant role in the economic affairs of the household. Agriculture, however, is no longer the principal means of subsistence and many Zunis now commute to jobs off the reservation in Gallup or as far away as Albuquerque.[32] They also go to these cities to shop and to sell their sometimes prize-winning jewelry and pottery at craft shows and ceremonials there. Jewelry making is now one of the principal sources of income for Zunis. Ladd describes the current economic activities, in order of their importance, as: "wage labor including federal, tribal, local industry, and off-reservation employment; arts and crafts; livestock; and agriculture."[33] Nevertheless, although most Zunis today enjoy a higher standard of living than in the past, unemployment is still a critical problem.

Historically agriculture was central to the Zuni subsistence economy and, given the harsh and sometimes desertlike climate of the region in which they live, it is not surprising that the ensurance of sufficient rain for the crops is the dominant focus of Zuni religious activities. Thus, one of the principal duties and responsibilities of the Zuni priesthoods and religious societies has been to act as mediators between the Zuni people and those beings, especially kachinas, who have the power to bring rain and, more generally, to confer prosperity in all areas of life. While many Zunis are affiliated with one or another Christian group, this generally neither precludes their continued membership in the traditional Zuni religious societies nor their participation in the ceremonies of those societies. The largest of these is the Kachina Society, into which most males are initiated at or about the time of puberty. The kachinas are masked gods, some of whom are the spirits of deceased Zunis; they have the power to bring rain and to confer other sorts of blessings on those who carry out the proper ritual activities. Divided into six kiva groups associated with the directions, the members of the Kachina Society are responsible for impersonating the kachinas and for conducting the ceremonies that implore these powerful beings to help the

Figure 4. "Zunis imitating dance of the 'Yebitchai' gods of the Navaho" (original caption to photograph). Photograph by Matilda C. Stevenson, 1896–1898. Courtesy of the Smithsonian Institution, National Anthropological Archives (Neg. No. 2356-c).

Zunis (Figure 4).[34] The impersonation of the most important of the kachinas, the kachina priests, is a deeply serious undertaking. It often involves memorizing lengthy prayers and participating in a year-long cycle of ritual activities such as the regular planting of prayer sticks at sacred spring areas. A good friend of mine, a young Zuni man whose father was a prominent religious leader for many years, has recently begun to take an active role in Zuni religion. He explained to me, however, that this is a difficult task for many reasons:

It's hard to be a Zuni.
There are so many prayers to learn,
you have to have a good memory.
Some of the prayers take hours to say.
I once asked my father
to teach me the shortest prayer he knew.
It took him twenty minutes
just to say it once.

Zunis who participate actively in the Kachina Society or in other religious organizations must devote a great deal of their time to ritual activities; they learn prayers and songs, spend many hours practicing dances and rehearsing Zuni ritual dramas, conduct a yearly series of visits to shrine areas, fast and meditate frequently, and refurbish masks, costumes, and other ritual paraphernalia. They often find that their religious duties make it impossible for them to undertake jobs that entail working a forty-hour week, a situation that Anglo employers are often unwilling to accommodate or even to try to understand.

In addition to the Kachina Society, the Zuni religious system includes twelve smaller societies, described by Matilda Stevenson as "esoteric fraternities."[35] Ten of these, affiliated with the Beast Gods, are concerned with the curing of illness; their members are said to have extraordinary knowledge of physical and mental powers.[36] Members of the more specialized orders within these societies have skills and powers that enable them to engage in activities such as sword-, stick-, and fire-swallowing, walking on hot coals (all without suffering serious damage), music-making, and clowning. Women may belong to these societies, although some orders or subgroups within the societies, such as the arrow-swallowing order, are closed to them; they may not hold positions of office in any of the societies. Besides these curing societies the "esoteric fraternal" group includes the all-male Coyote Society, whose patrons are the predators and game animals of the six directions; members of this society are experts in hunting. Another all-male group is the war society (Society of Bow Priests), whose patrons are the Twin War Gods. In the past, membership in this society was limited to men who had taken an enemy scalp.[37] Frank H. Cushing complied with this requirement in the 1880s when he was adopted into the tribe and became the head war chief of Zuni.[38] Two other war societies that were active in the past have ceased to operate.

The Zuni rain priesthoods, extremely important positions in the Zuni religious framework, are composed of smaller numbers than the societies; the Rain Priests pray for the welfare of all the Zunis and other beings as well. They have powers of divination, going into "retreat" or seclusion to resolve important questions. Their members include the six Daylight Priests who represent the six directions (they go into retreat following the pattern of a clockwise circuit of the four horizontal directions, then the zenith and the nadir), the ten Night Priests, and the assistants of both groups. Although certain clans must be represented in these priesthoods, membership is not automatically inherited—the determining factor is temperament: each priest must be "a really good Zuni" whose everyday life sets an example for all the people.[39]

Just as it is difficult to separate Zuni life into sacred and secular domains, in the past government and religion were closely intertwined in what was essentially a theocracy; religious leaders, acting as a unit, concerned themselves with all aspects of government. In the seventeenth century the Spaniards instituted a civil government, a form of which persists today. In many ways, though, they merely formalized a system that was already in existence. According to traditional practice, the Rain Priests were to remain uninvolved in violence; therefore, the enforcers of tribal laws were the Bow Priests, a society associated with war. It is likely that the Spaniards appointed the Head Bow Priest, the most obvious tribal leader, as governor. Since that time the system of tribal government has undergone considerable change. One of the most radical changes stemmed from the tribal decision in 1934 to institute a nominating committee and the election of civil officials by the entire tribe—prior to that time the members of the Tribal Council had been appointed by the Council of High Priests. Ironically in this matrilineal society, it was not until 1965 that women were given the privilege of voting and, hence, an official voice in determining the members of the Tribal Council. Recently, Zunis have begun to elect women to the formal governing body; in addition, women continue to wield considerable unofficial influence in tribal matters. The contemporary civil government consists of an elected Tribal Council made up of the Governor, the Lieutenant Governor, and generally, six other members. The laws passed by the Tribal Council are enforced by the tribal police force, the Zuni Rangers. As friction arose over issues such as the extent to which the tribe should permit or encourage outside influence, factions of "progressives" and "conservatives" were formed; these factions continue to play an important role in Zuni politics. Although the function of the Zuni governing body was initially somewhat limited, in 1970 the Zunis ratified their Constitution and the tribal government received the right to control the reservation and all functions of the Tribal Council. As a result, the control of agencies such as the Bureau of Indian Affairs over tribal matters has greatly decreased; currently there is an Indian agent who serves in an advisory capacity only.[40]

With the establishment of the Zuni Public School District as an independent state school district and the consequent reorganization of the schools on the reservation in the early 1980s, the tribe (or its representatives) gained greater control over matters of curriculum.[41] Prior to this, Zuni schools had been part of the McKinley County system; students from a variety of backgrounds, including Zuni, Navajo, and Anglo, filled the classrooms. Since the students are now almost entirely Zuni, the tribe is promoting the use of Zuni materials in the educational process. Zuni language learning materials and folktales emphasize the cultural background of the students. One important consequence of this orientation is that a staff of experts in the Zuni way of life frequently visits those classes to explain tribal traditions to the young people. Thus, as was a common practice in the past, the older members of the tribe are becoming involved in the education of the younger members. This by no means implies an exclusive focus on Zuni material but rather a switch from an all-English focus to one centering on bicultural education. For instance, especially since they are still fluent in the Zuni language, the Senior Citizens have been asked to take an active role in the Head Start Program for young children. This is an important formal recognition of the significant part that Zuni grandparents have traditionally played in the education of the young.

World War II marked an important point in Zuni history. A relatively large number of the men either were drafted or left the pueblo to engage in war-related activities; at the same time, funds for government programs were cut drastically. Once the war ended, tribal members made a great attempt to help returning soldiers readjust to the Zuni way of life, but these veterans experienced difficulty in making the transition back to the restrictions of the traditional life-style. A parallel problem is the increasing number of Zuni students who leave the reservation after graduation from high school to enroll in college or training schools. It is a tribal concern that many of these students do not return to live on the reservation. Certainly the experience these veterans and students gained of the world off the reservation has contributed to a number of changes in Zuni sociocultural practices, perhaps the most pervasive of which has been the increased dependence upon a modern cash economy for their needs. One Zuni aptly sums up the difficulties brought by cultural contact:

With the ways of the white man entering into our lives, perhaps it will not be long before our people become a wandering tribe, aimlessly roving the path of self-deterioration and destruction. But it is for our children to decide and work for. We cannot tell them of the way our people survived, for they would not believe us. We must just hope they, too, can survive what lies before them.[42]

Figure 5. Arlene Sheyka celebrates her birthday with a "Wonder Woman" cake. Zuni, New Mexico. Photograph by M. Jane Young, 1984.

Technological change may have come slowly to the pueblo, but it has had an inevitable impact on Zuni culture. Electricity was not introduced until 1950, and it was not until about five years later that most families began to use automobiles. Most Zuni children are bilingual in Zuni and English and have many experiences of the same sort that Anglo children do (Figure 5). They talk on the telephone, watch TV, listen to radios and stereos, and play video games. Their heritage, history, and religion are quite different, however, a fact that is a source of pride to young Zunis and sometimes a difficulty as well, especially for those who leave the reservation to pursue higher education or careers oriented toward members of "mainstream" society.

The physical look of the pueblo itself has been radically altered in recent years. While the "old village" with its stone and adobe structures remains much the same (Figure 2), it is surrounded by increasing evidence of change. Young married couples often have available to them a very different life-style than that experienced by their parents. Today, many couples with the economic resources to do so prefer to establish their own homes instead of taking up residence with the bride's family. They move to modern, single-family, wooden houses in the subdivisions located on the outskirts of the older part of the village. Such subdivisions are equipped with paved streets, streetlights, sidewalks, grassy lawns, central heating, gas, electricity, and other such accoutrements of modern life. Even those who live in the old village have running water, electricity, and frequently, telephones, television, modern appliances, and automobiles.[43]

Zunis today have considerable contact with the Anglo-American culture and there is every indication that the adoption of certain aspects of Anglo society will continue in the future. As per capita income and leisure time increase and as new business developments spring up on the reservation, more such changes will undoubtedly occur. Even Zuni religious leaders have made certain adjustments to accommodate a more "Western" mode of existence. For instance, major ceremonies such as Shalako are now held on weekends so that Zunis who live off the reservation can return; but this practice draws greater numbers of tourists as well. Furthermore, Zunis have recently formed organizations inspired by the pattern of Anglo society. Such associations include a Craftsmen's Cooperative Association, a Lions Club, an American Legion Post, and a Senior Citizen's group. Every August there is a Tribal Fair complete with a rodeo (Figure 6), performances of social dances and music, and a parade that includes the all-Zuni American Legion, the high school band and majorettes, dance groups, and elaborate floats (Figure 7). The highlight of the occasion is the coronation of Miss Zuni during the Saturday evening performance. Yet, it is of note that Miss Zuni is chosen not for her beauty, but for her knowledge of Zuni culture. She must prepare a traditional meal for the judges, answer ques-

Figure 6. Zuni Tribal Fair rodeo (Dowa Yalanne in background).
Photograph by Robert H. Leibman, 1980.

Figure 7. Zuni matrons dressed as olla maidens, Zuni Tribal Fair
parade. Photograph by Robert H. Leibman, 1980.

tions concerning the history and present situation of the tribe, demonstrate fluency in the Zuni language, and appear in traditional Zuni dress. In a culture so strongly matriarchal, it is significant that the young women are submitted to such a test, thus ensuring that the culture will be passed on.[44]

Despite the many obvious social and economic changes and the lamentations of some tribal members that the old ways are dying out, the core of Zuni religion and world view has held fast. The Zuni response to the meeting of cultures is one of syncretism: the adaptation to new conditions and incorporation of many Anglo-American elements into a vital and ongoing tradition.

2

Rock Art in the Zuni Area

Nancy, my assistant for the Zuni Rock Art Survey, and I have been at Zuni for almost three weeks. We leave the small trailer that we're renting for the summer very early each morning and spend the days photographing and keeping written records of rock art sites; sometimes the brief afternoon rain showers force an intermission and we duck for shelter. After a hasty dinner we drive into the village to watch the summer rain dances and then go to the old wooden building that is the base of operations for the Zuni Archaeology Program. There we type up our notes and read in the archaeological and ethnographic texts that are part of the Program's library. Sometimes there are no rain dances and we arrive at the archaeology office in the early evening; we sit on the steps outside and watch the setting sun tinge Corn Mountain and the eastern sky with dramatic purples and reds. The air is permeated with the heady smell from the wild rose bush on the west side of the building.

We have recorded three small sites so far and parts of a fourth one, *Kyaki:ma,* which is quite extensive and will require a considerable expenditure of time. Today we've decided to take a break from that site and look for one to the northeast of the pueblo that one of the archaeologists discovered during survey work. We have a roughly drawn map, but are otherwise on our own. We take a long time to find the side road; as drawn on our map, it seems to cut through the farming area of Pescado, running north from Highway 53. As we turn onto the side road, we pass an inhabited adobe house and hope that the residents won't think we are trespassing. We always carry with us a letter signed by the Tribal Governor that explains our project, but we have never yet been called upon to show it to anyone; perhaps people are accustomed to the archaeologists surveying sites all over the reservation. The map seems to indicate that the rock art site begins on big boulders close to the ground and then extends to the rock surfaces above that project steeply from the mesa. Nothing is carved on these boulders, however, so we begin to climb.

We climb for what seems to us like hours. The sun gets hotter all the time and we don't see a single rock carving or painting. Our legs begin to ache and we are aware that we're not in the kind of shape that would win us prizes for physical fitness—we are two students from the east who have spent most of the last year at seminar tables in classrooms or desks in the library. Still, we're more used to the climate and the activity than we were during the first week. Although the daytime temperatures in the summer are very hot at Zuni, the air is dry and the nights are cool and pleasant for sleeping. As if to mock our poor physical condition, a goat with a huge bell tied around his neck appears on the ledge above us. He eyes us with suspicion, turns and climbs with great agility up the steep and rocky side of the mesa, and then disappears over the top. Finally we decide that we've come to the wrong place and begin to climb down.

We manage to come down on the side of the mesa away from the car, and must walk on the edge of a cornfield to get back. The still air has given way to a light breeze, signaling an approaching storm, that causes a cacaphony from the cornfield. At intervals throughout the field the Zuni farmer who owns this land has tied empty tin cans and pie tins to fence posts; when the wind blows they rattle against one another to drive the crows away from the tender young corn plants. The farmer has placed scarecrows here as well. Made of tattered garments tied to sticks, they look like headless people, and in the sudden ominous darkness before the storm they take on a sinister appearance. As the raindrops begin to fall, we hurry for the car.

The next day, after getting clearer directions, we renew our attempts to find the site. This time Vance and Carlton, two Zuni high school boys who are working with us as part of the Rock Art Survey team, come along. They rush ahead and shout back excitedly that there is rock art everywhere; indeed, we can see it even from the ground. Hundreds of petroglyphs fill the wall of a rock ledge projecting above us. Once we reach that ledge we see that some of the figures are easily accessible, but some are so high overhead that we'll need to use a telephoto lens to photograph them. Even Vance and Carlton, who are much more agile than Nancy and I are, can find no way to climb up to the rock art; they suggest that the carvers of the petroglyphs must have used some sort of wooden scaffold or ladder.

Although we haven't yet established a relative dating scheme for the rock art of the Zuni area, it is apparent to us by now that most of these images were made in prehistoric times. In style, content, and technique they remind me of other prehistoric rock art I've seen in the Southwest. But these petroglyphs are unlike any of the others we have seen so far at Zuni. Geometric designs form the dominant motif; there are chains of diamond-like figures, rectangles (sometimes fringed on the sides and containing symmetrical designs), spirals, bird tracks, curved animal tracks (perhaps bear paw prints), lizardlike figures that look both human and reptilian, and a series of birdlike figures with fringed triangular or rectangular bodies and, sometimes, toothed beaks. All of these figures have been painstakingly pecked (a technique that requires using one stone as a hammerstone and another as a chisel); the creation of each one must have taken at least several hours. Some of the geometric designs look like pottery motifs and the fringed rectangles suggest blankets. Although we have no way of knowing what they really represent, most of the designs seem to evidence a concern with pattern, balance, and symmetry. (A year later, at Petrified Forest National Park in Arizona, I was to find strikingly similar birdlike figures and geometric designs carved on boulders near a habitation site that dates to about A.D. 1350.) On a rock face to the west of the ledge we have been looking at, we find geometric designs and hand-prints painted in colors that we never see again in Zuni area pictographs—pink, lavender, and gold. Because they are not very weathered, it seems likely that these painted figures were created much later than the carved images we have just seen.

As Nancy and I begin to photograph, Carlton, who has great aptitude with maps, draws a rough site map and Vance begins to make roughly-to-scale drawings of the less distinct figures that will not photograph well. We are all absorbed in our tasks and excited by the unusual petroglyphs. As it grows later in the day and the sun shines more directly on the dimly pecked figures, they practically disappear before our eyes, becoming impossible to photograph. We decide to come back early the next day to see if the morning sun will bring out contrasts between rock and image and enable us to take better photographs. We pack up our equipment and begin the descent.

On the huge boulders below—one of which has a fence built entirely around it for a purpose we cannot fathom—we find more rock art. There are geometric designs, another bird figure similar to those on the rocks above, a humpbacked fluteplayer, and a finely incised name that appears to have been executed much later with a penknife. Nancy, who has done research on the fluteplayer motif in Southwestern rock art, is very excited by the small carving of the fluteplayer.

As we walk to the car I mention that the archaeologists have told me the Zuni name of this site is *Heshoda Ts'in'a*. I ask Vance and Carlton what that name means, and they tell me "Place of Writing"; they guess that the word "writing" refers to the images carved and painted on the rocks. Later, a number of tribal elders concur with this interpretation. When we get to the car, we notice that Vance has run back to the big boulder and we wait for him, writing up our field notes and gulping water from the canteens that we had left behind on the floor of the car. When Vance joins us he has something in his hand. He holds it out to Nancy and we see that, on a piece of rock he found on the ground, he has carved a small replica of the fluteplayer that so interested her. He used a hard, sharp stone to make the carving, much as some of the early artists must have done. Nancy has that piece of rock still; a reminder of that summer and Vance's artistry.

For over a thousand years various peoples inhabiting or passing through the Zuni valley have carved and painted images on the mottled and banded sandstone cliff walls of the mesas that surround the present-day pueblo on three sides (see Map 2 for these various site locations; the Appendix contains detailed information on individual sites). The majestic rock formation, *Dowa Yalanne* (Corn Mountain), rises a thousand feet above the valley just east of the pueblo (Figure 8); several rock art sites have been created on that mesa, which plays a vital role in Zuni history and mythology. The sharply rising walls of nearby canyons (Figure 9) also form natural canvases for pictographs (rock paintings) and petroglyphs (rock carvings). Other rock art sites occur north of the pueblo at the base of the two mesas called *Kwili Yalanne* (Twin Mountains) (see Figure 10).

East of the pueblo, at El Morro, stands Inscription Rock, where early Spanish and Anglo explorers carved signatures, dates, and travel records (Figures 11, 12). Even earlier, Indians carved petroglyphs and painted pictographs on outlying boulders as well as on the rock itself. *Atsinna*, a thirteenth- to mid-fourteenth-century archaeological site situated on the top of the mesa, was so named during its excavation by Zuni workmen because of the "pictures on the rock" in the area of

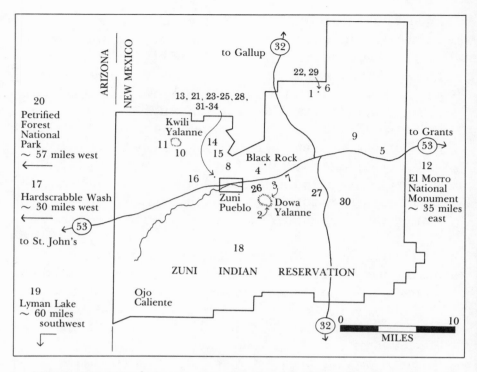

Map 2. Zuni Rock Art Survey site map. Numbers refer to sites, which are listed in the Appendix. Circled numbers refer to roads. Designed by Murray Callahan and Robert H. Leibman.

the ruin.[1] In the Zuni language, *atsinna* means writing or pictures.

To the west of the pueblo, in the Hardscrabble Wash area of Arizona, is a canyon that contains rock art covering a broad range of dates and styles. Some images here appear to date from before A.D. 400, earlier than anything found in the immediate surrounds of Zuni.[2] Others were produced quite recently; many of these are closely related in style and content to rock art located near the pueblo.[3]

Figure 8. View of Dowa Yalanne from ZRAS site 16 (taken west of Zuni Pueblo, looking east). Photograph by Robert H. Leibman, 1980.

Figure 9. Overview of canyon wall, ZRAS site 17 (petroglyphs faintly visible under rock overhang). Photograph by Robert H. Leibman, 1980.

Figure 10. Overview of ZRAS site 11. Photograph by Robert H. Leibman, 1980.

Techniques and Terminology

Some scholars have questioned the use of the term "rock art" because "art" implies aesthetic values and an emphasis on technical skill that may not have been intended by the cultural groups who originally produced this work. I use the term, however, because it is the most generally accepted and widely applicable.[4] By its use I do not mean to imply that the creators of these images were motivated exclusively, or even primarily, by aesthetic values; it is likely, though, that they did intend such values in most cases, whatever the primary reason for manufacturing the images.

Rock art images are, in general, created by means of two basic techniques: engraving (petroglyphs) and painting (pictographs). Specific engraving techniques include: *pecking*—striking the stone with a sharp piece of harder rock or using

Figure 11. Spanish inscription (note date, 1709), El Morro National Monument (ZRAS site 12). Photograph by M. Jane Young, 1979.

Figure 12. Anglo inscription (note date, 1866), El Morro National Monument (ZRAS site 12). Photograph by M. Jane Young, 1979.

Figure 13. Pecked lizardlike and anthropomorphic figures, 75 cm × 90 cm, ZRAS site 1. Photograph by Nancy L. Bartman, 1979.

a hammerstone and rock chisel (Figures 13, 23); *incising, gouging, scratching*—carving lines of varying depth in the rock with a sharp object (Figures 14, 15, 16); *abrading*—rubbing or scraping with a harder stone in order to create a smooth surface (Figures 15, 16); and *drilling*—rotating an object, often metal, to produce small round holes in the rock surface (Figure 17). Often these techniques are used in conjunction with one another. Figures 15 and 16, for example, depict rock art images that have been both abraded and incised. In the Zuni-Cibola region pecked figures are most frequently solidly pecked (Figures 13, 23, 24), whereas incised figures appear mostly in outline (Figures 15, 79). Pictographs are made by using many

Figure 14. Gouged shield or mask, 1 m × 80 cm, ZRAS site 2. Photograph by Nancy L. Bartman, 1979.

Figure 15. Incised and abraded shield-bearer, 35 cm × 25 cm, ZRAS site 2. Photograph by Nancy L. Bartman, 1979.

Figure 16. Abraded and incised lizardlike figures above pecked niches, 120 cm × 180 cm, ZRAS site 2. Photograph by Nancy L. Bartman, 1979.

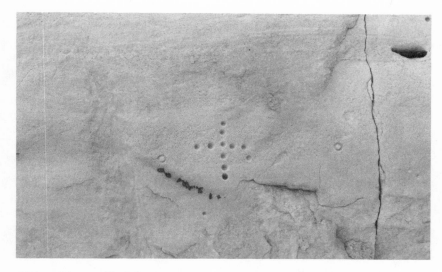

Figure 17. Drilled design, 8 cm × 7 cm, ZRAS site 11.
Photograph by Nancy L. Bartman, 1979.

kinds of brushes and drawing implements, including fingers
or hands (Figures 18, 48, 69, 70, 73–76). The splatter or "negative" design created by spraying paint or pigment around an
object is also common (Figures 29b, 52). Most of the rock art
at Zuni, especially that dating from the earliest periods, consists of engraved figures. Painted images, in contrast, appear
infrequently; perhaps because they have suffered the effects of
weathering, the earliest ones have long since disappeared.

  Rock art in the Zuni-Cibola region is either representational
or nonrepresentational in form.[5] Among representational design elements, those most commonly found include four-legged
animals, birds, insects, and human figures (Figures 26, 30, 32,

37, 38, 78, 79); nonrepresentational design elements are usually geometric forms such as spirals, zigzags, slashes, rectangles, and circles (Figures 33a, 33b, 33d, 33f, 39). Finally, there are a number of figures which, while lifelike, are also geometricized (see, for example, Figures 33c, 33e, 37c).

In describing this rock art it is difficult to make absolute or definite identifications, particularly for the older pictographs and petroglyphs. The names I give to such images are based on my own interpretation and on commentary from Zunis. As I discussed earlier, even contemporary commentary may not necessarily provide the original meaning of, or reason behind, the creation of an image over one thousand years ago. Many figures are ambiguous, perhaps intentionally so. The distinctions I make between mask and shield, human stick figure and lizard figure, animal figure and insect figure, for example, are tentative.

The Images: Size and Placement

Much of the rock art in the Zuni-Cibola area occurs near habitation sites for which archaeologists have established dates.[6] In some cases, pictographs are located on cliff faces high above ruin walls, as if they were executed from the rooftops of buildings; others, painted on rock surfaces forming the back walls of room blocks, could have been wall murals (Figure 18). Sheltered areas such as caves or places with rock overhangs are the most common locations for pictographs. In addition, one finds both pictographs and petroglyphs near spring areas, along trails leading to mesa tops, and in the vicinity of sheep camps.

The compass readings I took of individual panels within sites indicate that the rock faces on which images were painted or carved generally face south of east. Perhaps the various carvers and painters chose this orientation so that the morning sun would be behind them while they executed the artwork, avoiding the glare of sunlight in their eyes. Furthermore, sunlight would fall on rock surfaces facing the southeast during most of the day, enabling the artist to see his work more clearly

Figure 18. Red, yellow, and white painted elements (some pecked as well), 1.5 m × 3 m, ZRAS site 27. The rock art figures are located directly above a ruin, almost as if they had been painted on the back wall of a room block. Photograph by M. Jane Young, 1981.

than if the panel were most often in shadow. In the winter this orientation may have provided the carvers with the pleasant warmth of the sun on their backs. It is also noteworthy that rocks facing south, east, and west, generally have smooth surfaces as a result of the variable effects of weathering. They are, therefore, better suited for the production of petroglyphs than the surfaces of north-facing rocks, which are often deteriorated and have much more lichen because of the increased effects of moisture.[7]

In some cases the fact that rock art images "face the sun" may have ritual import similar to that apparent in other contexts. For instance, many Zunis today still face the rising sun each morning, offering prayers and sacred cornmeal; in the past, they designed certain houses with portholes or windows facing east so that the light of the rising sun would enter the house. According to Frank H. Cushing:

. . . many are the houses in Zuñi with scores on their walls or ancient plates imbedded therein, while opposite, a convenient window or small port-hole lets in the light of the rising sun, which shines but two mornings in the three hundred and sixty-five on the same place. Wonderfully reliable and ingenious are these rude systems of orientation, by which the religion, the labors, and even the pastimes of the Zuñis are regulated.[8]

In addition, Zunis generally locate the altars of ceremonial rooms in the west end of the room with the front of the altar turned toward the rising sun in the east, and they bring newborn babies outside and hold them to face the rising sun on the day they are to be named.[9] The last example illustrates the Zuni belief that the light of the sun will make newborn children into "finished beings," for prior to that moment they are still "raw."[10] This presentation to the sun is, therefore, a ritual reenactment of the travels through the four underworlds described in the origin myth and the people's subsequent "blinding" by the sunlight when they reach the surface of this world.[11]

It seems possible that the predominant southeasterly orientation of most rock art surfaces in the Zuni-Cibola area served both practical and symbolic ends. By the end of the field recording, my assistants and I could almost predict, while standing at some distance from a rocky area, which rock surfaces would contain rock art. This was in part due to the general tendency of the creators of such images to carve and paint them on rocks facing toward the southeast, but we had also learned to recognize that certain rock faces, those that were vertical and had a smooth surface with medium or dark patination (discoloration of rock surface due to weathering), almost invited rock carvings.

Vertical surfaces are not the only locations of rock art in the Zuni area. In the Hardscrabble Wash area (site 17), images are carved on horizontal rocks that lead, as if marking a trail, to the head of the petroglyph-filled canyon. At another site (site 1), a small carving on a flat rock on the ground served as a model for its replication, painted and enlarged, on the vertical rock above. Artists also commonly carved petroglyphs on the angle of two adjoining rock faces, creating the appearance of three-dimensional figures (Figures 19, 20). In most cases such images depict masks or faces.

Beyond this occasional use of specific features or contours of the rock surface, it is difficult to make any other generalizations about the placement of individual pictographs and petroglyphs, or even entire panel groupings on a rock face. There certainly is no general rule, no definitely established set of boundaries for the spatial ordering of such figures. On some panels, every available area has been used; on others, some elements are so close to the ground that the artists must have been kneeling (although, of course, the image's current relationship to the ground, due to the accumulation of mud and debris that has raised the ground surface, does not always reflect the relationship that existed at the time of its production); on still others, some figures are so high up that they are impossible to reach from the ground (Figures 21, 67). One can only speculate on how the artists produced these seemingly inaccessible images. In some cases the sites where they are located can be reached by climbing. In other cases, the artists may have constructed some kind of ladder or scaffolding. The latter is particularly likely for images painted on the high ceilings of caves.

The images range in size from the minute (for example, incised masks at site 30 are each only 5 centimeters high) to the extremely large (an incised and abraded serpent at site 11 is 6 meters long). Sometimes diminutive size must depend upon technique: the tiny masks would have been almost impossible to execute before the introduction of metal tools. Extremely large shields and masks are, in general, deeply carved or gouged (Figure 14).

The artists distorted the features of some images, giving

Figure 19. Pecked and eroded mask on corner of rock, 22 cm × 23 cm, ZRAS site 16. Photograph by Robert H. Leibman, 1980.

Figure 20. Incised and abraded figure, with antennae-like head projections, on corner of rock (note pecked niches below), 80 cm × 50 cm, ZRAS site 2. Photograph by Nancy L. Bartman, 1979.

Figure 21. Incised/gouged geometric fret design (high on rock surface), 180 cm × 40 cm, ZRAS site 11. Photograph by Nancy L. Bartman, 1979.

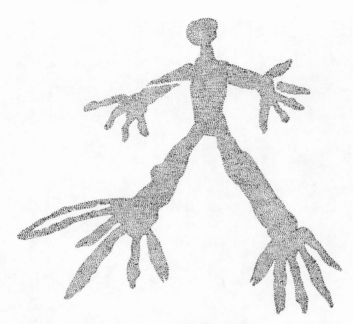

Figure 22. Black painted anthropomorphic figure (note oversized feet and hands, right hand has only four fingers), 55 cm × 40 cm, ZRAS site 3. Located about 50 cm above shield figures, Figure 36. Drawing by Murray Callahan.

them unusual size and perhaps power. The most frequent examples of such distortion are anthropomorphs with oversized hands and feet (Figure 22). As I discuss in more detail in Chapter 5, recent ethnographic work proposes that handprints and footprints served as signatures and also symbols of power for the Pueblo Indians, and by ethnographic analogy, for their predecessors as well. According to Polly Schaafsma, depictions that exceed the "realm of the ordinary" may have been intended as representations of supernatural beings or shamans.[12] Thus, rock art figures in the Zuni-Cibola region carved or painted with unusually large hands and feet may have been intended to represent such powerful beings.

Some panels consist of a grouping of several (often a considerable number of) images, all created during the same time period (Figures 23, 24, 72). Although I do not assert that such full panel groupings, most characteristic of the time period A.D. 400–1325, can be "read" as if they constituted sentences, it is likely that the rock art was indeed intended to be viewed as a whole.[13] Such panel groupings often include numerous superimpositions, but even the figures created at a later date frequently bear meaningful relationships to the earlier images on the same rock surface.

Certain pictographs and petroglyphs usually occur together or in close proximity to one another throughout the entire Zuni-Cibola region, suggesting that these are all repetitions of a common theme that, in some way, involves the juxtaposition of these images. Although the existence of such regularly co-occurring figures could be more conclusively established by means of a computer search for repeated pairs or clusters of images in the reports from all recorded panels, the enormous number of pictographs and petroglyphs makes this beyond the scope of the present work. An analysis "by hand," however, leads to some general comments concerning recurrent themes or motifs. For example, water-related figures such as frogs, toads, humpbacked fluteplayers, and spirals generally appear near one another (Figures 23, 86, 87). Animal tracks and human hand- and footprints often occur together, as do depictions of game animals, such as mountain sheep and deer. Also common is the association of certain game animals and their predators—deer and mountain lion, for example (Figure 52). Kachina figures, particularly those that are central to the same ceremonies, are often executed close to one another on the rock surface (Figures 69, 74, 76); sometimes they include the image of *Kolowisi*, the horned water serpent. This repetition of the same elements in close association may in fact relate to the function and symbolism of such images, but a conclusive statement is impossible. However, many of these themes are found in other artistic forms at Zuni as well. I point to this resonance, this repetition of certain themes, to

Figure 23. Arlen Sheyka and Robert H. Liebman in front of panel of varied pecked elements, 2 m × 350 cm, ZRAS site 1. Photograph by M. Jane Young, 1984.

suggest a relationship of some rock art to Zuni conceptions of power-invoking symbols—a topic that I discuss later with particular reference to imagery associated with water and with hunting.

One final generalization I make from my summers of recording is that pictographs and petroglyphs of the Zuni-Cibola region rarely include "literal" depictions of events, such as the detailed hunting scenes or battle scenes found in the rock art of other areas, although it is possible that some events and ceremonies are portrayed in the rock art. Some rock art figures, for instance, called forth a recitation of parts of myths and folktales and descriptions of ceremonies from Zunis; thus, the image or images seemed to stand for, rather than explicitly delineate, certain occurrences in Zuni myth and history.

Figure 24. Overview of full panel, numerous pecked elements, 220 cm × 9 m, ZRAS site 17. Photograph by Robert H. Leibman, 1980.

Description and Chronology

Although archaeologists use methods such as carbon 14 dating, pottery type, and tree-ring analysis to date sites and artifacts to within a specific time range, these methods are not directly applicable to the dating of rock art. In order to establish time frames for rock art, therefore, I have relied on the conjunction of a variety of other approaches.

While developing a relative chronology for the rock art of the Zuni region I found discussions with tribal members quite helpful in dating contemporary examples, but these conversations proved less valuable for dating older elements. For the latter, the rock art itself often provides clues for determining age. Evidence that proves useful in producing a relative chronological ordering includes: differential weathering; the superimposition of one figure over another; and the relationship of a pictograph or petroglyph to the boundaries and other physical features of the surface on which it is located or to surrounding images on the same or neighboring panels. Rock art may also be dated by reference to some already existing temporal framework. Nearby datable habitation sites, for example, suggest limits to the time period in which an image was produced. Features of style and content have also proved useful in this respect, particularly when found in the rock art of a neighboring area for which a relative chronology has already been established or in other, more datable visual art forms such as pottery, jewelry, and kiva murals.[14] Technique can also aid in dating rock art; for example, finely incised figures were most likely produced after the introduction of metal tools by the Spanish in the mid-sixteenth century.

A necessary step toward constructing a temporal framework for the rock art of the Zuni-Cibola region is the recognition and definition of various stylistic influences. I use the term "style" to refer to an overall quality of expression encompassing technique, content, and form, concurring with Schaafsma that it "signifies participation in a given ideographic system and, in turn, in a given communication network."[15] Because generally only one style or a limited range of styles pertains to a given period of a culture, style can be used as a tool to determine time and place of origin of a work of art as well as to delineate influences from surrounding groups.

Just as I have found a general temporal framework adequate for the purposes of discussing Zuni perceptions of rock art, I also find this general framework sufficient to sketch an outline of the Zuni-Cibola rock art style. As might be assumed, given the relationship discussed above between style and time period, Zuni-Cibola rock art from A.D. 400 to the present displays evident changes through time and cannot be treated as having a single style. The general stylistic distinctions that can be made, however, correspond with and inform the temporal framework discussed below. Furthermore, I am not suggesting that the Zuni-Cibola style is radically different from that of surrounding areas. It shows clear affinities with San Juan Anasazi to the northwest, Mogollon to the south, Rio Grande to the east, and Hohokam to the west; occasionally elements of more recent Navajo, Hopi, Mexican, and Anglo origin also occur in the rock art of the Zuni-Cibola region. Nevertheless, there are some distinctive elements, particular to the Zunis and their antecedents, that should be pointed out.

Most of the sites I recorded in the Zuni-Cibola area are characterized by elements so stylistically similar to those of nearby areas as to be reasonably assignable to the same time periods.[16] For example, some of the elements at the Hardscrabble Wash site (site 17, see Figure 25), also occur at a site recorded by Schaafsma approximately sixty miles south of Zuni in the Quemado area.[17] These figures are, in turn, extremely similar to those in other parts of the Southwest described by Schaafsma as "late Glen Canyon Linear style" from the Basketmaker II period. This style complex includes deeply pecked, rectilinear outline human and animal forms that are occasionally filled with horizontal or vertical hatching. Abstract geometrical figures are also common, especially wavy lines, long lines of dots, ticked lines, rakes, zigzags, and connected circles. Often a large number of these figures are crowded close together on a single rock face.[18] The primary difference between the rock art in the Zuni-Cibola and Quemado areas and that in the Glen Canyon area is the occurrence in the Zuni and Quemado regions of a number of stylistically abstract masks or heads (Figure 25).

From Basketmaker III through Pueblo III, the Zuni-Cibola rock art style appears to be a substyle of the more general Plateau Anasazi style described by Schaafsma as consisting of ". . . a wealth of solidly pecked figures which usually occur in panel groups on cliff faces."[19] Characteristic elements of the earlier part of this style complex include stick figure anthropomorphs with their arms hanging down, birds with crescent-shaped bodies, and simply rendered animal figures. There are

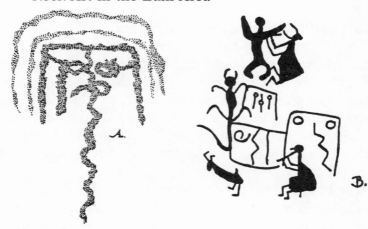

Figure 25. Pecked masks or heads, from 20 to 25 cm high, located in chamber at head of canyon, ZRAS site 17. Figure 25a has pecked arcs above the head that may indicate hair. Fluteplayers and insect figures surround and are superimposed upon masks in Figure 25b. Drawings from slides: (A) by Murray Callahan; (B) by M. Jane Young.

fewer abstract elements, but forms such as wavy lines, concentric circles, and simple dots and spirals do occur. According to Schaafsma, the later part of this period is characterized by a "general interest in formal patterns, and, to this end, a tightening of form."[20] The human figure in this later period is smaller in size and is frequently portrayed as a highly formalized rectilinear stick figure with arms held up as well as down. A greater number of abstract designs appear, and geometric designs resemble those from pottery and textiles. There are large numbers of mountain sheep, handprints, and sandal tracks. A long-tailed animal resembling a mountain lion also has wide distribution, and the ambiguous lizard-man figure emerges as an important element. In contrast to the earlier part of this period, in later depictions the fluteplayer is both humpbacked and phallic. All of these elements, characteristic of the Plateau Anasazi style complex, occur in the rock art of the Zuni-Cibola area during the same time period.

As described below, the Rio Grande style began to influence the rock art of the Zuni-Cibola region around A.D. 1325.[21] More representational human and animal figures as well as kachina figures and shields are usually attributed to this new style complex. Furthermore, the techniques of incising and abrading occur with greater frequency, particularly after the mid-1500s when the Spaniards introduced metal tools. Characteristics that link the rock art created during this time in the Zuni-Cibola area to that of surrounding areas include the large, deeply gouged shields or mask figures (Figure 14), the elaborate, sometimes fringed, rectangular designs ("rug and blanket designs," Figure 39), and the plethora of ceremonial and kachina figures and masks (Figures 26b, 26c, 26d, 26e, 34, 35).[22] Rock art of the Zuni-Cibola region is distinctive, however, because of the large number of full-figure kachina dancers and kachina masks depicting figures specific to Zuni religion that occur after A.D. 1325, both as petroglyphs and as pictographs (Figures 26c, 35e, 69, 70, 73–76, 80). In addition, this rock art contains a number of figures that are very similar to those typical of Zuni pottery, such as images of Kolowisi, deer with heart lines, tadpoles, dragonflies, horned toads, and cloud altars (Figures 37d, 49, 50, 51, 52, 56, 63, 74j, 86, 87).[23]

In sum, although some of the rock art at Zuni is characterized by culture-specific figures and themes, like modern Zuni culture it reflects communication networks and contacts—a participation in the broader Pueblo spectrum.[24] On the basis of changes in style, technique, and content, I have established the following general temporal framework for the rock art of the Zuni-Cibola region.

The first period, prior to A.D. 400, is primarily represented by elements that are abstract in style (rare in the Zuni-Cibola region), including wavy lines (meanders), circle chains, rakes, and mask- or headlike rectangular forms with circles, lines, and zigzags inside. The early date is suggested partly because these elements are similar to those classified as Basketmaker

II for surrounding areas. This rock art, which includes perhaps the earliest depictions of masks/heads in this region, occurs in part of a mile-long canyon west of Zuni Pueblo in Arizona's Hardscrabble Wash district (site 17). The site itself plays an important role in Zuni mythology and has been linked to Zuni by archaeological studies of the area.

The oldest rock art at this site is found at the head of the canyon and is characterized by the repeated occurrence of many stylistically similar masks or disembodied heads (Figure 25).[25] Thirteen of these figures, ranging from twenty to twenty-five centimeters in height, are found within an area approximately thirty-four meters in length. As a result of the protection of the cavelike shelter, the images remain visible despite their great antiquity. Some of them are, however, heavily patinated and it is possible that even more such depictions, as yet undetected, occur in this area. The masks/heads exist on closely adjoining panels, and, in some cases, even on the same panel. They and most other elements at this site were produced almost entirely by pecking. Later superimposition of more lightly patinated forms such as Anasazi style fluteplayers (i.e., humpbacked and sometime phallic), insects, quadrupeds, and anthropomorphs over several of the masks is further evidence of their early date.

The period from A.D. *400 to 1325* (Basketmaker III–Pueblo III) is often divided into finer segments, but that is not relevant to the present discussion. Most of the figures dating from this time are solidly pecked and often form panel groupings on cliff faces (Figures 23, 24, 72).[26] Characteristic anthropomorphic figures are stick figures with slightly rectangular bodies, small heads, and sometimes feathered headdresses (Figures 23, 26a, 26g). Although some types of anthropomorphs are depicted with their arms raised or lowered, others have arms and legs bent in an attitude of motion. Hand-holding pairs and figures in rows also occur (Figure 27).

The fluteplayer is a common design element during both this and the following time period, appearing in human, animal, and insect form (Figures 23, 25b, 28, 86). Frequent attri-

Figure 26. Human figures: (A) pecked, 30 cm × 20 cm, ZRAS site 17; (B) incised, 25 cm × 15 cm, ZRAS site 2; (C) incised, 50 cm × 25 cm, ZRAS site 2; (D) pecked, 60 cm × 35 cm, ZRAS site 5; (E) incised, 35 cm × 20 cm, ZRAS site 2; (F) pecked 25 cm × 15 cm, ZRAS site 11; (G) human figures from several sites. Drawings by Murray Callahan.

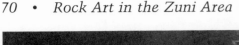

Figure 27. Pecked elements, including lines of figures holding hands, 80 cm × 95 cm, part of panel in cave area, ZRAS site 17. Photograph by M. Jane Young, 1980.

butes are a prominent phallus, hump, flute, and sometimes projections from the head.[27] Some of the fluteplayers at the Hardscrabble Wash site have triangular humps with interior designs (Figure 28b). In general, these figures are seated or reclining, sometimes with legs kicking in the air.

Human handprints and footprints occur during this period, as well as in the later time period, demonstrating a variety of techniques (Figure 29). They are generally painted (some are negative prints) or solidly pecked. Elaborately patterned handprints and sandal prints occur at the Hardscrabble Wash site.

Mountain sheep are the animal figures perhaps most characteristic of this time period (Figures 23, 30, 67, 68). They are depicted singly, as well as in rows so that they appear to be running one after another. Their bodies range from rectangular to crescent-shaped with straight legs, curved horns, and some-

Figure 28. Humpbacked fluteplayers. All pecked and from ZRAS site 17: (A) 45 cm × 30 cm; (B) 30 cm × 23 cm; (C) 50 cm × 35 cm; (D) 12 cm × 9 cm. Drawings by Murray Callahan.

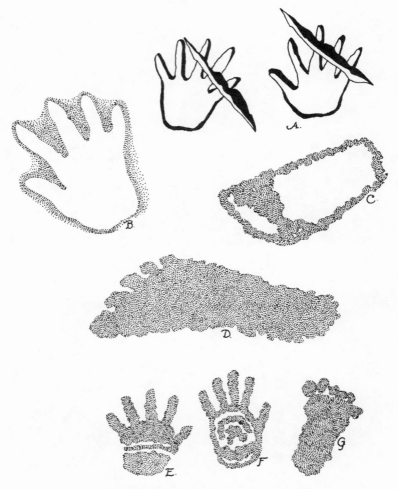

Figure 29. Handprints and footprints: (A) incised, 15 cm × 30 cm, ZRAS site 12; (B) "negative" print (red), 22 cm × 19 cm, ZRAS site 2; (C) pecked, 15 cm × 25 cm, ZRAS site 17; (D) pecked, 12 cm × 25 cm, ZRAS site 17; (E) pecked, 17 cm × 15 cm, ZRAS site 17; (F) pecked, 19 cm × 12 cm, ZRAS site 17; (G) pecked, 20 cm × 13 cm, ZRAS site 17. Drawings by Murray Callahan.

Figure 30. Mountain sheep, all pecked. The body of figure 30c has been pierced by a pecked spear or atlatl: (A) 20 cm × 30 cm, ZRAS site 19; (B) 45 cm × 40 cm, ZRAS site 19; (C) 25 cm × 17 cm, ZRAS site 17; (D) 15 cm × 35 cm, ZRAS site 20. Drawings by Murray Callahan.

times hooves. Occasionally they display interior body decoration, particularly with a geometrical design. Spears or arrows often project from bodies of mountain sheep, indicative perhaps of a wish for success in the hunt (Figure 30c). At some sites these figures have been riddled with bullet holes (Figure 68).[28] Other animals represented include images of deer, generally small and stiffly portrayed. However, several larger deer figures with rounded bodies and clearly defined antlers do occur. Animals with long tails bent over their bodies (often identified as mountain lions) are also particularly prevalent (Figure 72).

As with handprints, it is possible that the frequently carved animal and bird tracks also serve as a signature—perhaps representative of particular clans. Among the tracks identified by Zunis are those of deer, bear, coyote, mountain lion, and wolf. They typically identify bird tracks as turkey or crane. Deer tracks often frame other elements as though the animal walked around the design; this may indicate a symbolic or mythic function, rather than the depiction of a clan animal. Animal tracks occur in the greatest numbers at the Hardscrabble Wash site (Figure 31). Although their tracks appear repeatedly, full bird figures are not so common. When they do occur, they are usually small with crescent-shaped bodies and stiff legs.

Other popular elements include lizard figures (often with their legs straight out from their bodies), snakes (sometimes horned), and horned toads (Figures 13, 23, 86, 87). Among insects, pecked centipedes are the most recurrent and easily identifiable (Figure 32c). Corn plants are rare, but at one site (site 16) they appear to be anthropomorphic, with humanlike heads instead of tassels.[29] Complex geometric designs, spirals (Figures 33a, 33f, 87), concentric circles (Figure 57), and wavy lines also characterize this rock art. Most of the figures of this time period are solidly pecked.

From around A.D. 1325 to the present the Rio Grande style had considerable impact on the rock art of the Zuni-Cibola region, although elements of the older Anasazi influence re-

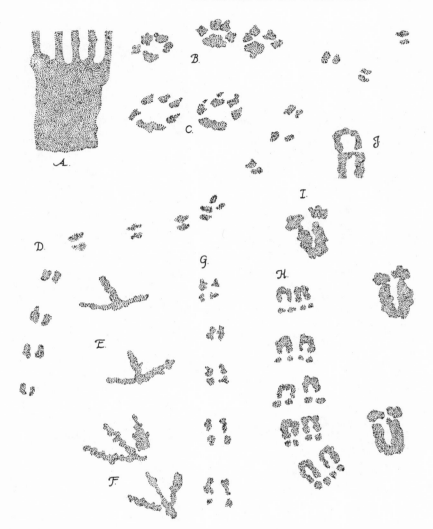

Figure 31. Animal tracks, all pecked and from ZRAS site 17: (A) bear track, 17 cm × 12 cm; (B) mountain lion tracks, 7 cm × 8 cm; (C) coyote tracks, 9 cm × 10 cm; (D) rabbit tracks, 4 cm × 5 cm; (E) crane tracks, 7 cm × 9 cm; (F) turkey tracks, 5 cm × 5 cm; (G) deer tracks, 5 cm × 6 cm; (H) deer tracks (stylized), 5 cm × 8 cm; (I) elk tracks (stylized), 9 cm × 5 cm; (J) mountain sheep tracks, 9 cm × 5 cm. Drawings by Murray Callahan.

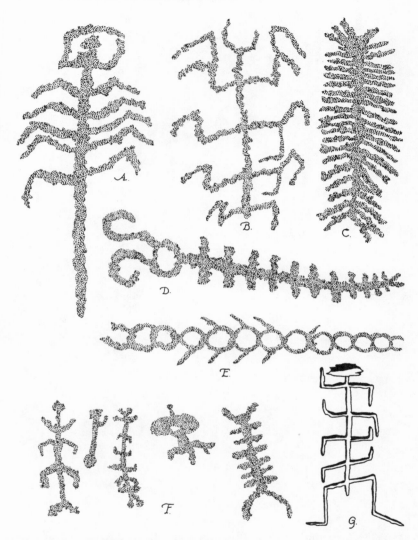

Figure 32. Insect figures: (A) pecked, 41 cm × 20 cm, ZRAS site 17; (B) pecked scorpion, 50 cm × 35 cm, ZRAS site 9; (C) pecked centipede, 30 cm × 10 cm, ZRAS site 17; (D) pecked, 15 cm × 50 cm, ZRAS site 19; (E) pecked, 17 cm × 110 cm, ZRAS site 5; (F) pecked red ants and other stinging insects, 50 cm × 70 cm, ZRAS site 1; (G) incised, 25 cm × 13 cm, ZRAS site 11. Drawings by Murray Callahan.

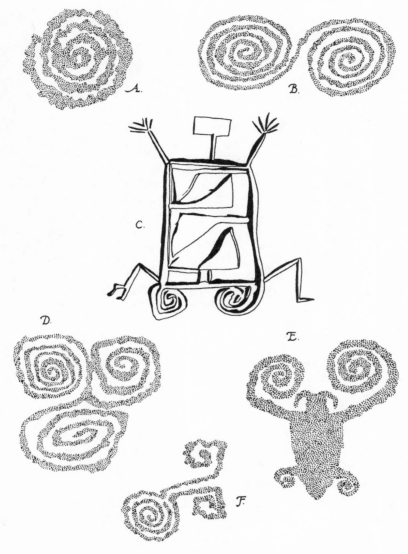

Figure 33. Spiral figures: (A) pecked, 30 cm × 30 cm, ZRAS site 1; (B) pecked, 25 cm × 50 cm, ZRAS site 11; (C) abraded and incised, 50 cm × 30 cm, ZRAS site 11; (D) pecked, 30 cm × 30 cm, ZRAS site 11; (E) pecked and abraded, 60 cm × 50 cm, ZRAS site 10; (F) pecked, 30 cm × 30 cm, ZRAS site 1. Drawings by Murray Callahan.

Figure 34. Incised kachina figures and masks. This section of the panel is approximately 50 cm × 60 cm, ZRAS site 21. Photograph by Robert H. Leibman, 1981.

mained.[30] This new artistic tradition brought with it increasingly representational human and animal forms, as well as kachina figures, masks, and shields (Figures 34, 36, 69, 74). In contrast to the deeply pecked images of earlier periods, the predominant techniques of this time period are incising, abrading, and drilling, as well as some lighter pecking.

Although human stick figures are still produced during this period, most depictions of the human form have fuller, rounded or rectangular bodies, explicitly depicted fingers, arms raised at the elbow, and legs bent at the knees. There are also a number of human figures with oversized hands and feet (Figure 22). Particularly characteristic of this period are representations of kachinas, especially the *Shalako* kachina (Figures 26c, 35e, 69d, 80), *Koyemshi* (perhaps depicted in Figures 26f, 60), and dancers (Figures 26b, 26e, 34, 69, 74). Figures with obvious headdresses or masks are also common. While most of these kachina figures have been incised rather than pecked, those few kachina images (especially depictions of *Shalako*) that were pecked suggest by their style, content, and degree of patination that they, too, were made after A.D. 1325. Flute-players continue to be depicted in this period, but generally with a more rectangular body and rounded hump than in earlier times.

Square and circular mask forms are also prevalent, some appearing in elaborate detail (Figures 35b–35g). At several different sites masks are carved on the angle of two adjoining rock faces, giving them a three-dimensional appearance (Figures 19, 20). Also of interest is a series of masks at the site near *Kyaki:ma* (site 2) that occur on five adjacent panels at approximately right angles to one another. While the masks themselves are each relegated to single rock faces, a horizontal line cut with vertical slashes runs the entire length of the five panels, linking them together. These masks, most often symmetrical about a central vertical axis (Figure 14), are abraded and deeply incised in a way that, especially in the early morning and late afternoon sunlight, accentuates their design.

Circular shields are frequently depicted in Southwestern rock art and kiva murals of this time period. Although when first introduced to the Southwest shields were primarily used for defensive purposes, shortly thereafter they acquired a greater ceremonial importance; there is ritual symbolism on a number of the shields in rock art and in kiva murals that date from after the thirteenth century.[31] Designs on Zuni area shields, for example, include plantlike depictions (Figure 36). In this book I define a shield as a circular image without distinctive facial features, thus distinguishing it from a mask. Striking examples of carved or painted shields occur in the Zuni region. At the site near *Kyaki:ma* (site 2) there are a number of elaborately incised shields and at least one shield-bearer—that is, an anthropomorphic figure holding a shield in front of his body (Figure 15). Shields also appear on the flat side of a prominent stone monolith on the northern face of *Dowa Yalanne*

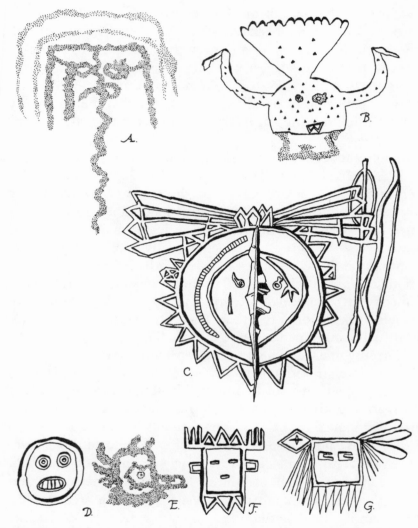

Figure 35. Masks: (A) pecked, 20 cm × 15 cm, ZRAS site 17; (B) abraded and pecked, 50 cm × 60 cm, ZRAS site 11; (C) incised and abraded, 25 cm × 35 cm, ZRAS site 16; (D) incised, 23 cm × 21 cm, ZRAS site 2; (E) pecked Shalako mask, 20 cm × 15 cm, ZRAS site 8; (F) incised, 35 cm × 30 cm, ZRAS site 10; (G) incised, 25 cm × 40 cm, ZRAS site 11. Drawings by Murray Callahan.

Figure 36. Abraded, incised, and painted shields (one with an animal's head), a snake-like figure, and an animal with its tail bent over its body, 85 cm × 80 cm (dimensions of shield to left), ZRAS site 3. Drawing by Murray Callahan.

(Figure 36). Close examination shows that these shields were abraded and painted, then later reabraded and incised. One of these shields has the same design motif as that of three shields recorded near Albuquerque: two are rock art depictions, the other is a kiva mural.[32]

Handprints and footprints occur in this period as well as in the earlier one. At the site near *Kyaki:ma* there is a negative handprint in red (Figure 29b). The Pescado area (site 5) exhibits handprints in a variety of colors: yellow, white, and lavender. The latter are impressions rather than paintings; the artists covered their hands with paint and then pressed them firmly against the rock surface.

Of note is the general absence of mountain sheep among the animals depicted within this style complex. Animals with their tails bent over their bodies, however, continue to appear

(Figures 36, 37a, 37b, 62). Deer, antelope, and rabbits are frequent and are usually carved in profile. In many cases the deer has a "heart line" from its mouth to its interior (Figure 37d, 74j); in pictographs the heart line is generally red. Similar depictions of deer with heart lines are also found on Zuni pottery water jars (Figure 63). The heart line is a symbolic representation of the source or "breath" of the animal's life.[33] In the rock art, arrows sometimes project from the bodies of the deer as if they had penetrated the heart portrayed at the end of this line (Figure 66). Sometimes pictographs and petroglyphs of bears and horned or plumed serpents also have heart lines. Since horses were introduced to the Southwest by the Spaniards, depictions of horses, generally running and sometimes with riders, clearly date from after the Spanish Conquest. At one site there is a finely incised horse with two tails (perhaps indicative of a moving tail). Rock art images of brands, which appear on horses and cows and also separately, can be useful tools for dating, since ranchers often have records that tell when certain brands were used (Figure 78b).

Animal tracks occur with less frequency than during the earlier period, but various types of bird figures are now found more often (Figure 38). Birds are carved and painted in both profile and frontal view. Most common is a bird with fringe-like wing and tail feathers (Figures 38b, 38c). Several Zunis have suggested that this figure represents the Zuni Beast God of the zenith, variously identified as eagle or 'Achiyalataba ("Knife-Wing").[34] Some bird figures have the long legs characteristic of wading birds; others are distinguished by several long tail feathers (Figures 38a, 38f). An unusual panel at Petroglyph Canyon (site 11) consists of a turkey and a two-headed bird (Figure 38d). Other common elements include crosses (often outlined), stars, crescents, cloud-altar shapes, insects, and snakes. Stars are usually four-pointed, but five- and six-pointed stars also occur.

Concentric circles, spirals, wavy lines, and frets are typical geometric designs. Spirals appear alone or in joined pairs. At several sites spirals form the hands or feet of human and an-

Figure 37. Animal figures: (A) incised and abraded mountain lion, 25 cm × 50 cm, ZRAS site 2; (B) incised and abraded scorpion, 23 cm × 33 cm, ZRAS site 11; (C) painted (white) geometricized animal figure, 20 cm × 40 cm, ZRAS site 15; (D) incised deer with heart line, 15 cm × 20 cm, ZRAS site 10. Drawings by Murray Callahan.

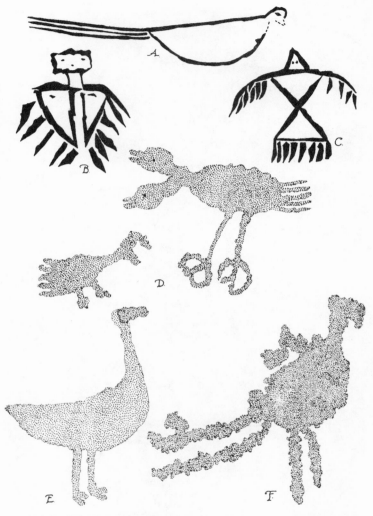

Figure 38. Birds: (A) incised macaw, 15 cm × 55 cm, ZRAS site 11; (B) incised image of Knife-Wing, 15 cm × 14 cm, ZRAS site 2; (C) incised image of Knife-Wing, 15 cm × 16 cm, ZRAS site 2; (D) pecked turkey and two-headed bird, 33 cm × 60 cm, ZRAS site 11; (E) pecked wading bird, 40 cm × 30 cm, ZRAS site 20; (F) pecked macaw or parrot, 25 cm × 27 cm, ZRAS site 17. Drawings by Murray Callahan.

imal figures (Figures 33c, 33e). Rows of diamond designs are common at the site near Pescado Springs (site 5), in one case constituting the body of a human figure. Complex geometric rectangular designs, perhaps pottery and blanket designs, are also particularly prevalent (Figures 39b, 39c).

Deeply incised gouges or slashes occur most often near temporary sheep camps dated to the 1700s. The arrangement of some of these slashes in a seemingly ordered sequence would support the hypothesis that these were counting devices. Other gouges, however, have an extremely random appearance, suggesting an activity such as the sharpening of metal tools.

Contemporary Rock Art. Tribal members and others continue to create rock paintings and engravings around Zuni Pueblo. The rock art produced in the past one hundred years or so reflects both a continuation of earlier styles and the impact of Western graphic art, as for example in the use of three-quarter frontal perspective, foreshortening, and shading to create the illusion of three-dimensional, dynamic form (see, for example, the *Shalako* kachina in Figure 69d). Predominant techniques are painting, with a wide variety of colors, and incising. Modern tools make it possible to execute elaborate detail with more ease than in earlier times. Full figures are often highly representational and executed with great detail (see, for example, Figure 78c). The most frequent animal figures are horses, cattle, and deer, sometimes shown in motion. Generally they are portrayed with rounded bodies, flexible legs, and an overall "fluid" form (Figures 78, 79). These figures are usually carved in profile, sometimes with the head turned to give a three-quarter view. Recent elements also include names, initials, and dates, which are generally scratched, incised, chalked, and painted (Figures 82, 83). Sometimes they are carved on top of older elements, obliterating the designs beneath.

Thus, the engravings and paintings on cliff faces surrounding the Pueblo of Zuni represent a tradition that dates from before A.D. 400 and continues to the present day.[35] This rock art displays considerable variation in style, technique, and subject matter, ranging from the elaborate shields, masks, deer, insects, kachina dancers, and geometric designs depicted on rock outcrops near old occupation sites to the more recent spray-painted names, dates, and initials on boulders along Highway 53. My particular focus here will be on those images in the rock art that contemporary Zunis regard as myth-evoking, power-invoking, or, simply, beautiful; many of these images appear in other Zuni artistic forms as well. Such images are often linked with the predominant theme of Zuni ritual life: the desire for increase, whether it be rain for the crops, success in the hunt, many children, or a long life.

Contemporary Zuni Perceptions of Rock Art

During my fieldwork at Zuni I not only documented the actual rock art images and compiled a variety of other data concerning the sites but also began seeking Zuni commentary on these images and their possible meanings.[36] I was particularly interested in eliciting categories of related images and, to this end, asked Zunis to sort cards bearing rock art figures into groups of images that seemed to "go together."[37] When the sorting was finished I asked my Zuni colleagues to identify the individual images and to label each group or to explain why they had put those particular images together. In response they often referred to distinguishing features also associated with the graphic depiction of these same images in such other media as fetishes and pottery designs. Mountain lions, for example, were the animals with tails bent over their bodies; turkeys had clustered tail feathers; and kachinas wore dance kilts and had feathers on their heads.

Sometimes those who participated in the card-sorting experiment were able to name or describe the category to which figures in a particular group or pile belonged, as, for example, "images that go on pottery"; at other times they could only say that "they seem to go together," and some groups simply consisted of those elements that were unknown or anomalous. Individual Zunis varied considerably with respect to the num-

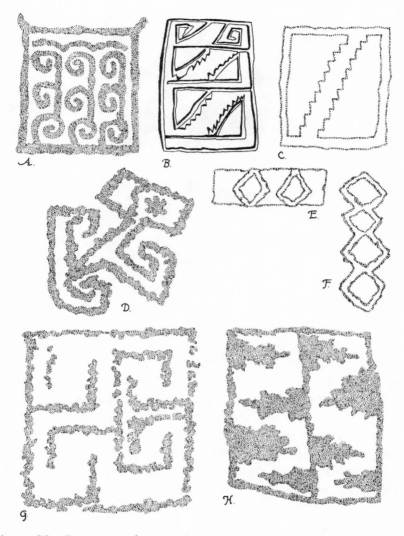

Figure 39. Geometric designs: (A) pecked, 45 cm × 40 cm, ZRAS site 19; (B) incised, 60 cm × 40 cm, ZRAS site 11; (C) pecked, 75 cm × 60 cm, ZRAS site 5; (D) pecked, 25 cm × 17 cm, ZRAS site 17; (E) pecked, 15 cm × 40 cm, ZRAS site 5; (F) pecked, 45 cm × 15 cm, ZRAS site 5; (G) pecked, 40 cm × 35 cm, ZRAS site 20; (H) pecked, 25 cm × 17 cm, ZRAS site 20. Drawings by Murray Callahan.

Figure 40. Deer figure used in card-sorting. Abraded and incised, 15 cm × 13 cm, ZRAS site 2. Drawing by M. Jane Young.

ber of groups they created, their criteria for grouping figures, and the size of their category of unknowns. For example, an elderly man once active in tribal civil affairs and the descendant of famous tribal chiefs had only two categories: images that he knew and regarded, in some sense, as "well-formed" and images that were either unknown or, although quite recognizable to him, in some way or other "not complete." For example, he said that Figure 40, a card in the animal category, was a deer, but that it was not complete because the antlers had not been finished. Similarly, he said that Figure 41, a card in the anthropomorph category, would be a man except that the hands were not finished: "one hand has four fingers and the other only has three." Three young women potters (student potters) focused primarily on those animal figures that might be found on pottery, leaving the rest to form a single large category of unknowns, which contained the majority of the images. Another young woman potter, to the contrary, made numerous groups of a few images each and found no figure

Figure 41. Anthropomorphic figure holding staff, used in card-sorting. Incised, 25 cm × 12 cm, ZRAS site 11. Drawing by M. Jane Young.

for which she could not provide some sort of interpretation. An elderly and quite famous woman potter had no category of unknowns, nor even a single unknown figure; she did have many divisions for each major stack. Although she identified certain images as "those that go on pottery," she most frequently responded by telling a story or reciting part of a myth, thus locating that image in the corpus of Zuni mythology and folktales. One well-known and well-educated painter divided figures by time period, such as "contemporary images" and "old images," and by their corresponding style, for example, "having primitive characteristics." Another painter examined the cards over and over again, deliberating carefully on those that he grouped together and often changing such groupings after he had thought about them for a while. His sorting thus had a "fluidity" as he returned to groups and changed their composition upon further reflection. This man also said that certain rock art depictions, generally painted images that were not in the card-sorting categories but that he remembered from his childhood, had been painted by his father, a noted mural and mask painter. Three fetish makers all divided the animal category into "those that could be made into fetishes," whereas their major identifications of the anthropomorphs were as kachinas or unknowns. Several of the older men, in particular the religious leaders, identified specific kachinas in the anthropomorph category, and predators (or Beast Gods) and game animals (deer and mountain sheep) in the animal category.

Such varied approaches to rock art imagery reflect individual interests and, in some cases, diverse artistic pursuits. Some of the potters, for instance, clustered figures according to the way they might be organized into a pattern on Zuni pottery, while some fetish makers created categories according to what could or could not be made into a fetish. An analysis of all of the clusters together reveals a strong thread of individualism (idiosyncratic interpretations) and an inclination to relate rock art to Zuni religion and the important concerns of daily life. Over fifty years ago Ruth Bunzel came to a similar conclusion regarding the identifications Zuni potters made of pottery designs. She sums up the various responses as "the tendency at Zuni to invariably associate decorative designs with ideas of a religious character," and adds that this "is not a personal peculiarity of one woman, but is a general pattern of Zuni thought."[38] At the same time, however, Bunzel found a high degree of individual variation in identifications of all but the most representational of pottery designs. While no one disagreed on what constituted a deer, the more abstract and geometrical designs that might be flowers, different types of clouds, lightning, wind, rain, and so on, gave rise to a variety of interpretations, even from one woman who interpreted them twice over a period of one year. Bunzel concluded from this: "The same name is applied to designs having no objective resemblance; the same design is differently named by different individuals, and by the same individual at different times."[39] This lack of correspondence in naming designs led her to suggest that Zunis do not generally explicitly name designs, and that they experience such images as sensual rather than intellectual phenomena.[40] While this may be so, one should not overlook the fact that Bunzel was working through an interpreter, in many cases asking women who did not speak English fluently to name designs in Zuni that the interpreter would then translate into English. Some of the variation in names for designs may have been due simply to the problem of rendering concise Zuni meanings into equally concise English meanings.

Certainly the Zunis with whom I worked often found it difficult to render their identifications of rock art imagery into English; fortunately, my knowledge of the Zuni language made it possible for me to understand the Zuni terminology in such cases. But even this situation doesn't change the fact that while Zunis may *recognize* designs in pottery, religious paraphernalia, or rock art, they may have no culturally consistent terminology to apply to such designs—there may be no tradition of *naming* the designs. Variation applies to more than just the names of images. The differing Zuni responses to rock art suggest that a diversity of practices, purposes, and meanings applies to this particular medium of expression. This leads me to hypothesize that, within the panoply of forms of Zuni aesthetic activity and expression, the strictly memorized texts of ritual prayers constitute one pole, which in ideal terms is invariable, while the creation and identification of rock art figures constitute another pole characterized by "the organization of diversity."[41] This is entirely in keeping with the location of ritual at the center of the physical community of Zuni and of rock art at the periphery. While no individual could alone undertake to perform a ceremony, an individual could alone undertake to bring rock art into being.

My Zuni colleagues reached nearly unanimous agreement on some images, especially those identified as deer, mountain sheep, and certain specific kachinas. Their identifications of others varied much more, and most found some images they simply couldn't identify. Even my categories of "human" and "animal" were not inviolable. Occasionally Zunis would identify a "human" image as an "animal" or vice versa, and less frequently they would identify some image in one or the other category as a plant, insect, prayer stick, altar, or design. Zunis tended to group animals according to content (e.g., there were groups of deer, mountain sheep, birds, Beast Gods, and "animals that go on pottery"). However, with certain exceptions, they grouped human figures on the basis of form (e.g., round bodies, simple bodies, solid figures, and outlined figures). This may reflect the fact that with the exception of kachinas, human figures, unlike animal figures, rarely appear in any of the other Zuni art forms. Consequently, they may be less recognizable as specific beings.[42] It might, therefore, be more accurate to say that while Zunis grouped and labeled *known* images by content, they grouped *unknowns* by form. Furthermore, according to the general chronological framework I developed, many of the unknown depictions are from the older Anasazi rock art tradition, dating prior to A.D. 1325. The known images, on the other hand, tend to be from the more recent Rio Grande tradition characterized by more representational animal and human figures as well as kachina figures and masks. With the exception of certain highly representational figures such as fluteplayers, deer, and mountain sheep, Zunis were generally unable to identify older Anasazi pictographs and petroglyphs. In the card-sorting experiment these images often constituted a residual category of unknowns. Of particular interest to me was the way that the Zunis often related rock art images to various facets of their religious practice and/or to the myths describing the emergence of the Zuni people into this world.

3

Zuni Cosmology
and Cultural Symbolism

During the part of my fieldwork that focused on the interpretations the Zunis offered for various rock art images surrounding their pueblo, I found that certain visual images evoked
similar and sometimes formulaic verbal responses. My attempt to understand the reasons for this evocation has led to
a more general consideration of the relationship between verbal and visual communicative codes among the Zuni. The
research conducted by Claire Farrer and Barbara Tedlock in
the American Southwest, as well as Nancy Munn's studies in
central Australia, have been of particular importance to this
endeavor.[1] Farrer posits an underlying metaphor involving the
principles of balance, circularity, directionality, and the number four as the organizing basis for much of Mescalero Apache
life and ritual. This base metaphor in turn generates verbal
and visual metaphors described by the Mescalero as "the same
thing." This is the same phrase that Munn uses to describe
the Walbiri practice of representing "different-meaning items"
with one graphic element; these items are "the same thing"
and together they form one complex entity.[2] Tedlock regards
Zuni expressive forms, whether they be visual forms such as
pottery, or verbal forms, such as rain-dance songs, as integral
to an aesthetic system that is characterized by two principles:

"the beautiful" and "the dangerous." Rather than describe the two as purely oppositional or mutually exclusive, Tedlock suggests that one may be incorporated in the other: ever since the time of the beginning when the choices that determined these principles were made, "the beautiful has had the dangerous somewhere near or even bursting into the midst of it."[3] Taken together, these analytic frameworks contribute to an understanding of the rules or cultural categories underlying Zuni artistic behavior. Although based on investigations of somewhat different phenomena among different peoples, these hypotheses need not be regarded as opposing or contradictory. Indeed, it seems that the two characteristic aesthetic qualities discerned by Tedlock operate within an overall framework of cultural symbolism similar to that described by Munn and encompassing the same sort of principles as those delineated by Farrer—balance, circularity, and directionality.

The rich ethnographic record compiled by scholars studying the Zunis over the last one hundred years is valuable to those of us who are conducting research with contemporary Zunis: their high degree of cultural continuity makes it possible for us to develop new hypotheses while at the same time complementing our research with data collected by earlier scholars. Although there is no doubt that my own work at Zuni has been influenced by my interest in Native American astronomy (thus I offer a somewhat different perspective than that of other scholars investigating the same culture), it is nevertheless a perspective that is quite consonant with earlier results, a "working hypothesis" that fits with other lines of evidence.[4]

In the past twenty years or so, knowledge of indigenous astronomical systems has become increasingly important in studies of Native American cultures. A number of scholars are discovering that for certain groups, cultural perceptions and ways of organizing the world are greatly influenced by, perhaps even derived from, native perceptions of cosmological phenomena. For instance both Gary Urton, who recently conducted fieldwork in Peru among the Quechua-speaking occupants of Misminay, and Von Del Chamberlain, who studied ethnohistorical records of the Skidi Pawnee, found that these respective peoples perceive the celestial and terrestrial spheres as patterned after one another: the Skidi Pawnee sometimes arranged their villages to mirror the groupings of stars in the sky, while the people of Misminay construct canals and footpaths to reflect the intersecting axes of the Milky Way.[5] Furthermore, the Skidi regarded themselves as literally conceived by the stars and developed a complex star theology that became the pattern for all other aspects of Skidi life—political hierarchy, village layout, agricultural practices, socio-religious activities, and the embellishment of material culture. Similarly, the people of Misminay organize their world so that every terrestrial object is a counterpart of one in the sky, establishing a one-to-one correspondence; they incorporate not just the stars, but all observable celestial phenomena into this scheme.

Directionality as a Conceptual Model for Zuni Expressive Behavior

Research such as that discussed above, as well as my own fieldwork, suggests that one way to make entrance to the Zuni culture is to investigate the hypothesis that their cosmological outlook—that is, their perceptions of the motions of the sun, moon, and stars, as well as concepts of time and space—form an organizing principle for much of their expressive behavior. These ideas about the cosmos contribute to the way in which Zunis respond to graphic forms such as certain rock art images, whether or not those graphic forms themselves refer explicitly to cosmological phenomena. I suggest that the order apparent in the cosmos acts as a paradigm for the Zunis, a model for conceptually ordering their verbal and visual art. They do not, however, consider all cosmological phenomena to be equally important in this respect; as is common with agriculturalists, the Zunis devote most of their attention to the apparent recurrent motion of the sun. The preeminent position of "Our

Father the Sun" in Zuni thought is illustrated by the fact that the Zuni word for "life," *tek'ohannanne,* is the same as the word for "daylight."

The Zunis appoint an officer whose main function is to watch the sun's daily points of rising and setting from a special sun-watching station and to announce the times for events—he is, therefore, the keeper of the calendar.[6] This does not imply, however, that the other members of the pueblo pay no attention to the sun. Incidents are known in which the sun watcher erred and the other townspeople ably corrected him.[7] Every member of the community prays to the Sun Father each morning as he rises in the east. They believe that when the sun rises he inspects the character of the prayers and offerings addressed to him and takes them with him when he goes in the evening to his home in the west. To keep track of the sun's motion, the Zunis have constructed certain buildings in the pueblo so that the sun shines through windows or port-holes at calendrically significant times of the year. Frequently they embed markers in the walls to act as indicators of these events; often the events so recorded are the solstices.[8]

Although the Zunis note the sun's daily motion—its rise and set positions along the horizon—with keen interest, it is the yearly motion of the sun that forms the conceptual model that I discuss here. Zunis regard the extreme "swings" of this annual cycle—the winter and summer solstice rise and set positions—as the most critical times of the year, for it is then that the sun appears to stand still for four days during his journey along the horizon. To encourage "Our Father the Sun" to move again, particularly to assure that he turns around and continues his journey back along the horizon, the Zunis perform complex and vitally important rituals. The most elaborate of these occurs at the winter solstice when the sun is at its southward pause, perhaps because if the sun did not move northward again the fields would stay frozen and unsuitable for planting. The ceremony occurring at this time marks the beginning of the calendrical year and the cycle of ritual performances for the Zunis. The summer solstice ceremony is an abbreviated version of the winter solstice ceremony. A practical explanation of this is that during the summer months much agricultural work needs to be done, whereas in the winter the agriculturalist is unemployed with ground working and has time to devote to more extensive ritual activities. But the symbolic value with which the Zunis imbue the time of the winter solstice indicates that there are reasons other than sheer pragmatism for its prominence.

The apparent annual motion of the sun along the horizon serves to divide the Zuni year into two parts, each lasting for six months and each beginning when the sun reaches the solstice position and turns around. The winter and summer solstice ceremonies that occur at this time are both called *'itiwana* (the Center), although it is the winter solstice that marks the starting point of the new year cycle. In a kind of symbolic economy, the Zunis repeat the names of the months so that the first month of the winter season has the same name as the first month of the summer season, and so on, counting only six names in all. Winter and summer are thus more than complementary; they are reflections of one another. Nevertheless, distinctive ceremonies and activities characterize each half of the year. There are, for instance, a winter cycle and a summer cycle of ritual dances; certain narratives may be related in the winter but not the summer, and so on. These examples illustrate that the idea of duality or balance is important in Zuni thought, a duality that is expressed in dichotomous terms such as: morning/evening (sunrise/sunset), summer/winter, above/below. Although I have focused on the yearly motion of the sun, it is of further note that the Zunis consider the Sun Father to have two houses that he visits in the course of his daily journey: one in the eastern ocean and one in the western ocean. They associate this morning/evening duality with two deities who play a central role in the Zuni origin myth: the Twin War Gods. They are sons of the Sun, the Morning and Evening Stars, one going before and one following the Sun. Taking pity on the people and desiring their prayer offerings, the Sun asked these Twins to lead the people

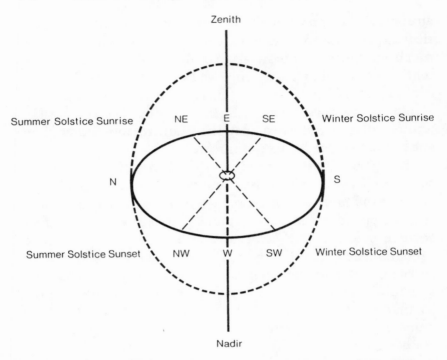

Figure 42. Schematic drawing of the circle of the earth's horizon with solstice rise and set points marked (the inner circle and dotted lines could represent the heart and legs of the Water Skate described in part of the Zuni origin myth). The inclusion of the zenith and nadir extends the circle into a sphere. Drawing by Murray Callahan.

from the four underworlds to the surface of this earth back in the time of "the beginning." The principle of duality is significant not only in and of itself, however, but also because it gives rise to the Zunis' quadripartite view of the world, achieved by combining the solar positions—yearly and daily motion, winter and summer solstice sunrise and sunset—so that the entire annual cycle is represented (Figure 42).

The number four, associated with the solstices as well as sunrise and sunset, and hence directionality, is both sacred and ubiquitous in Zuni mythology and cultural symbolism.[9]

According to the Zuni origin myth, the people traveled through four underworlds to reach the surface of the present world where they were, at first, blinded by the light of the sun. Then they spent four years (or, in some versions, four days) searching for the Center. It is significant that the Zuni word for this surface of the earth or Earth Mother (that is, the ground in which seeds are planted), *'awitelin tsitta,* derives from the word for four, *'a:witen,* for it is here that the four directions begin to take on significance. Directionality, or location in time and space, was not a feature of life in the sunless underworlds. Furthermore, as noted above, Zunis perceive the sun as standing still at the solstices for four days rather than three or five. One Zuni colleague even suggested that a single handprint in the rock art represented the forecasting of some event four days hence, and several handprints together referred to a predicted event four times that number of days hence. Such an interpretation ignores the thumb and counts only the four fingers. The number four is also central to Zuni ideas about reincarnation: they believe that, with the exception of young children and certain priests, each Zuni person is born four times and dies four times. After the fourth death Zunis either return to the hole where they emerged from the four underworlds to this earth in the time of the beginning, or find that they have descended one of those underworlds with each death, arriving with the fourth and last death at the lowest of the four underworlds where the Zunis originated. At this point they may become a member of one of the species of animals (raw beings) they had an affinity for in life and return to the world of the living.[10] Finally, the number four serves as an organizing principle for most other aspects of Zuni life. According to Ruth Bunzel, four is the major literary and ceremonial model (important events are repeated four times; ritual actions are often carried out in a four-part sequence) as well as an ideal pattern in pottery decorations: when discussing their painting, Zuni potters "express a preference for the number four," but it is an ideal that is not always realized.[11]

In Zuni ritual practice, too, this number is significant. For

instance, when praying to the sun, Zunis scatter sacred cornmeal in the direction of the four solstice points. These are the
four points on the horizon approximating the semicardinal
directions of northeast, northwest, southwest, and southeast
(their usual ritual order), where the winter and summer solstice suns rise and set and appear to stand still.[12] Located at
these four points are four oceans that encircle the earth so
that it becomes their Center; each ocean contains a mountain
that is the color of that particular direction. The importance
of these directions is established in the origin myth: the Center
Place was finally found when the Water Skate, given magical
powers of extension by the Sun Father, stretched out his four
legs to those same four solstice points (Figure 43). The place
where his heart and navel then rested marked the Center, the
heart and navel of the Earth Mother. This is the place where
the present-day Zuni was built.[13] Finally, at the center of the
village itself, directly under the spot where the heart or navel
of the Water Skate rested, lies yet another center. On a permanent altar in the fourth underground room of the house of
the chief priesthood is a heart-shaped rock, "the heart of the
world," which has within it arteries reaching toward the four
solstice positions, just as did the legs of the Water Skate.[14]
One can conceive of these various centers, then, as a series of
concentric circles, all surrounding this ultimate center, "the
heart of the world." In addition, the Zuni view the universe
as consisting of a definite number of vertical layers: there are
four underworlds, oriented toward the nadir, and each associated with a tree; then comes the surface of the earth (the
world currently occupied); finally, there are four upperworlds,
oriented toward the zenith, and each associated with a different kind of bird. Although totaling nine levels, Zunis perceive
them as four on either side of the central layer: the familiar
world, the beginning point in the cycle of reincarnation.[15]

With the addition of these various "centers" to the sacred
number four, we now have the number five—four plus the
Center. One may say, in fact, that the number five is derived
from the two major cosmological principles of the Zuni: 'iti-

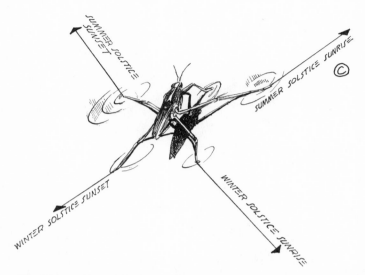

Figure 43. Water Skate finding the Center. Drawing by Snowden Hodges.

wana, "the center," and *'a:witen,* "four." The directional scheme of four plus the Center can be represented visually by the same diagram that illustrates the sun's apparent annual motion (Figure 42). Stretched with limbs extending to the solstice points, the Water Skate appears to form a figure X, with his heart at the center (Figure 43). Any X, therefore, can be seen to symbolize this. One Zuni man saw a representation of the story of the Water Skate finding the middle place in an image of a mask with feathers across the top (Figure 35c), perhaps by ignoring most of the image and focusing on the X made by the lines representing the long sides of the outermost feathers.

As with the number four, the number six is ever-present in Zuni ritual. Its origins lie in the Zunis' recognition of the three-

Figure 44. Dry painting, fetishes, and wall decoration of the Sword Swallower Fraternity, an esoteric society of the Zuni. By an unknown artist, 1893. Published as Plate 108 in Matilda C. Stevenson's "The Zuñi Indians." Courtesy of the Smithsonian Institution, National Anthropological Archives (Neg. No. 2359-C-2).

dimensional nature of the world in which they live. Thus, the zenith and nadir are combined with the four solstice points located on the horizon that form the seemingly planar surface of the earth. For instance, the Zunis associate each of the six sacred kivas with one of these directions. They link the six *Shalako* kachinas (major figures in the "coming of the gods" ceremony that occurs prior to the winter solstice) and six pairs of *Salimobia* ("warrior" kachinas, two of whom accompany the Shalako kachinas) to those kivas. When these kachinas come to the pueblo at the time of the Shalako ceremony, they dedicate the six houses (called Shalako houses) that have been built or remodeled in the past year. Furthermore, the Zunis relate the directions to life-bringing water, as well as to the sun: this cosmological scheme includes six rain priests of the six directions "who take the form of clouds, rainstorms, fog and dew when they leave their homes,"[16] six rain-bringing winds, six bow priests who make lightning and thunder, and six different varieties of "water bringing birds."[17] Finally, associated with each direction and symbolizing it is a color.

Animals, too, are drawn into this network of symbolic relations. According to Zuni mythology, six Beast Gods (*wema:we*) guard the world. Each of these animals is positioned at one of the four solstice points as well as the above and the below, and is colored accordingly. They are the yellow mountain lion of the northeast, the blue bear of the northwest, the red badger of the southwest, the white wolf of the southeast, the speckled or all-colored eagle of the zenith, and the black mole of the nadir (see Figure 44). Sometimes Knife-Wing (the mythic being with wings and tail of knives) rather than the eagle is associated with the zenith.[18]

Although the number six is significant in itself, there is an implied center in all of these examples; with the addition of this center, the ritual number becomes seven. This can be seen in Figure 42, but one must imagine that the circle of the horizon is a slice of a sphere, the axis of which runs through the center with the zenith and nadir as its end points; thus zenith and nadir both lie on a line perpendicular to the center point. The Center represents not only the contemporary Zuni village, but also the place found in the myth time by Water Skate, the middle of any place, the time of the winter solstice, a person's navel or heart, that person as the center when observing the six directions or offering prayer meal, and so on, all encompassed by the six directions oriented toward that center.[19] Which specific center is being referred to at any time depends upon the context; at the same time, the Center is a multivocal or condensed symbol that can represent all of these centers at the same time.

I stress here that the annual motion of the sun (shown schematically in Figure 42) constitutes a base metaphor similar to that described by Claire Farrer and Bernard Second for the Mescalero Apache. A major difference, however, is that the visual metaphor they illustrate is a quartered circle (referring to the cardinal directions), whereas the visual representation of directionality, circularity, and balance for the Zunis is frequently a semiquartered circle (discussed above as forming an X and symbolizing the semicardinal directions) plus the zenith and nadir. Thus, the Zuni model is spherical rather than circular; it is based on three rather than two dimensions. Furthermore, for the Mescalero Apache, the quartered circle and the designs it generates form the observable basis of most ritual symbolism. In contrast, although one Zuni man did find a representation of directionality in a rock art figure, the Zunis seldom visually depict the semiquartered circle as a design in itself, either in the rock art surrounding the pueblo or in other graphic media.[20]

Instead of constantly rendering this symbol as a design on ritual paraphernalia, making its concrete visual representation a focus, Zunis employ the directionalism it dictates as the basis for patterns of *arrangement* in ritual. When they constructed the six sacred kivas they aligned them to the solstice directions plus the above and the below (they regard these latter two as symbolically associated with the above and below, not actually aligned to the zenith and nadir). They frequently assign roles in ritual drama so that certain participants represent the six directions (taking on a personality, acting in a manner that is seen as in accordance with these directions).

They include symbols on kachina costumes, as well as on the painted bodies of the kachina impersonators, that refer to the directions, painting these symbols in the appropriate directional colors. They position altars in ceremonial rooms, as well as the objects on those altars, so that they are incorporated in a four- or six-directional scheme. They perform ritual actions in a directional pattern, and so on. Thus, the semiquartered circle with the zenith and nadir constitutes a design that operates implicitly, rather than explicitly; as a symbol its basic structure is copied in visually perceivable arrangements and actions. For instance, it is mimed in ritual activity by the gestures of the person who scatters sacred cornmeal to the six directions. It is a metaphor that is acted out, or sketched in the air, but seldom codified in graphic art. Finally, although the model of directionality may be cited as the ideal principle of organization, the Zunis do not always consider it necessary to follow this pattern rigidly in actual practice. The arrangement of the six kivas, for instance, is at best an approximation of the six directions; what is important is the symbolic relationship to those directions, not the actual precision of directional alignments. Further, as alluded to earlier, Zuni potters state that, ideally, pots should be painted in a four-part pattern, but they divide the design field on many pots into threes instead. Perhaps if one recognizes the overall conceptual importance of the pattern, one need not feel strictly obliged to adhere to it.

The allusive yet uncodified property of the base metaphor gives it a dynamic quality, a characteristic permeability or fluidity that adds to its generative power. Indeed, the vast network of symbolic associations to which it gives rise is not amenable to concretization; as one Zuni man said when discussing the various animals, plants, and natural phenomena contained in the six-directional scheme: "It includes everything." But the very generality of the metaphor lends it ambiguity—an ambiguity quite characteristic of the Zuni view of the world. Zuni ritual symbols, whether expressed verbally or visually, are frequently multivalent or multireferential, standing for both themselves and something else *at the same time;* yet all of the meanings are bound together, so that the Zunis say, as do the Mescalero Apache: "They're all the same thing."[21] This system of multiple possible meanings is part of a general pattern in Zuni thinking about the nature of the world, a pattern that is integral to the verbal and visual symbols devised to refer to this world. For example, the various "centers" mentioned earlier, all embedded in the base metaphor of directionality, are linked together by the generalizing concept of the Center; a reference to one can evoke all of the others, yet each has its own distinctive characteristics as well.

For the Zunis, these centers are not simply concrete objects or mental constructs but, rather, powers; although they may be thought of separately, they are also perceived as a single unified power—the Center—derived from conflating all of the powers inherent in the activities, objects, relationships, and ideas it represents.[22] But, as I will discuss further in Chapter 4 with reference to visual images that have the efficacy to evoke the past, the boundaries of time and space are also collapsed in the base metaphor, giving it the ability or power to refer to many disparate concepts simultaneously. The Center, a nuclear or condensed symbol that is integral to the conceptual model of directionality, is both a temporal and spatial center; yet it transcends time frames, such as past, present, or future, as well as transcending the limitations of physical space. Significantly, the Zunis' name for their village, their "center," *'itiwana*, is also their word for the winter solstice; one is a center in space, the other a center in time, yet both are "the same thing."

The multireferential quality of Zuni nuclear symbols relates to Zuni principles of aesthetics as well. In the article in which she discusses the two principles, "the beautiful" and "the dangerous," Barbara Tedlock uses the prefix "multi-" over and over again in referring to "the beautiful." "The dangerous" is dark, plain, muffled, and indistinct, whereas "the beautiful" is dynamic, chronomatic, varied: multilayered, multilingual, multisensory, multitextured, and multicolored.[23] I suggest that another way to describe "the beautiful" is as a Zuni "aesthetic of accumulation," an elaborate redundancy of symbolism in

Zuni sacred and secular environments.[24] Zuni costumes, altars, religious paraphernalia, ceremonial rooms, pottery, wall murals, and the ritual activity itself are all replete with sensory images—objects, sounds, colors, and so on—repeated over and over again, all resonating, all dense with meaning, frequently referring to "the same thing." Although I have listed examples that relate to religious life, my observations of "secular" activities such as the Zuni Tribal Fair lead to the same conclusions. Secular costumes, exhibit rooms for the fair, the fairground itself, floats in the parade, social dances and music, all are characterized by layers and layers of symbols, colors, and sounds, all bound together metaphorically.

"The same thing" in these instances, the metaphoric base that connects all these facets of Zuni cultural symbolism, is conceptually linked to the motion of the sun along the horizon and to the rain- and snow-bringing winds of the six directions. Indeed, the multiplicity inherent in the Zuni aesthetic of accumulation is also revealed in the generative power of the base metaphor of directionality; it gives rise to a plethora of symbolic associations that extend to include "everything." Further, this concept of multiplicity or accumulation is related to the predominant theme of Zuni religion: the desire for increase, whether it be rain for the crops, success in the hunt, many children, long life, or the sale of much jewelry. Significantly, the central request of most Zuni ritual prayers is that the people may experience increase or prosperity, but this is linked to the more general petition that the Sun Father continue in his appropriate journey and that the rain fall in sufficient abundance; for it is the sun's light, equated by the Zuni with life itself and coupled with water, that provides the subsistence base for all beings. This request is repeated continually, expressed in various but similar ways in Zuni verbal and visual modes of expression.

Cosmological Principles in Verbal Art

To this point in my discussion of the Zuni cosmological outlook, I have emphasized that the annual motion of the sun forms an implicit rather than explicit model in the ritual process. Similarly, the yearly travels of the sun and, sometimes, the recurrent phases of the moon, serve as organizing principles in much of Zuni verbal art, but they are principles that operate in a covert manner.

It is evident that the number four and the number six prevail in Zuni sacred narrative. For instance, in the origin myth the people travel through four underworlds then journey for four years or four days; the Water Skate stretches out his legs to the four oceans (also the four solstice positions); the six Beast Gods, serpents, winds, and so on, which reside at the solstice positions, zenith, and nadir, are mentioned repeatedly in reference to their directional associations (again, the idea of the Center is embodied in these directional schemes, so that the numbers could be described as five and seven, as well). The number four especially is prevalent in other Zuni narratives, too: significant events occur four times; important questions are asked four times; journeys last for periods measured by fours, whether it be days, months, or years. Although this repeated use of numbers associated with directionality is quite clear, the numbers also serve to structure Zuni narrative in ways that are not so readily apparent. For instance, Dell Hymes suggests that certain Zuni narratives consist of measured verses ordered on a four-part pattern, and Ruth Bunzel states that for the Zuni "the literary pattern is always four."[25]

In my work with Zuni poetics I have delineated verbal units larger than verses and have also found that the number four is frequently a pattern number for those sections of many lines that might be called stanzas. The pattern number is not always four, however. Just as the number associated with the directions can be five, six, or seven instead of four, depending on the dimensional perspective one takes, the patterning in verbal art corresponds sometimes to those other numbers as well. I describe the patterning as covert because it is not immediately obvious to anyone who reads or hears the poetry that the strikingly similar lines divide it into parallel sections. Ruth Bunzel, an expert linguist and ethnographer familiar with all aspects of Zuni life, does not acknowledge this fact in her translations or explications of Zuni ritual poetry; although she describes four as the pattern number in Zuni verbal art, pattern for her seems to mean the number of times an event occurs in the narrative. Of course, in the 1920s and 1930s when she conducted her fieldwork at Zuni and wrote up the results, the interest in Native American ethnopoetics that is prevalent among folklorists and socio-linguists today was not so widespread, and scholars did not devote much attention to parallel lines, measured verse, patterns of intonation, and breath pauses in Native American oral literature.[26]

In retranslating some of the Zuni ritual poetry collected by Ruth Bunzel in the 1930s, I find that astronomical motifs (for instance, in this case the movements of the sun along the horizon and the appearance of the moon near the winter solstice) often serve as major organizational elements. The following lines are from my retranslation of "Sayatasha's Night Chant," the major ritual poem recited during the Shalako ceremony at Zuni.[27] Shalako is the final ceremony in the annual cycle of ceremonies of the kachina priests, and it represents the coming of the gods to Zuni. This ceremony also signals the approach of the winter solstice, which marks the New Year for the Zuni, the time when the sun "turns around" in its journey along the horizon and a new ceremonial cycle begins.

Because the appearance of the moon is significant to the structure of the poem, it is of note that the Sayatasha impersonator who chants this ritual poem has chief responsibility for observations of the moon. He also "plants" the first prayer sticks (places them upright in the ground as an offering) at the first full moon after the close of the winter solstice ceremony. The major phase of the Shalako ritual during which the poem discussed below is recited begins at sunset, after a period of ten full moons and forty-eight days have passed since the last winter solstice or new year. It ends with the rise of the morning star and sunrise on the forty-ninth day. Prior to this, an all-night ceremony takes place during which Sayatasha recites his night chant—an event lasting for almost six hours.

The first part of "Sayatasha's Night Chant" is divided into

five major sections by parallel lines that are strikingly similar in construction and wording, referring to the movements of the sun along the horizon and the appearance of the moon near the winter solstice.[28] Interestingly, however, the four parallel stanzas relating to the motion of the sun are completed by a fifth parallel stanza that refers to the moon. Furthermore, both the solar and lunar motions described in the poem occur at or near a time that is a "center" or "beginning"—the sun at the winter solstice and the first full moon after the winter solstice. The initial lines in each stanza serve to establish the framework for the rest of the lines in the stanza. In other words, the beginning lines indicate the time of year and the location in the ceremonial cycle. I have represented here only the astronomically significant initial lines of each stanza. The drawings in Figure 45 are a graphic representation of the verbal message. At the left of the drawings is my translation of the Zuni phrases; I have indented the lines to indicate parallelism and repetition. Below are the Zuni phrases set out to show that parallelism, followed by brief descriptions of the meaning of these initial lines:

```
    hon yatoka tach ilab a:te'ona                          (I-1)
            li:wanem yam weshikanem telhashinakwi
                itiulhatuntekwin kow antewechikwi
    hon yatoka tach ilab a:te'ona                          (I-2)
            yam telhashinakwi
                i:muna kwatokaba
    hon yatoka tach ilab a:te'ona                          (I-3)
            yam telhashinakwi
                i:muna kwatotuntekwi kow antewechikwi
    hon yatoka tach ilab a:te'ona                          (I-4)
            yam telhashinakwi
                ye:lana kwai'ikaba
    hon ya'onaka tsit ilab a:te'ona                        (I-5)
            li:wan kalishiankwin tana
                kowilhana yetsakana
        teluankwin tana
            itiulhana
                ho'i ya:kanaka tewanan ashaba
```

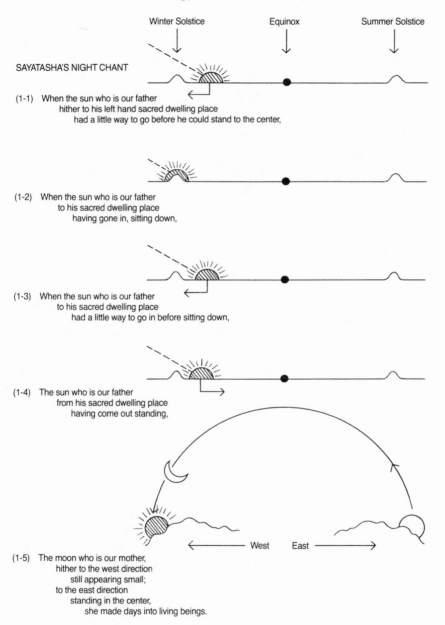

Figure 45. Sayatasha's Night Chant, translation by M. Jane Young. Drawing by Murray Callahan.

(*I–1*) The location is sunset, facing west. The time is just prior to the winter solstice. As is shown in the drawing, the left-hand sacred dwelling place indicates the position along the horizon at which the sun appears to stand still during the winter solstice. "A little way to go before he could stand to the center" refers to the time of Shalako, the ceremony that takes place just before the winter solstice.

(*I–2*) The time is sunset of the winter solstice. "Sitting down" refers to the sun's appearance as it sets in the same place for four consecutive days at the winter solstice.

(*I–3*) Just before sunset of the winter solstice. At this point the poem goes back in time to describe the ritual activities made in preparation for the solstice.

(*I–4*) Sunset after the winter solstice. The four days during which the sun appears to "stand still" have passed; the sun has "turned around" and will continue his journey northward along the horizon.

(*I–5*) The first part of this line indicates that the moon is not yet full, and therefore it is not yet time for the planting of prayer sticks. The moon's position at this time may be near sunset in the west. As the month progresses, the moon appears to slip eastward among the stars each night until it becomes full; at that time, the moon and sun appear to be opposite each other. Thus, the second part of the line depicts the first full moon after the winter solstice, the signal for the Sayatasha impersonator to plant the first prayer sticks of the year at a spring area.

Although I have discussed only one example, astronomical motifs form major organizational elements of much Zuni ritual poetry. Similarly, cosmological order serves to structure the ritual itself. The Zunis determine the time for specific ritual activities throughout the year on the basis of the apparent recurrent motion of the sun, moon, stars, and planets; similarly, events during a specific ritual are timed by astronomical phenomena as well. For instance, the moon, Orion, the Pleiades, and the Big Dipper frequently serve to mark divisions in rituals that occur during the night; their rising or passage over the uncovered hatchway in the kiva roof signals the culmination of ceremonies or specific phases of those ceremonies. Ritual activities occurring during the day are frequently demarcated by events such as the rise of the morning star, sunrise, and sunset.[29] Thus, the entire ritual cycle as well as individual events within that cycle are timed or structured according to astronomical phenomena.

Furthermore, just as astronomical motifs serve as paradigms in Zuni verbal art, so are they essential to both the symbolic content and the order or arrangement of visual art. The kivas and ceremonial rooms in which the most formal genres of Zuni verbal art (prayers and origin myths) are performed, the costumes of the participants in the performance, and the ritual paraphernalia, are all decorated with visual symbols representing the same cosmological beings as those predominant in the ritual poetry: sun, moon, morning star, evening star, Orion, the Pleiades, the Big Dipper, the Milky Way, the Beast Gods and snakes of the six directions, and so on (Figure 44). As discussed earlier, these symbols are generally arranged according to an overall pattern of directionality.

The central request of this ritual activity reiterates a theme of increase or multiplicity that is linked to directionality. The sun and the rain- and snow-bearing winds that emanate from the solstice positions are of central importance to the Zunis, not only because they cause the crops to grow, but because, in a more symbolic sense, they represent life. The solar motions, especially the four critical solstice positions, are implicit as organizing factors of Zuni expressive behavior. One may say that, just as the Zunis structure certain buildings and the rooms within them to incorporate the motion of the sun, so do they structure the rituals that occur in these rooms, as well as their accompanying verbal and visual art forms, according to principles of directionality derived from the apparent solar motion.

Zuni Perceptions of Space and Time

Zuni cosmology is shaped by a belief in the unity and sacred nature of all life, the above *and* the below. The Zunis speak of the Sun Father, Earth Mother, and others who reside in these realms as living beings; furthermore, the zenith and nadir are integral to their conceptual model of directionality, extending the two-dimensional scheme into three-dimensional space. In contrast to the "Western" view of outer space as consisting of inanimate objects in motion, the Zunis see themselves as intimately related to the sun, moon, and stars—major figures in their traditional narratives who, particularly because of these ties of kinship, ought to be treated with respect. It is not surprising, then, that the Zunis perceive the actions of "Western" scientists and astronauts toward these cosmological beings as not only disrespectful, but highly dangerous.[30]

The Zuni attitude toward the "persons" who inhabit the sky world, as well as their perceptions of space and time more generally, are aptly illustrated by stories several Zunis told me about certain clown performances that occurred at the time of the first U.S. moon shots. One man described a memorable summer rain dance during which the clowns in the plaza gave a good rendition of the particular walk that the astronauts in their cumbersome space suits exhibited. Then the clowns climbed to the rooftops and walked on top of one of the sacred kivas. The purpose of these actions, he said, was to object to the behavior of the astronauts who heedlessly walked on the body of the moon mother and pierced her with metal instruments in order to bring back samples for study.[31] This performance was not only a critique of the moon shots, however, but an enactment of Zuni cosmological principles— that the clowns equated the moon with sacred space in this instance was not arbitrary. This coupling suggests a merging of space and time in a ritual context such that the kiva, a ceremonial chamber, sometimes located underground and symbolically associated with the emergence from the underworld, becomes equivalent to the moon, one of the Zuni deities who travels across the sky.[32] Outer and inner space thus occupy the same place at the same time.

The group of Zuni clowns who portrayed the astronauts not only provides comic relief, easing tension through laughter, but also embodies disorder through ritual reversals. In addition, their performances often become vehicles for criticizing the actions of both Zunis and non-Zunis alike. The Zunis regard these clowns as extremely powerful, potentially dangerous beings who play a central role in their ceremonies. Between "sets" of the sacred rain dances they mimic the stately kachinas, make sexual overtures to the highly respected matrons of the tribe, and even walk on the moon; yet none of these activities constitutes appropriate behavior in day-to-day life. The disorderly behavior of the clowns, enacted in a ceremonial context, contrasts with the order by which people should govern their lives. Significantly, Zuni and Hopi clowns include impersonations of anthropologists and government bureaucrats, as well as astronauts, in their repertoire—perhaps an indication that all of these roles are characterized by the exploitative nature of the Anglo-American.[33]

Interestingly, one Zuni man who told me about the clowns' performance of the first moon walk mentioned it within the context of a discussion about the ability of the clowns to predict, and hence, control, future events. His description of the event tallied with the others I had heard, with one striking difference: he said the event took place a year *before* astronauts first walked on the moon. Certainly this example underscores the perceived power of the clowns, but it also serves to link this event with other ominous events foreseen in the future. This man associated the story of the moon walk with one the grandfathers used to tell long ago, predicting that a time would come when their children would begin to drink dark liquid and quarrel and that eventually the world would end in a shower of hot rain.[34] Finally, just as the clowns' equation of the moon and the kiva constituted a collapsing of inner and outer *space* in ritual activity, so does this example reveal a similar collapsing of *time:* present and future coalesce as the clowns ritually enact an event that has not yet occurred.

These examples illustrate a Zuni ethos in which time as well as space can be seen as being inner- rather than outer-directed. According to Zuni mythology, which the Zunis themselves regard as history, the people back in the time of the beginning lived in the fourth underworld, below the surface of the earth. This time of the beginning had no beginning; it simply *was*, before the time of the emergence. Similarly, Zunis believe that existence after death is not situated in the sky but rather inside the Earth Mother, back in the time of the beginning. In the Zuni origin myth, as the people search for the Center after they have emerged from the underworld, they undertake geographical travels that steadily spiral inward until they reach their destination. Their search for knowledge is synonymous with their search for the Center. The vehicle for attaining this knowledge, for finding the Center, for reaching the moon, is ceremonial activity, not travel in a space ship.

Also apparent in these examples is the Zuni emphasis on process rather than product; on the unity of all beings in the act of harmonious existence. For the Zunis, the moon, like the sun, is not an object to be walked on or traveled to but a living being whose light is drawn through the kiva hatchway during certain rituals. This perception of the sun and moon as living beings who enter sacred space at ritually significant times of the year is a phenomenon similar to that described earlier: the behavior of the clowns during a Zuni rain dance that served to equate the kiva with the moon for a circumscribed period of time. Both instances are part of a sequence of ritual activities in which a condensation and intensification of experience occur—a fusing of "inner" and "outer" into one entity. Thus, the Zunis do not view space and the beings who reside there as external to ceremonial life, nor do they regard them as material objects that they can own, control, or overcome. According to this perspective, there are no rigid boundaries between the spiritual and the physical; or, if such boundaries exist at all, they are fluid and permeable. The cosmos is one entity; the beings within it operate according to the principles of continuity and similarity—principles evident in the unification of inner and outer space in the context of ritual activity.

For the Zunis, this continuity applies to time as well as to space. Although they may introduce a myth as having occurred "a long time ago" or "in the beginning," they do not envision the events of the myth as over and done with, situated at a single point in a linear flow of time; instead, they perceive them as ever-present, informing the here and now. It is this perspective that accounts for the "presentness" of the beings of myth and folktale in Zuni life.

This view of time and space is perhaps closer to that of relativist physics, in which space and time exist as a single continuum that is relative to the observer, than it is to the linear perspective of the average member of Western society.[35] For the Zunis, time is *cyclical*, apparent in the orderly and regular motions and "returns" of the sun, moon, and stars, and both time and space are *organic*, continuous entities. One may say that time for them is reversible; past, present, and future are coexistent. They believe that when people die four times, they return to the time and place of the myth, completing the human cycle of reincarnation; yet they may return to the present in another form if they so desire. Further, in the context of sacred performances, the gods return again and again. The kachina dancers in the plaza do not *represent* the gods, they become the gods, and the time of the myth is one with the present. The efficacy of ritual activity is the result of the merging of the here and now with the myth time and space. Thus one might describe the Zuni view of the universe and its dimensional aspects as a unified and orderly phenomenon, symbolized by the directional model that links a complex web of associations, extending to include "everything." It may well be that the power of myth, the power of certain visual images, and the power of the ritual process inhere in this world view as well.

Although I have discussed Zuni spatial and temporal per-

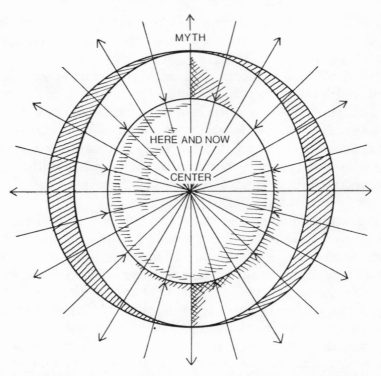

Figure 46. Schematic diagram of the dialectic between the "here and now" and the myth time. The concentric spheres revolve about a common center or radius (the Zuni *'itiwana*). Drawing by Murray Callahan.

ceptions in terms such as the "merging," "collapsing," and "coalescing" of boundaries between the here and now and myth time and space, I do not mean to imply that this results in a permanent condition so that the two states (time and space; myth and "here and now") are unified in every aspect from that moment on. Rather, the relationship between the two is best expressed as a dialectic interaction made possible by the fluid boundary that exists between the two. Figure 46 illustrates this movement back and forth across a permeable boundary: the here and now validates the myth and the myth validates the here and now. In this diagram the two states are depicted in three-dimensional space—they are represented by concentric spheres. The Center from which both spheres have been generated is the nuclear symbol discussed earlier: *'itiwana,* the center of all time and space. The "here and now" sphere is congruent with the model of the world depicted in Figure 42, but this directional scheme does not include the myth time and space that extend beyond the limitations of the present. Furthermore, the volume of neither sphere portrayed in Figure 46 is constant. Given certain circumstances, either sphere may expand or contract such that the conceptual distance between the two becomes greater or less. For instance, the rituals that occur near the time of the winter solstice (such as the "coming of the gods" to Zuni), the most critical period of the year, draw human time closer to myth time so as to intensify the relationship between the two (depicted schematically, this would mean that the inner sphere in Figure 46 expands and moves toward the outer sphere). The recitation of ritual prayers and reiteration of myths during this period contribute to this intensification, acting as catalysts in a world renewal rite, bringing the beings and events of myth time close to hand.[36] Similarly, visual images that are conceptually linked to the realm of myth, the time of the ancestors, also serve as catalysts. Certain rock art figures have the power to evoke the past and are thus perceived by the Zunis as "signs from the ancestors."

4

Metonyms of Narrative

Metonymic Rock Art Images

Contemporary Zunis regard many of the pictographs and petroglyphs in the landscape surrounding the pueblo as meaningful signs from the past that were made by the ancestors. For example, one man told me that most Zunis believe the figures were drawn on the rocks during the time when the rocks were still soft—back in the time of the beginning, before the earth was hardened. He described the earth at that time as *'awitelin kabin,* meaning "raw earth." Certain depictions, generally among the more ambiguous in design and dating from the earliest time periods, stimulated the narration of excerpts of Zuni myths and tales about creatures or events called to mind by these images.[1] Especially frequent were those stories about the mythic period when animals and people did not look or act the way they do now. As one Zuni woman described it: "All the animals and bugs used to speak way back then." These narratives or narrative segments were generally not prefaced by any introduction such as "I will explain it this way," or "it means this." Rather, they were simply begun as a direct response to particular images. Thus, these graven figures were transformed into narrative events; products were

121

transformed into process. Rock carvings and paintings that evoke parts of tales and myths and the emotions associated with these vitally important "texts" operate, then, as "metonyms of narrative": the visual image stands for and calls forth the verbal recitation.

One such group of images consisted of varieties of "lizard men," which are lizardlike, anthropomorphic figures prevalent in the rock art of the Zuni-Cibola region (Figures 26a, 47, 48). Several Zunis identified these figures as "the way the Zunis looked at the time of the beginning" or "in the fourth underworld," often adding, "when we still had tails." A few people even launched into telling the part of their origin myth in which these creatures, "moss people," are described as having tails and webbed hands and feet.[2] That this sort of reaction to certain images is consistent with a traditional Zuni ethos is supported by Matilda Stevenson's report of a similar response by her Zuni guide to one such figure she photographed near Zuni in 1879.[3]

According to most versions of the Zuni origin myth, the people did not behave in a properly "human" manner at the time of the beginning but did the reverse of what they should have done. They were dirty beings, somewhat similar in appearance to the salamander; they did not worship their father the sun and in other ways did not behave correctly. They were not "finished," "ripe," or "human" beings, but rather "raw" or "non-human" beings.[4] They lived an orderless life, lacking location in time and space; in the underworld there was neither linear time nor geographic location, for the people did not yet have a Center.

Taking pity on these poor creatures and also wanting their prayer offerings, the Sun Father sent his sons, the Twin War Gods, to lead the people to the surface of the earth. When the people reached this surface after having traveled through the four underworlds they were dazzled by the light of the Sun and were made human by the Twins. They were washed, their tails were cut off, their webbed digits were separated, and the genitals were removed from the tops of their heads. They were

Figure 47. Pecked "lizard man," 20 cm × 14 cm, ZRAS site 17. Photograph by Robert H. Leibman, 1980.

Figure 48. White painted lizardlike or anthropomorphic figure (with webbed appendages, but no tail), 25 cm × 20 cm, ZRAS site 15. Photograph by Nancy L. Bartman, 1979.

also hardened or finished in the same fire with which the Twins hardened the soft surface of the earth. Thus, the myth describes the existence of the Zuni people in the underworld as a period of inversion that ended when they reached the surface of the earth.

As portrayed in rock art, these lizardlike figures, part reptile, part human, are quite ambiguous—perhaps intentionally so. Ambiguity is certainly characteristic of Zuni verbal art, which abounds with word play and metaphor. It is not surprising, therefore, to find similar ambiguity in Zuni visual art as well. In fact, as I elaborate below, this ability to operate at different levels of meaning is partially responsible for the power of such images. In any case, younger Zunis, especially those involved in pottery making, generally tended to see these depictions as lizards, frogs, and toads rather than as anthropomorphic figures, grouping them with other similar images as "things that go on pottery." Such animals are considered to be "raw beings" with special powers whose origins are also described in the Zuni emergence myth. After the people had emerged from the underworlds and were wandering the earth looking for the middle place, a brother and sister committed incest near the place that later became Kachina Village (which, according to Zuni belief, is where some of their dead go, becoming kachinas who have the power to send rain). As a result of their transgression, the brother and sister were transformed into beings of hideous appearance. The brother and nine of the offspring of this incestuous union became the *Koyemshi* who, in Zuni ritual, are represented as grotesque clowns, the Mudheads (Figure 3). Furthermore, the sister was so outraged that she created a river dividing a mountain to separate herself from her brother. One Zuni man described the subsequent events as follows:

As the people were searching for the center place,
    they had to cross a river near the Kachina Village.
Although the mothers held tightly to their children,
    they turned into water beings in their mothers' arms—
        and, many of the mothers dropped their children into
                the water.
Those who were dropped swam to Kachina Village
    and joined the kachinas there.

Zunis believe that young children become such creatures— turtles, frogs, water snakes—when they die. Because they have not lived long in the "finished" world, they are still close to the "raw" world; hence, it is unnecessary for them to pass through four cycles of birth and death in order to return to the earliest stage of existence. Thus, they become raw beings similar to the salamander-like creatures who were Zunis at the time of the beginning.

These animals are water beings in both a literal and a metaphorical sense. Not only are they creatures who live in or near the water, but their images are used in several ritual activities aimed at bringing water to Zuni in the form of rain.

Figure 49. Zuni jar. Note figures of tadpole, dragonfly, horned toad, and Kolowisi. Courtesy of the School of American Research Collections in the Museum of New Mexico (catalogue # 8125/12). Photograph by Robert H. Leibman, 1981.

Frogs, toads, tadpoles, and representations of Kolowisi are painted on pottery water jars so that they will fill with water (Figures 49, 50). Such figures are also painted in kiva murals (Figure 51) and on the backs of kachina masks to ensure that there will be rain for the crops—examples of what Ruth Bunzel has called "compulsive magic."[5] Similarly, Zunis identified certain rock art figures as toads, frogs, and insects that live in or near bodies of water, adding that they were carved or painted on the rocks surrounding the pueblo in order to bring rain to the area (Figures 52, 86, 87). The animals depicted by these pictographs and petroglyphs, and through them the images themselves, derive their power from their association with certain vital aspects of the physical world such as water and rain. Because toads live near the water, and a toad can be

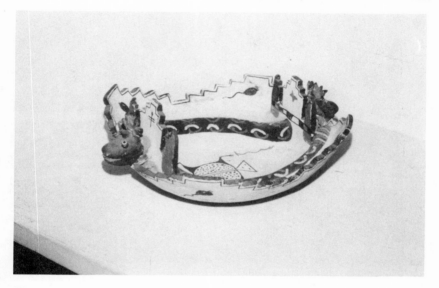

Figure 50. Zuni bowl. Note figures of tadpole, dragonfly, horned toad, and Kolowisi. Courtesy of the Museum of New Mexico Collections (catalogue # 37114/12). Photograph by Robert H. Leibman, 1981.

represented by its carved or painted image, the production of this figure is an important part of those ritual activities aimed at encouraging rainfall. This associative power is not, however, limited to images. Some kachina impersonators, for example, carry living turtles in their hands as they perform the summer rain dances.

As described earlier, Zunis believe that when their ancestors emerged from the four underworlds onto the surface of this world they were transformed from the "raw" beings they had been into "made," "finished," or "ripe" beings. According to Zuni belief, all inhabitants of the world vary along this rawness-completeness continuum and, furthermore, one's power is directly correlated with one's degree of rawness. Raw beings, such as the kachinas, have more power than others, and all

Figure 51. Wall painting of Kolowisi and the "sacred toad."
Published as plate 36 in Matilda Stevenson's "The Zuñi Indians."
Courtesy of the Smithsonian Institution, National
Anthropological Archives (Neg. No. 86-10120).

beings are ranged along a hierarchy with respect to rawness
and power. Rawness here seems to imply closeness to the
world of the myth and the events that transpired then, and it
is those beings for whom this rawness is an attribute who
have the ability to effect change in the physical world. The
"moss people" were infused with a particular kind of potency
that they lost when humans became "finished beings." Since
that time, humans, the most finished of all creatures, have
also been the least effective, located at the very bottom of the
taxonomy. Having little influence themselves, humans have
had to rely on more powerful, raw beings to act as mediators
between themselves and the most powerful beings, especially
the kachinas, and to convey to the latter their prayers for rain.
Such mediation is often effected by means of visual representations of the mediators in a variety of forms including masks,

Figure 52. Painted (yellow-white) deer, toad or frog, mountain lion, "negative" handprint, 150 cm × 2 m, ZRAS site 30. Photograph by M. Jane Young, 1981.

fetishes (figures carved in stone or, sometimes, made out of clay), images on pottery, and, perhaps, rock art as well (e.g., the previously mentioned uses of depictions of various water creatures).[6]

Both identifications of these lizardlike figures ("Zunis at the time of the beginning," and "things that go on pottery") refer to the same category of beings: creatures who are raw and hence powerful, associated with the time of the beginning and, because of their physical attributes, linked to water. Furthermore, these are multivalent depictions; although Zunis tended to articulate one identification rather than another, it is highly likely that in certain situations these images might call both interpretations to mind at the same time.

Another such group of powerful (raw) mediating beings often called upon to carry the spirit of Zuni prayers to the kachinas are the Beast Gods of the six directions. They are located at the solstice points, and Zunis believe them to have the power to send rain- and snow-bearing winds from these directions. Images of the Beast Gods are painted on the walls and altars of the kivas and medicine society rooms (Figure 44). Generally all six beings are painted, for as one Zuni man said: "It would not be right to leave any one out." They are an important component of the ceremonies that take place in these rooms, and Zunis refer to them in the words of their prayers and in the act of scattering sacred cornmeal to the six directions.

In sorting through my drawings and photographs of rock art figures, many Zunis found images they identified as the various Beast Gods, often describing their associations with specific colors and directions. Owing, perhaps, to their close association with the semicardinal directions, in more than one instance a description of the Beast Gods occasioned the telling of the story of the Water Skate who, by stretching his legs to the solstice points, helps the people find the Center. Because all six Beast Gods go together in many other contexts, some Zunis were perplexed if they could not find depictions of all of them either while sorting through my photographs and drawings or while visiting a particular rock art site at which one figure identified as a Beast God appeared; others seemed to make a point of finding them, looking back over the site or the photographs and drawings until they found something "close enough."

The six Beast Gods, however, rarely appear together in rock art. Only those identified as the mountain lion (Figure 37a, 52, 62), Knife-Wing or eagle (Figure 38b, 38c, 54), and bear track (Figure 31a) commonly occur, and even these three seldom appear together on the same rock face. This also appears to be true with respect to Beast God fetishes, perhaps for the same reason. Because the Beast Gods are all predators, Zunis believe that their fetishes have great power in bringing success in the hunt, and nearly everyone at Zuni has a fetish of one or another of these beings (Figure 53).[7] The potency of the fetishes is derived by analogy from the efficacy that their

Figure 53. Modern Zuni fetishes. From the collection of M. Jane Young.

Figure 54. Incised and abraded rabbit, bird (eagle or Knife-Wing), sun figure, 70 cm × 150 cm, ZRAS site 2. Drawing by Murray Callahan.

animal counterparts have in the "natural" world, so each fetish has greatest power with respect to the particular game animals that are its prey. Thus, a hunter usually takes with him only the fetish that has the most power over the game he wishes to hunt.[8] In rock art, too, images of a Beast God and the animal over which it has power, such as the mountain lion and the

Figure 55. Painted wall decorations in the "animal room" at Zuni, a ceremonial chamber. Among other animals depicted are deer, mountain lions, a rabbit, and an eagle (or Knife-Wing). Numerous painted pots are on the floor. Photograph by Adam Clark Vroman, 1899. Courtesy of the Smithsonian Institution, National Anthropological Archives (Neg. No. 2296-B).

deer (Figure 52), or the eagle (or Knife-Wing) and the rabbit (Figure 54), are sometimes found near one another on the same rock face. An example of this sort of occurrence in another graphic form is Figure 55, a Zuni mural that depicts this deer/mountain lion and eagle/rabbit association.[9] Of related interest, the division between game animals (deer, elk, antelope, rabbits, and mountain sheep) and predators (Beast Gods or *wema:we*) appears to have been an important conceptual distinction in the interpretation of rock art figures by at least some Zunis.[10]

Although other animals are the subject of fetishes and their images were also often grouped together, only the Beast Gods evoked stories and descriptions. Perhaps this was because of their significant role in Zuni mythology and ceremonialism. Recognizing that the animals of prey were more powerful than humans and would devour them, in the time of the myth the Twin War Gods changed many of them, including those that became Beast God fetishes, into stone. Cushing describes this transformation thus:

. . . it happens that we find, here and there throughout the world, their forms, sometimes large like the beings themselves, sometimes shriveled and distorted. And we often see among the rocks the forms of many beings that live no longer, which shows us that all was different in the "days of the new."[11]

Some of the features of the landscape, then—huge boulders and rock outcrops that look like animals of prey—are, in fact, these fossilized animals, as are some of the smaller stones strewn on the ground that are animal-like in form. Zunis search for these stone images, considering them to be the most powerful of fetishes: they not only resemble the Beast Gods, they *are* the early Beast Gods, encapsulated in stone but still alive with the spirit, and hence the power, of these animals. Although fetish makers also carve figures of the Beast Gods from lumps of turquoise, obsidian, and so on, the Zunis do not perceive these images, which show evidence of human artifice, to be as powerful as those that "by nature" have the form of the Beast Gods and are found in the environs of the pueblo. These fetishes are three-dimensional images rather than two-dimensional depictions on rock faces; nevertheless, they reveal a Zuni tradition of venerating images in stone.

Many Zunis associated the Beast Gods with a group of images labeled "snakes," including *Kolowisi*, the plumed or horned water serpent, which is an important figure in Zuni mythology (Figure 49, 50, 51, 56). Fetishes of these snakes, like those of the Beast Gods, are among the most powerful. In the context of ritual activity, Zunis offer prayers not only to the Beast

Gods of the six directions but also to the snakes (sometimes described as rattlesnakes) and ants of the six directions. According to Matilda Stevenson, some of the medicine men who came to this world from the fourth underworld were transformed into the six Beast Gods, and "the others were converted into rattlesnakes and ants to preside with wisdom over the earth."[12] The Zunis have both a Snake Society and a Red Ant Society—curing societies whose powers are attributed to their association with red ants and rattlesnakes. Red ants are also linked to the Warrior Society (the Priests of the Bow). According to an elderly Zuni woman, the sting of the red ant represents both power to kill the enemies of the Zunis and fertility because the blood of the dead enemy fertilizes the earth. (Zunis said Figure 85, for example, depicted insects that gave the Zunis power in war by stinging their traditional enemies, the Navajo). This commentary illustrates a significant connection between death-bringing and life-giving powers. A picture in Stevenson's report of a mural in the meeting place of the Wood Society shows all six Beast Gods plus six snakes colored in the hues characteristic of the six directions (Figure 44).[13] Kolowisi and the rattlesnake also share certain physical attributes. In rock art, pottery, and fetishes, images of Kolowisi (distinguishable by the medial horn and/or feathers on the head of its serpentine body) often depict the rattle of the rattlesnake at the tip of its tail as well (for this figure in rock art, see Figure 56).[14] At one pictograph site, in addition to portrayals of six Shalako kachinas and the Council of the Gods, there are also six painted Kolowisi, one in each of the colors related to the six directions.[15] Thus, Zunis incorporate the Kolowisi, other snakes, red ants, and the Beast Gods in their complex system of symbolic relations, connecting them with each other as well as with particular colors, directions, and segments of society. It is this network of symbolic associations, involving both verbal formulae and visual forms, that makes the physical environment as a whole, and the elements within it, meaningful to the Zunis.

Other types of images in stone also evoke stories that de-

Figure 56. Incised Kolowisi (with rattle tail), 10 cm × 110 cm, ZRAS site 21. Drawing by Murray Callahan.

scribe Kolowisi's actions in the time of the myth. According to one Zuni man:

> . . . the great water serpent caused the flood in ancient times,
>   forcing the people to flee to the top of Corn Mountain.
> The children of the high priest—
>   they were virgins—
>   saved the people by going into the water.
> The serpent was satisfied and the waters went away,
>   leaving marks on the sides of the mesa.
> Two stone pillars came into being
>   where the children went into the water.
>   One is a woman
>   and the other is a man.
> So these are used in the fertility rites of the Zunis.[16]

During hikes to rock art sites near these stone pillars other Zunis provided similar descriptions, adding that Kolowisi is the guardian of spring areas and other bodies of water. Once again, images long ago fixed in stone had the power to evoke a story in which information is passed on about their relationship to the Zuni world.

Two geometric designs that occur frequently in the rock art surrounding the pueblo and sometimes elicited narratives about the myth time were the spiral and concentric circle (see Figures 23, 27, 33, 57, 87). Of note is the similarity in form between the figures (when these rock art images have eroded due to weathering it is often quite difficult to tell them apart);

additionally, both forms are generated around a central point. Identifications of the two are sometimes linked to solar motion, although, as I will discuss in Chapter 6, such identifications seem to have been introduced by non-Zunis during visits to the pueblo. The spiral figure in particular has a number of related meanings, for both the Zunis and the Puebloans in general. The historic Puebloan peoples described spirals as representing wind, water, creatures associated with water such as serpents and snails, and the journey of the people in search of the Center.[17] The most frequent interpretation of this figure I heard at Zuni was "journey in search of the Center"; less often the figure was described as representing snails or snakes. Those who identified the spiral figure in rock art as representing the "search for the Center Place" referred the figure back to the myth time, frequently narrating the part of the origin myth that describes the travels undertaken by the Zunis as they searched for that location as well as its discovery by the Water Skate. The Center Place, then, is represented by the central point of the spiral.[18] The spiral could be described as referring to this event from two different perspectives. The central point of the spiral is itself a condensed symbol, but so is the rest of the figure; years of travel and hardship are encoded in the inward-turning coils. It is of interest that the Zunis with whom I worked perceived a figure that could be seen as "opening out" as "turning inward" instead. They described the journey in search of the Center as motion through time directed inward, often following the coils of the spiral in toward the center point with their fingertips. This perspective is quite consistent with the inner- or center-directed ethos of the Zuni people.

The concentric circle occurs much less frequently than the spiral in the rock art of the Zuni-Cibola region: Zunis generally equated it with the spiral, identifying it as "journey in search of the Center Place" (especially in instances in which the concentric circle was badly eroded and appeared to be a spiral instead). Although this symbol has been interpreted by

Figure 57. Pecked spiral and concentric circle figures above a depression in the rock that frequently collects water, 120 cm × 115 cm, ZRAS site 17. Photograph by Robert H. Leibman, 1980.

members of Eastern Puebloan groups as representing the sun, I never heard this interpretation at Zuni.[19]

Photographs of geometric designs, as well as visits to actual sites where they were depicted, often elicited comments that linked these figures to "the time of the beginning." With the exception of spiral and concentric circle figures, such comments generally did not involve specific identifications; instead, Zunis frequently described the most elaborate geometric designs (e.g., the design to the right of the panel in Figure 23) as having been "done by our ancestors" and as conveying "some sort of message that we no longer understand." One may say that these images, too, are metonymic but in a broader sense than was true of the pictographs and petroglyphs and other landscape features discussed earlier. Zunis describe them not only as the creations of the ancestors but as images bearing some special (if undecipherable) message from them to the contemporary Zuni people; they are signs from the ancestors. Rather than recalling any specific event of the myth, these figures represent or recall the time of the myth in its entirety. These are the kinds of depictions that both the Zunis and early ethnographers most often referred to as "hieroglyphs."[20] Many Zunis regard such images as powerful because they are links with the past; this is another example of the Zuni view that the past is constantly informing the present. They see these mysterious signs, carved by their ancestors but now unintelligible, as important messages demonstrating the direct involvement of the ancestors in the present-day, even if that involvement cannot be precisely articulated. One might contrast this view with that of Westerners who see Stonehenge in England as the work of ancestors, mysterious and powerful, but having no particular meaning for contemporary society.

To this point I have been discussing rock art figures that evoked similar interpretations and responses from the Zunis with whom I worked, focusing in particular on those that Zunis perceived as relating to certain figures and events located in the myth time. Thus the visual images eliciting narratives from Zunis are those that are *recognized* as significant aspects of Zuni cultural symbolism. Despite the ambiguity of meaning of some of the depictions, they are nevertheless familiar and identifiable in some manner. Of the other pictographs and petroglyphs in the corpus of rock art sites surrounding the pueblo, some were consistently described as "unknown"; for others there was less consensus in identification—few such images evoked stories or descriptions of their role in Zuni cultural symbolism.

One major exception was the group of images labelled "kachinas" (see, e.g., Figures 26b, 26c, 26d, 69, 70, 73–76). Zunis generally agreed upon the identification of individual kachinas, but such images tended to evoke descriptions of the particular ceremonies in which they take part rather than stories of the "time of the beginning." Nevertheless, depictions of kachinas are always metonymic of the past because they are representations of the ancestors. Zunis identified certain kachina images in the rock art by name (i.e., *Shalako* or *Sayatasha*, see Figures 69, 74); others they simply classed as "dancers" or "kachinas." Interestingly, the "named" kachinas, or kachina priests, were generally those who appear in the winter night dances that begin prior to the winter solstice ceremony with the Shalako or "The Coming of the Gods" ceremony. These are the kachinas with whom the majority of Zunis are most familiar; thus the Zunis most easily recognize them in various media and also create representations of them more frequently than of those kachinas classed more generally as "dancers." Although not mentioned by the Zunis themselves, it is noteworthy that almost all of the images identified as specific kachinas were incised, gouged, or painted and date from post-A.D. 1325 (Figures 26c, 69, 74). This suggests easier identification (and less ambiguity) for images produced after A.D. 1325. It is, of course, not surprising that Zunis are most familiar with images that date from more recent times; further, these kachina images are linked to the elaboration of artistic expression and ceremonialism (the Rio Grande style) derived from the Jornada Mogollon and probably ultimately from Mexico, which reached the Western Puebloans around A.D. 1325.

Figure 58. Abraded fluteplayers and anthropomorphic figure, 140 cm × 250 cm, ZRAS site 26. Photograph by Robert H. Leibman, 1981.

Many of the male Zunis added the labels "warrior gods" and "whipper kachinas" to kachina images in the rock art described as *Salimobia* (see, for example, Figures 74g, 74i); frequently, they amplified such identifications with a description of that part of the initiation ceremony in which whippers play the greatest role. Each male who, as a young boy, is initiated into the Kachina Society, undergoes this whipping with yucca wands. During the initiation, which is supposed to occur every four years, the initiates first discover that the kachinas who dance in the plaza are not, as they have always thought, the real kachinas but only their impersonation by men. In a dramatic moment, while the eyes of those too young to be initiated are covered, they see the kachina masks removed and recognize the men who impersonated the kachinas (the fathers, uncles, brothers, and so on, of the boys being initiated).

Once initiated, the young boys are threatened with having their heads chopped off if they describe this impersonation to the younger children. This is thus a dramatic and powerful moment in the young boys' lives. The older men remembered it vividly and, when discussing it, dwelt most on the descriptions of being whipped—"hard"—by the Salimobia.

The rock art depiction of another frightening kachina, *Atoshle*, often called the "scare kachina," was specifically identified and described by a number of Zunis (see Figures 26d, 69a, 69e). Atoshle appears in male and female guise, and sometimes both were represented near one another in rock carvings and paintings. This kachina is particularly feared by young children, who are told they will be eaten by Atoshle if they are disobedient.

A figure prevalent in rock art of the Zuni area, as well as in the Southwest more generally, is the one described as the "humpbacked fluteplayer," a depiction belonging to a ritual complex in the Southwest that preceded the kachina cult (see Figures 23 far right, 25b, 27 far left, 28, 58, 86). Most Zunis said that this image represented a Hopi kachina but also noted features that were similar to those of certain Zuni kachinas. For instance, a flute-playing "culture hero," *Paiyatamu*, is prevalent in Zuni mythology, but he is not humpbacked. (Despite the humped back, the figures on the left in Figure 58 were most frequently linked with Paiyatamu by Zunis who looked at my photographs.) He nevertheless has a flute and, like the Hopi kachina, is associated with fertility and rain. Some Zunis described the kachina *Owiwi* as humpbacked; others said he carries a pack full of fetishes on his back. Finally, Zunis mentioned a phallic kachina who has no hump but was the central figure in a ceremony that involved flute playing (on flutes described as belonging to Paiyatamu) and the grinding of corn by men dressed as women. After some embarrassment, due probably to the fact that past experience shows outsiders to be notoriously critical of such performances, three Zuni men identified the two images in Figure 59 as "female with metate and *Ololowishkya*." The men described the cere-

mony in fairly similar terms, summarized in the following
statement by one of the men:

It's embarrassing,
    but it was for religious doings.
        Some males dressed like females
            and stretched out with grinding stones.
There were fluteplayers and rain dancers.
Ololowishkya had a dingaling made out of a gourd.
    He peed a sweet syrup into a big pot
        that had sweet corn in it.
    He peed to the directions of the earth six times.
    He made balls of the juice and corn
        and gave it to everyone.
            It tasted good.
This ceremony was done so there wouldn't be any problem
    with men's urine.
            We don't do this now because white people watch.

The closing sentence of this description reveals the negative
impact that value judgments of both tourists and some of the
early anthropologists have had on certain aspects of Zuni ritual life. The man who described the ceremony sadly concluded: "I don't think we'll ever see that dance again . . . only
certain people could do it. They're dead now." It is of note that
ritual actions involving the six directions are employed. Furthermore, in this particular ceremony, as in others at Zuni,
the ejection of fluid (urine/sweet syrup) is an omen: if it flows
evenly, things will go well for the Zunis; if it flows in a jerky
manner, sickness will occur.[21]

A final group of frequently identified kachina images in the
rock art was the category of "clowns"; within this category
those identified as Mudheads sometimes evoked the story of
their origin from an incestuous act as the people were searching for the Center. Zunis suggested that Figures 26f and 60
were Mudheads because of the apparent belly button; the Mudheads or *Koyemshi* often go bare-chested (Figure 3), and sometimes the dance kilt is worn low enough to reveal the belly

Figure 59. Pecked (and chalked) anthropomorphic figures, 30 cm × 30 cm, ZRAS site 11. Photograph by Robert H. Leibman, 1980.

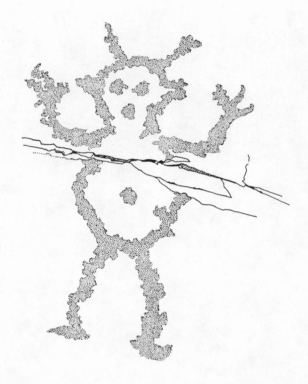

Figure 60. Pecked anthropomorphic figure, 22 cm × 12 cm, ZRAS site 11. Drawing by Murray Callahan.

button. Also, all of the figures so identified had projections from their heads, a characteristic of both groups of clowns at Zuni, the Koyemshi and the *Newekwe*. Zunis say that the knobs of mud on the heads of the Koyemshi contain butterfly wings and "bits of soil from the people's tracks about town," while the projections from the heads of the Newekwe are squash blossoms.[22]

All of these images evoke the past because they are representations of the ancestors; some, such as the Koyemshi and

Paiyatamu, are doubly evocative because they serve to recall parts of the origin myth in which they performed significant actions. While the Koyemshi originated from an act of incest, Paiyatamu, the flute-playing God of Dew and patron of the Newekwe, was a handsome but clownish figure who fell in love with the Corn Maidens and caused them to flee. Furthermore, Zunis link the kachinas to the predominant theme of their religion: the request for increase. As the above-described ceremonies indicate, the kachinas are central to rituals that relate to human health and fertility, but because they bring rain to the village, they are also associated with the growth of the crops. Kachina images, then, are figures of central importance to Zuni cultural symbolism; they are reiterated in a variety of graphic forms and are integral to the Zuni concept of multiplicity or accumulation.

Metonymic Features of the Landscape

Just as certain images carved on the rocks surrounding the pueblo evoke the myth time, so do various features of the landscape serve as vehicles by which Zunis "recall" events of the myth. These markers, some of which are beings preserved in stone since the time of the beginning, refer specifically to those events that take place after the emergence of the people from the fourth underworld to a world in which they are located both spatially and temporally.

With the emergence of the ancestors from the underworlds and the beginning of their journey in search of the Center, the origin myth takes on a more "historical" character involving notions of linear time (though clearly still mythic) and travels to places the Zunis identify with actual geographic locations.[23] For instance, they say that a river in Arizona is the site of the act of incest that created the Koyemshi, and they identify a nearby lake as the location of Kachina Village. Several Zunis told me that the actual place of the ancestors' emergence from the underworlds to the surface of this earth was located "somewhere in the Grand Canyon," and that later in those travels the second set of Twin War Gods (often called "the diminutive war gods") were created, and the clans were given their names at *Hanlhibinkya,* a place in Arizona near the reservation. They claimed that the petroglyphs on one very large and densely covered rock surface at this site were those clan symbols, although they seldom offered identifications of the specific images. Describing that mythic event, Stevenson writes, "Each name was chosen from some object seen at the time, and the totem of each clan was cut on the rocky walls; many of them are to be seen at the present time."[24] In some instances such places have even been incorporated into Zuni rituals. For example, Kachina Village in Arizona is the destination of an important pilgrimage undertaken every four years.

Some Zunis regard their ability to identify points named in the myth with actual geographical locations as a validation of the myth. One man expressed this in the following way:

These so-called legends
  are all based on actual facts
    as they are recited in the creation stories—
    the migrations of our people.
So, therefore, all these are based on fact
  and, this is the part
    that the whiteman never understood—
    the missionaries and others.
In the excavation of the ruins of our ancestors
  a lot of our priests
    told these white people in charge
      stories of how these cities, villages came into being,
      how they were settled,
      how they were abandoned.
A lot of these people said
  "Well, those are very interesting stories
  but there's no grounds for them."
Frank H. Cushing, an anthropologist
  from the Smithsonian Institute, I think,
    came out here—
      to Zuni—in 1879.

And for five years he spent his life
 living and studying the Zunis.
  He mastered the Zuni language—
   both the old and the new one,
  the prayers, everything.
And in time he was initiated
 into the warrior cult,
  or the warrior priesthood as we call it,
   of the Zuni people.
And in time he was second in command
 of these warriors.
But because of this knowledge
 of the Zuni language
  he was able to get
   all these facts from the Zuni people,
    according to their migrations
    and everything.
In listening to the migrations,
 and the villages where they settled,
 and the *landmarks* in the area of the villages.
He came back later on
 with the Hemenway expedition, I think,
 and while he was with this expedition
  he made a survey
   of this—ah—country here.
And using these landmarks
 described in these so-called legends
  he found them just where,
   where the Zunis said they were.
He found the ruins
 in the area of these landmarks
  and he followed these ru—
   line of ruins clear into Mexico,
    bearing out the traditions of the Zunis.
And so this shows that—
 that all of this
  as it pertains to our oral traditions
   is based on facts.
And a lot of this,

I later found out,
   this ties in with what
      the archaeologists have found.
So—I think—
   the archaeologists working
      with the Zuni people
         in *this* part
will—will maybe in time
   be able to find the key
      that's gonna solve the mystery
         of where we came from
            who we are
               and *everything.*[25]

Yet the actual geographic location of mythic places may not be as important as their location within the time and space of the myth. For instance, although most tribal members are familiar with the name "Hanlhibinkya" and consider it to be a shrine area that should be visited by certain religious groups, many do not know its precise location. On one occasion when I visited the site with an elderly religious leader he commented, somewhat noncommitally: "Maybe this is where I should have been bringing those prayer sticks."

Zunis do not believe that all events within the myth happened at places some distance away, however. They identify a number of places with distinctive physical features in and about the pueblo as the locations of various mythic events. For instance, I have heard some Zunis describe certain lopsided boulders just east of the village as marking the path of Salt Old Woman when the people desecrated her and she fled in anger. They associate the mesa called Corn Mountain with the time of the flood, partly because they attribute the banding of the sandstone to the different water levels as the water receded. They also say that the two stone pillars at its base represent the children who were sacrificed to the Horned Water Serpent so that the waters would dry up (Figure 61). They refer to a rocky outcrop on a mesa near Ojo Caliente as Sand Hill Crane, one of the Zuni clan animals fossilized in stone. Fur-

Figure 61. Detail of Dowa Yalanne (three miles southeast of Zuni Pueblo) showing "the Chief's son and daughter." Photograph by Adam Clark Vroman, 1899. Courtesy of the Smithsonian Institution, National Anthropological Archives (Neg. No. 2327).

ther, they describe certain oddly shaped rocks as the monsters that were solidified into rock in the fire that the Twin War Gods used to harden the surface of the earth after the emergence. All of these features of the present-day landscape evoke and are identified with events that took place at the time of the beginning. Hence, like rock art images, these landscape features can serve to evoke narratives. According to Robert J. Smith, whose characterization of visual images in a festival procession as metonymic of narrative has greatly influenced my own analysis: "Mountains, springs, trees, anything in the landscape may serve as such once it has been identified with a narrative. This fact explains the difference in meaningfulness of a landscape to people who live in an area and to those who are only passing through."[26] A similar linking of sacred locations and other features to mythological events has been described by Travis Hudson and Georgia Lee in a paper that focuses on the function and symbolism of Chumash rock art. The authors state:

Such locations were not only given placenames, but many quite probably also received some form of visual identity—a prominent symbol or symbols ... linked to specific myths and First People, and recognized by the community. Such sites must clearly have served to connect the greater community with its sacred past. Their specific location within the community served as a "story display" of their past and present within the total realm of the universe.[27]

The relationship between visual forms and traditional narratives is not one-sided; narratives can evoke the image of a visual form. For example, the mention of a place name in reciting a portion of the Zuni origin myth can evoke an image of the place named, both as an important point in the ancestors' quest for the Center and also as a known place in the physical world. Hanlhibinkya, where the clans were named, not only has mythic existence in the past but physical existence in the present as the specific place in Arizona to which the Zunis make periodic pilgrimages. Thus, past and present coexist; the time of the myth is one with everyday existence.

In a discussion of narrative presuppositions in the performance of Eastern Pomo myth, Sally McLendon suggests similarly that the reference to "real geographical areas functions to call forth an image of the area itself," adding that "the assertion of locational and directional detail involves the presupposition that the myths are true."[28] At Zuni, such areas often have well-recognized markers—for example, the skewed boulders identifying the path of Salt Old Woman. In other instances no such marker or even place name exists to specify or recall the purported site of an event. Nevertheless, the location of the site is "known" with no less certainty. In a discussion of the conflict the Twin War Gods had with a monstrous snake that whipped them with its tail, one old man told me: "It happened over there, just beyond the place where the elementary school is now." Certainly this ability to locate an episode from a myth, despite the lack of an obvious physical marker, serves to validate the myth. Here, too, McLendon's work is relevant. She describes driving around with an Eastern Pomo myth teller who pointed out to her the specific locations where episodes in a myth took place, "despite the fact that none of the significant landmarks remained!"[29] Similarly, the merging of present with past at Zuni is a validation both of everyday experience and of the myths, linked in some instances to visual features and in others to verbal formulae.

The examples in this chapter illustrate two types of visual elements in the Zuni environment that evoke traditional narratives: figures carved on the rocks, mesa walls, and in caves, surrounding the pueblo, and natural features of the landscape itself. I designate certain of these images as metonymic of the myth time because they have the power to symbolize and recall that time.[30] These are the sorts of images described earlier as those that contribute to drawing the world of the myth closer to the human world during ritual activities. Although my visits to rock art sites with Zunis were never framed as relating to ritual (indeed, I was generally prohibited from going near shrine areas), it is difficult to divide the Zuni world into secular and sacred activities or attributes of experience. Despite the existence of situations during which the myth time is closer to the present or human time than it is on other occasions, it is never very far away; Zuni religion is an integral part of Zuni daily experience. The immediacy of the myth time is partly demonstrated by the power of these metonymic images. Not only do they call forth stories about the time of the beginning, but they do so in an affective manner, also evoking the emotions associated with these stories. They project the past into the present, condensing experience, and they are frequently multireferential, standing for a number of things at the same time; thus, they intensify the experience of those who perceive them as signs from the past. No Zuni who responded to such images by reciting a portion of the origin myth remained unmoved by the experience, nor for that matter did I. In addition, the telling of part of the myth was itself a metonymic act, for that part stood for and evoked the entire world of the myth. Sometimes, when the evocative depictions were rock art figures, Zunis demonstrated their involvement by gently touching the figures or standing in front of them in silence for a long period of time; at other times they simply described them as "important." Furthermore, most Zunis regard at least some of the pictographs and petroglyphs in their environment as part of their cultural heritage, reacting with dismay when they are destroyed by vandalism.

The older Zunis with whom I talked were those who most frequently referred to certain figures as linked with the time of the beginning, perhaps because they and people of their generation know most about the mythical world and most readily find its presence in such visual imagery. Younger Zunis, especially when they did not know something themselves, indicated that it was the more elderly members of the tribe who knew most about myths, tales, and the meanings of things in general; it is the "old people who are the experts" about such matters. For instance, one man in his late fifties said that he only knew a few of the rock carvings and paintings and did not recognize the others but added: "They used to tell us that a long time ago they were made to represent clans and stuff like that—but, most of them I couldn't say that I know. I'm not that old."

Zunis relate the imagery of other material forms to the time of "the ancestors" as well. In fact, they surround themselves with symbols that represent important beings and events of the myth time; these symbols serve conceptually to link the two states of experience, the here-and-now and the myth. Fetishes, symbols on pottery, kiva murals, religious paraphernalia—all reiterate this connection in Zuni life.[31] While this may be a means by which Zunis validate their beliefs and ritual practices, it also reveals much about the Zuni attitude toward time. Zunis are constantly aware of the presentness of the past; this awareness is facilitated by symbols, prevalent in every aspect of Zuni life, that evoke their past.

The pictographs and petroglyphs and features of the landscape that operate as metonyms of narrative refer to past and present *at the same time,* contributing to an intensification of experience. This collapsing of time periods is similar to the verbal/visual interaction described by Robert J. Smith that results in a "tremendous compression of both emotion and concepts in the metonym."[32] It is, I believe, this compression of emotion that accounts for the affect and, hence, the power of these depictions. Indeed, such rock art images fit Robert Plant Armstrong's description of "affecting presences": works with "indwelling" power "which own some kind of ability— of efficacy of affect."[33] Affecting objects must be regarded in a dynamic way, as both processes and products, things and events. According to Armstrong, such objects are those in any culture that are accepted by its participants "as being purposefully concerned with potency, emotions, values, and states of being or experience—all, in a clear sense, *powers.*"[34] For the Zunis the power of certain visual images, their affecting presence, lies in their ability to evoke stories of the myth time and consequently to make the past coexistent with the present.

Some of the rock carvings and paintings that I have described as metonymic refer to the past in a doubly potent and quite explicit manner. The lizardlike figures described as "Zunis at the time of the beginning," for example, not only represent the ancestors (that is, the people who lived in the fourth underworld looked like this) but were also created by the ancestors back "in the time of the beginning." Thus these images are not only vehicles for talking about or representing the past, they are part of that past. Similarly, Zunis described spiral and concentric circle figures both as representing the "journey in search of the Center" and carved on the rocks by the very ancestors who made that journey. Unlike the lizardlike figures and the spiral and concentric circle figures, the more elaborate geometric designs are undecipherable—no one knows exactly what they represent, yet there is no doubt that they constitute some sort of "message from the ancestors," intentional communications from the past to the present.

The power of these images derives not only from their ability to project the past into the present, but also from their ambiguity.[35] All of these figures can refer to a number of meanings at the same time, an attribute inherent in the underlying principle of directionality as well. Depending on factors such as the age and involvement in Zuni religious life of the interpreter, the lizardlike figures can be either "Zunis at the time of the beginning," or "things that go on pottery"; the spiral and concentric circles give rise to a number of different meanings that were detailed earlier; the more elaborate geometric designs elude identification, but their very undecipherability lends itself to multiple but related meanings, all encompassed in the designation "signs from the ancestors." Furthermore, this dynamic ambiguity relates not only to the cultural meaning attributed to the figure but to its form as well. For instance, any spiral, no matter how large or small, no matter how many "turns" it contains, may embody a number of conceptually linked meanings. The particular meaning articulated at a given moment—i.e., water, wind, journey in search of the Center—depends on the context, the situation in which that meaning is given voice, not the form of that specific spiral. But there may be a meaning in the appearance of the figure as well. In this respect it is highly significant that all of these evocative rock art images ("lizard men," spirals and concentric circles, geometric designs) were pecked before A.D. 1325. Although clearly discernible, all are a bit eroded and, through the process of patination, have begun to take on the coloration of the rock surface on which they were carved. Thus their appearance on the rock is somewhat ambiguous: compared to the rock carvings created in the past fifty years or so, their form is rather blurred and indistinct. This very indistinctness may also relate to the perceived power of the images.

I have discussed two types of metonymic rock art images in this chapter. Lizard men, spirals, concentric circles, and geometric designs are those that most clearly call forth narratives—they are powerful, ambiguous, and related to the myth time. Depictions of the Beast Gods, Kolowisi, and kachinas, while also evocative, operate in a somewhat different manner—they more frequently elicit descriptions of their role in Zuni cultural symbolism than recitations of traditional narrative. The first group of metonymic figures are most specific to rock art; they are not well-known symbols repeated in other graphic media per se. Rather than referring to beings and events portrayed in other forms of Zuni visual art, they relate to beings and events "pictured" in Zuni verbal art. One might argue that lizardlike forms do appear on pottery, but they are identified as toads and frogs, not "Zunis at the time of the beginning" (nor is the form of such creatures in the pottery quite like that in the rock art). It is this latter meaning that I describe as calling forth the mythic past. Spirals and concentric circles seldom appear in other graphic media and, although geometric designs are prevalent in Zuni pottery, they are different from those in the rock art that are regarded as messages from the ancestors. The latter category of figures, those that represent the Beast Gods, Kolowisi, and the kachinas, occur frequently in other graphic media at Zuni and are generally highly representational. Significantly, most of these images have been gouged or incised—a technique dependent

Figure 62. Abraded mountain lion with five legs and tail bent over body, 50 cm × 110 cm, ZRAS site 26. Photograph by Robert H. Leibman, 1981.

upon the widespread use of metal tools, which began in the 1600s—and are often deeply carved, quite distinct in outline. Thus, these petroglyphs are generally not so ambiguous in form as those that have been pecked, nor have they been subjected to so much erosion; furthermore, they are characterized by distinguishing features that relate them to depictions of the same sorts of beings in other media. For instance, whether portrayed in rock art or a kiva mural, the mountain lion is characterized by a long tail bent over the body of the quadruped. (Zunis consistently identified the image in Figure 62 as a mountain lion, unperturbed by the existence of the five legs—the most significant feature was the tail bent over the animal's body.) Kachinas, whether dancing in the plaza or carved on mesa walls, are identified by dance kilts, masks, and head feathers, while individual kachinas are recognized by particular features such as the one long horn that denotes

Sayatasha, and so on. These depictions still evoke the myth time, but they do so less ambiguously than those more mysterious and older images that were made by "the ancestors."

These various characteristics, coupled with Zuni responses to a range of pictographs and petroglyphs, suggest a taxonomy that has as its broadest categories "old," "new," and "somewhere in between." This taxonomy also roughly corresponds to the relative dates of the rock art: "old" refers to those images created prior to A.D. 1325; "new" to those created in the last one hundred years; "somewhere in between" to those created during the period from A.D. 1325 to the late 1800s. Interestingly, one of the distinctions made by several Zunis who looked through my drawings and photographs of rock art figures, dividing them into categories, was complete/incomplete. The complete images were highly representational and created since A.D. 1325, whereas those categorized as incomplete were older and more ambiguous in form. Thus, this temporal taxonomy relates to perceived power as well: the oldest carvings and paintings are those that are most powerful because in their very ambiguity they relate most strongly to the time of the ancestors.

This taxonomy also relates to the Zuni aesthetic principles delineated by Barbara Tedlock: "the dangerous," which is powerful, dark, plain, muffled, and indistinct; and "the beautiful," which is dynamic, chromatic, varied, multicolored. It is quite possible that the old, blurred, ambiguous, and metonymic rock art images—those that evoke the past—embody the aesthetic of "the dangerous," whereas the more recent highly representational rock art figures, some of which are painted in a variety of colors with distinct outlines and, sometimes, a three-dimensional perspective, are part of an aesthetic of "the beautiful." Those depictions discussed as "in between," figures of the kachinas, Kolowisi, and Beast Gods, for example, partake of both characteristics: they may be dangerous and beautiful, powerful and dynamic (although some of the kachina pictographs were probably painted in the last fifty years, the greatest number of these images fall within the time period post-

A.D. 1325 to the late 1800s). Thus I do not suggest, nor do I think Tedlock means to imply, that "the beautiful" is not powerful. One cannot separate Zuni sacred from secular life, nor can one simply divide the beings that inhabit their world into powerful and powerless. The hierarchy of rawness/finished that I discussed earlier, however, makes it clear that some beings are more powerful (raw) than others (less raw, or finished). In any case, Zuni perceptions of rock art images are integral to the Zuni way of conceptualizing the world along continua defined by qualities such as unfinished (raw) and finished; dangerous and beautiful. These qualities are not entirely mutually exclusive, however; certain of the kachinas, for example, are beings that are both raw and beautiful. Just as Zuni temporal and spatial perceptions are characterized by fluid boundaries, so are their perceptions of other qualities or aspects of existence; it is this very permeability that makes possible the dialectic interaction between present and past.

5

The Power of Image and Place

Iconic Power: Power by Similarity and Association

In the previous chapter I discussed certain rock art images and environmental features that were evocative of, or perceived as formed in, the time of the myth. I now wish to explore the related issues of why rock carvings and paintings are produced and the function of certain rock art sites at Zuni in the present day or the recent past. Underlying both concerns is the concept of power, whether it be the power *evoked* by certain images that recall the time of the beginning or the power *invoked* through the depiction of particular figures. On the one hand, the power inherent in those images I previously discussed as metonymic is frequently related to their ambiguity of both form and meaning. On the other hand, the power inherent in those images that depict beings associated by the Zunis with vital aspects of the physical world is related to their specificity—their ability to "represent" those living beings. The *meaning* of these latter images may at times be metaphorical or ambiguous, but their form rarely is. Furthermore, these more representational images were generally produced in more recent times than those that are evocative of the myth time.

One way in which to answer the question of why pictographs and petroglyphs are produced by the Zunis is to see if the same figures are prevalent in other media as well. If so, one would then ask if the production of such similar figures across various media is motivated by the same factors. Certain categories of efficacious rock art images, such as those depicting Beast Gods and creatures associated with water, do appear in other graphic forms at Zuni. Perhaps this is because the Zunis would most naturally surround themselves with those elements regarded as potentially powerful and capable of bringing benefits to them, whatever the artistic mode. The use of such imagery may be an instance of what Bunzel has called "compulsive magic"; that is, the attempt to attain desired events or outcomes by their ritual depiction, either in the form of graphic illustrations or by means of their dramatic enactment.[1] In semiotic terms, these images may be said to invoke power because of their iconicity, their resemblance or similarity to living beings that are potent in and of themselves or associated with some efficacious aspect of the natural world.[2] Previously mentioned examples include painting water-related creatures on prayer meal bowls so that rain will fall (Figures 49, 50)[3] and carrying the fetish of a Beast God while hunting its natural prey.[4] Likewise, Bunzel reports that Zuni potters often painted deer enclosed in a "house" on their pottery so that their husbands would have good luck in hunting (Figure 63).[5]

It is quite possible that Zunis created some rock carvings and paintings for similar reasons. For instance, the following descriptions of insect figures in rock art link the carving of the image to beneficial results, such as stinging the enemy with poison or making Zunis invisible to their enemies. The latter power is derived from insects whose protective coloring and shape render them invisible to their predators. As illustrated by the story of the Water Skate finding the Center as well as by the association of ants with the six directions, insects play a major role in Zuni cultural symbolism; like the Beast Gods, they form another category of raw beings whose potency humans can accrue to themselves through ritual ac-

Figure 63. Zuni jar. Courtesy of the Smithsonian Institution, National Anthropological Archives (Neg. No. 2266B).

tivity. Although they did not necessarily associate them with events that occurred in the myth time, Zunis frequently identified insectlike rock art figures as beings with special efficacy; their depictions evoked descriptions of their important position in the Zuni hierarchy of powerful beings.

The identification one Zuni woman offered for Figure 64 illustrates the use medicine men make of the special powers of insects:

I don't know its name,
        but it is a gray insect.
It draws its legs next to its body
        and then looks like a stick.
Medicine society men who go to war crush up
        and eat these insects
                so that they will be invisible to their enemies.

Figure 64. Incised figure, 14 cm × 9 cm, ZRAS site 11. Drawing by Murray Callahan.

Similarly, according to many Zunis, a panel of insect petro-glyphs at the Village of the Great Kivas site was carved there for purposes of warfare (Figure 85). They said the panel depicted poisonous insects that were carved on the rocks by the war chief so that they would sting the enemies of the Zunis. Such belief in the potency and wisdom of insects is echoed by one man who said the following about ants:

> They are so wise,
>   they always remember where their home is.
> They travel great distances,
>   but always find their way back.
> We make offerings to ants for their wisdom,
>   so that we will have the ability
>   to keep the prayers in our memory.

These descriptions and identifications reveal the particular powers Zunis attribute to insects and their belief that, if they perform the proper ritual procedures, they can invoke the help of these creatures.

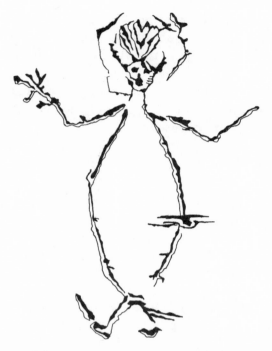

Figure 65. Incised figure identified frequently by Zunis as a stink bug, 30 cm × 22 cm, ZRAS site 2. Drawing by Murray Callahan.

Not only does the portrayal of certain images effect desired outcomes—that is, a result occurs because of the iconic power of the figure—so, too, can such portrayals lead to the prevention of undesired outcomes. A petroglyph identified as "stink bug" (Figure 65) evoked the following story from one man who described its role in Zuni beliefs about reincarnation:

> My grandfather told me not to kill stink bugs,
>> because in Zuni belief when you die the first time
>>> you go to Kachina Village.
> Then you go through four reincarnations.
> The last one is a stink bug.
> If you kill that there is no more life,
>> that is the end of the cycle.

This man concluded that the rock carving was produced to remind Zunis that they should respect all living beings and, in this case, the stink bug in particular. Other Zunis said that one could become a variety of raw beings after the fourth death, not just stink bugs; nevertheless, this example serves to underscore the prominent place of this particular insect in the Zuni taxonomy of raw beings.

Just as powerful insects are carved on the rocks to effect desired outcomes, so are other images depicted because of their association with certain powerful characteristics of the species represented. For instance, according to a number of Zunis, water-related creatures such as frogs, toads, and hump-backed fluteplayers were carved and painted on the rocks in some areas to bring rain to the village (see Figures 86, 87), and the depiction of game animals not only recorded a successful hunt but propitiated the spirits of the animals that had been slain, ensuring more such success in the future (see Figure 87, deer figure). Other representations of game animals in rock art, especially the many carved images of mountain sheep struck with spears (Figure 30c) and deer with arrows projecting from their bodies (Figure 66), may also have been created in the hopes of assuring good luck in the hunt. Although most of the animal figures in rock art of the Zuni-Cibola region are not so explicitly related to hunting, a number of them may have been produced for this reason. Figure 67, for instance, is a pecked figure of a mountain sheep that has been carved with a hole in the center of its body, perhaps indicating the heart that the successful hunter's arrow will strike. In any case, whatever the original motive for their production, such images, once made, might very well have been used in ritual activities aimed at ensuring the success of the hunt. For example, in her major work on Zuni published at the turn of the century, Stevenson states that men sometimes shot rock art depictions of game animals, especially deer, with arrows before they set out to hunt.[6] Some evidence suggests that suitable pictographs and petroglyphs are still used in this way, at least on a limited scale, although the weapons are now guns

Figure 66. Incised and gouged deer with arrows in their bodies, 50 cm × 35 cm, ZRAS site 2. Photograph by Nancy L. Bartman, 1979.

Figure 67. Pecked mountain sheep (pecked hole near heart), 45 cm × 65 cm, ZRAS site 17. Photograph by Robert H. Leibman, 1980.

Figure 68. Pecked mountain sheep, actual bullet holes, 45 cm × 40 cm, ZRAS site 19. Photograph by Robert H. Leibman, 1980.

rather than arrows, spears, or atlatls. Whether shooting at rock art figures is motivated by a belief in the efficacy of ritual activity to ensure a successful hunt or by a simple desire for target practice, the bullet holes and disfigured images are mute testimony to the fact that such shooting occurs.

When I initially undertook the project of recording rock art at Zuni, I assumed that bullet holes, like spray-painted, chalked, and carved graffiti, were examples of vandalism. Now I have come to believe that, at least in some cases, the bullet holes are the visible remains of the modern version of the sort of ritual activity described by Stevenson rather than the result of vandalism. The choice of targets, generally game animals such as mountain sheep, bear, buffalo, and deer, supports such a conclusion (Figures 68, 70, 74, 76). My re-examination of two panels of painted masks and animal figures at the site called the Village of the Great Kivas reveals that while none of the other kachina masks had been used as targets, some masks and paintings of game animals had been disfigured by bullet holes.[7] In Figure 74 the deer figure to the far right is riddled with bullet holes, as are the bear (also identified as coyote) and buffalo masks.[8] The only image marked by bullet holes in the other panel of masks (Figure 69) is a deer (this is most obvious in Figures 75 and 76). Overall, at this site only the masks and figures of the buffalo, bear, and deer have been shot at. It would appear, then, that some Zunis are less concerned with the preservation of these pictographs as "art" than with their use toward more practical ends. This is quite in keeping with the numerous accounts in the ethnographic literature describing the purposeful "destruction" by Zunis of pottery, baskets, sand paintings, and kiva murals in rites of cleansing, renewal, and purification.[9] Zunis even place the sacred images of the Twin War Gods in open shrines on mesa tops so that they are slowly eaten away by weathering—a process that, in this case, Zunis regard as desirable. While an outsider might consider the destruction of such material culture items to be a deplorable loss to the scientific community that seeks to preserve and study such things, the Zunis place a high value on newness and do not necessarily value their old things as others do. Barbara Tedlock points out this emphasis on change and newness in her description of kachina dance songs, many of which are made new for every dance. Although these songs are tape recorded by many Zunis, they are not preserved for posterity but taped over and replaced by newer songs when they have become old.[10] This attitude may change with increased emphasis on the preservation of the "old ways" by many tribal agencies and individuals, but for the present it certainly remains.

At the same time it should be clear from the previous chapter that many Zunis do value "old" rock art because of its presumed great antiquity, which is related to their perception of it as having been made by "the ancestors." This is a somewhat different situation from that of the rain-dance songs created last week or last year or even pots made fifty to one hundred years ago. Nor are all songs created for particular rain dances and then forgotten. For example, Barbara Tedlock distinguishes between songs that should be new each time and those most sacred prayers and ritual activities that should never be changed but must be learned word for word and carried out in the same manner from year to year.[11] Thus, both the new and the old can be valued for different reasons or in different contexts and one needs to pay attention to such contexts, particularly given the emphasis on preservation that is a contemporary concern, in certain situations, for both Native American and non-Native American peoples.

Finally, though some Zunis may shoot at rock art images, others are disturbed by this practice, stating that it is "a shame" and attributing it to "young kids who don't know any better." Figure 70 illustrates this point. Whatever the reason for the shooting of the bear mask (mask on left), it is apparent that since the time of the shooting someone has tried to repair the damage. The lines of the mouth have been repainted over the bullet holes.

Although I have made use of Bunzel's term "compulsive magic," I dislike the sense of causality and legerdemain it

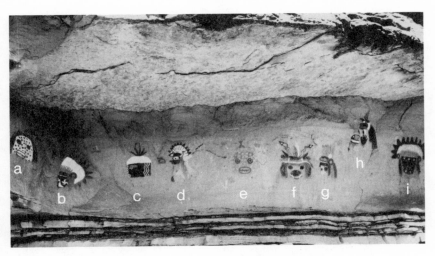

Figure 69. Panel of painted masks and figures, 1.5 m × 8 m, ZRAS site 1. Images from left to right are: (A) *Atoshle*—Male Scare Kachina; (B) *Kumance*—Comanche; (C) *Hehe'a*—Blunderer; (D) *Shalako*—Courier of the Rain Gods; (E) *Suyuki*—Female Scare Kachina; (F) *Wo'latana*—Bear; (G) *Wilatsukwe*—Apache; (H) *Wa:kashi*—Cow; (I) *Kumance*—Comanche. Photograph by M. Jane Young, 1980.

seems to imply. The relationship between the action and the desired result is not conceived of by Zunis as causal in the Western scientific sense of the term. As already noted, Zunis do not believe themselves to be so endowed with power that they can make things happen. Instead, they consider that they are relatively weak beings who must consequently depend on the aid of more efficacious mediators to gain desired ends. In return for this help Zunis make appropriate offerings both to the mediators and to those even more potent beings to whom such mediators convey their prayers. Zuni religious belief is thus based not on a notion of the ability of humans to cause things to happen but on the idea of reciprocity between humans and other more powerful beings who do have the ability to effect change in the physical world.

Figure 70. Enlargement of bear mask with bullet holes and Comanche mask, 70 cm × 120 cm, ZRAS site 1. Photograph by Nancy L. Bartman, 1979.

An interesting illustration of the way in which Zunis view religious activity as couched in a framework of reciprocal activity, a dialectic between humans and the gods, is provided by an examination of the structure and texts of Zuni ritual prayers. Frequently the main body of these often lengthy prayers consists of a recitation, in the past tense, of all of the ritual activities undertaken during the year; special emphasis is given to the places where such activities were carried out, including spring areas and sites marked by rock art depictions. The prayers are concluded with a request section, in the future tense, which could be summed up as meaning: "we've done our part, now you will do yours." The specific Zuni verb used to make this "request," *shema* (translated most often as "ask for"), has more accurately the meaning of "demand." In the context of the prayer, the use of this word does not strike an arrogant chord but instead expresses the Zuni belief that certain actions must inevitably happen upon the completion of others—because A has been accomplished, B surely will follow.[12]

Conversely, activities intended to ensure successful hunting, such as painting a deer enclosed in his "house" on a piece of pottery or carving deer with arrows through their bodies on rocks, are not simply magical acts, believed to be sufficient to produce the desired outcome. Rather, the creation of those depictions is only one part of the ritual activity believed necessary to achieve the desired end, albeit the most explicitly communicative of what is being asked for. To be effective, such depictions must be accompanied by the appropriate prayers and offerings, and the entire ritual must be carried out by one who has a "good heart."[13] When those prayers are not answered—if, for example, the dry spell continues despite the rain dances—the Zunis attribute this inefficacy to the involvement in the ceremony of someone who has a "bad heart."[14] Thus, the core of Zuni religion may be said to be a belief not in magic but in the potency of reciprocal relations, the belief that if ritual activities are carried out in the proper manner, with a good heart, the desired result will be obtained. The central issue here, then, is the power of ritual activity and related visual imagery, but only as they exist within this framework of reciprocity.

Similar power is invoked in ritual activities that consist mainly of the enactment of a desired event. This is illustrated in Stevenson's description of hunters shooting arrows at rock art depictions of deer. More recently Zuni colleagues told me that when Mudheads throw water on one another and on the dusty ground of the plaza during summer rain dances, they do so to encourage rain to fall. A further example is provided by an event that occurred while I was visiting a rock art site located near a pool of water with an elderly Zuni religious leader. It had not rained at Zuni for over a week, and people were worried about their crops. The site we visited, however, was thirty miles west of the pueblo, just across the Arizona border; the wet ground there, as well as the greatly enlarged pool, were evidence of a recent rainfall. Stating that there was something he needed to do before we looked at the rock art, the old man took a pinch of sacred cornmeal from a pouch he always carried and scattered it to the six directions. Then he waded to the center of the pool and prayed. Afterward, turning so that in effect he had his back to the direction of the pueblo, he leaned over, cupped his hands, and proceeded to throw water over his right shoulder toward Zuni. Later, he said the purpose of these actions was to encourage the rain to move to the New Mexico side of the border, to the village and fields of Zuni. He also filled his canteen with water from the pond to bring back and sprinkle on those fields, another act performed to move the rain over to Zuni. After looking at the rock art we started back to the pueblo and encountered a mild summer shower that did, indeed, extend all the way to Zuni, supplying the crops with much-needed water. The old man said: "I guess my prayer was answered."

The aim or request of most such activity is traditionally expressed in terms of a number of related goals, such as rain for the crops, success in the hunt, many children, and a long life. These, however, are often metaphors for the broader goals of increase, prosperity, and well-being in general or for the satisfaction of a variety of specific needs relating to particular situations. These interrelated goals, all encompassed in the concept of increase or multiplicity, form what I described earlier as the Zuni aesthetic of accumulation. The metaphoric rather than directly literal nature of such requests is underlined by the interesting adaptation to modern circumstances reported by Barbara Tedlock.[15] Traditionally, summer rain dancers have carried corn kernels and seeds of important crops in their belts as the "heart" of their request.[16] As the economy of Zuni has shifted from a reliance on farming to a heavy dependence on the sale of jewelry and pottery, many dancers now carry a lump of turquoise instead of the seeds in their belts. Although the song text is couched in terms of the traditional request for rain, it is clear that rain is used here as a metaphor for prosperity in general and the increased sales of jewelry in particular.

Another example of such metaphoric activity is the ritual smoking during the ceremonies in kivas and medicine society rooms. In this ritual, one sends smoke to the six directions so that the gods of those regions may, in return, send their "smoke" in the form of clouds, and hence rain. In the text of the prayer, the same word—*shipololon*—is used to denote "smoke," "mist," and "rain," an intentional ambiguity that is characteristic of Zuni verbal art.[17] Central to this example is the metaphoric transformation by which smoke becomes equivalent to rain clouds; herein lies the power of the ritual.

Indexical Power: Interaction of Image and Site

If rock art depictions such as those mentioned earlier (water beings that bring rain, insects that render one invisible or sting the enemy, and game animals and their predators that relate to successful hunting) may be regarded as powerful or capable of invoking power, does this efficacy extend to the places where such figures are found? In other words, is the potency of the imagery an index of the power of the site to which it is integral? Many early anthropologists and archaeologists have suggested that pictographs and petroglyphs were often used to mark shrine areas.[18] But what exactly is a shrine area? Can a clustering of rock art images be sacred in itself? Can it make the place where it is found powerful? It may be impossible to separate in this manner the power of the place and the power of the images found there or to distinguish one or the other as being prior or prime. This is because rock art characteristically brings together both the power of place and the power of imagery, juxtaposing the natural world with the human creative world. Nevertheless, a discussion of certain places where rock art occurs in the Zuni-Cibola region will be useful at this point.

At Zuni, rock art is found beyond the confines of the pueblo proper, beyond the central dwelling place and in potentially dangerous areas less controlled by the people—areas in which raw, powerful beings dwell. Pictograph and petroglyph sites include cliff walls and caves, places where game animals and predators roam, and places where Zunis say even the powerful kachinas sometimes assume animal form and walk about. Perhaps inaccessibility itself may be a power-producing attribute of such sites. Certainly the location of a number of rock carvings and paintings far above the ground on a seemingly sheer cliff wall or high on the ceiling of a cave often led my Zuni colleagues to muse: "How did they get up there?" (see, for example, Figures 21, 67). Although they speculated on the use of devices such as scaffolds, ropes, or arrows dipped in paint, the reasons for employing such methods remained perplexing and intriguing to contemporary Zunis. Nevertheless, images that were produced in recent times, especially those images that relate to the central themes of Zuni religion, are sometimes also located in out-of-the-way places. An obscure or hard-to-reach location is not the only means by which to render rock art inaccessible to the casual observer; diminutive size can be a contributing factor as well. One site contained finely incised and highly detailed depictions of the masks of the Council of the Gods (a group of kachinas who play a central role in the Shalako ceremony); each mask was only five centimeters high and the entire group could be easily overlooked by someone who did not already know they were there.

Not only are rock art sites located in the rugged mesa lands surrounding the pueblo; so too are sacred shrine areas. Sometimes the two even co-occur. Mesa tops and other high places signify the special haunts of the Twin War Gods in the time of the beginning. The shrines located there today are dedicated to those gods and contain figures of them carved out of wood. Spring areas are also sacred, not only as sources of water but because they are the domain of Kolowisi, the Horned Water Serpent. The Zunis believe that all bodies of water—springs, lakes, ponds, rivers, and so on—are connected by a system of underground waterways to the surrounding oceans; Kolowisi travels through these underground waters to reach the various bodies of water that serve as outlets to the surface of the earth.

Pictograph and petroglyph sites are often located near, and may even be an integral part of, these sacred shrine areas where prayer sticks are deposited during the yearly round of ritual activities. In his recitation of all the ceremonial duties he has performed that year to ensure rain for the crops, *Sayatasha* (the Long Horn Kachina) mentions the names of twenty-nine spring areas where he left prayer sticks; several of these places are rock art sites.[19] One such spring/shrine area is the previously mentioned Hanlhibinkya. The name of another of these spring areas, *Atsinakwi,* translates as "the place of the writing." Zunis told me that "writing" in this case referred specifically to the rock art images located there.

Sometimes the cultural meaning of rock art relates to its particular location. At one site, for example, a spiral and a concentric circle were carved in the rock face at a point that is directly above several connecting pools of water (Figure 57). One Zuni man suggested that this placement was due to the fact that the spiral figure sometimes represents water. On the day we visited this site the sun shining on the water was reflected onto the petroglyphs above, almost in a spiral design; it is possible that the figures were carved to depict this phenomenon, as well as to symbolize water. Significantly, Zuni ceremonialism and mythology link sun and water. According to the Zuni origin myth, the Twin War Gods were born of the union of the sun and a waterfall; hence they represent two of the most important aspects of Zuni ritual: prayers to the Sun Father asking that he allow the crops to thrive and prayers to the ancestors that they may send rain.[20] The connection between the meaning of a rock art depiction and the place where it is located is illustrated further by the comment made by a Zuni man who was very familiar with a number of the rock art sites when we were looking at projected slides. Even though I had not grouped these slides by site and was not asking for any sort of information concerning location, this man quite accurately accompanied his identifications of images with descriptions of the sites where they occur. Every now and then, however, he encountered a figure he hadn't seen before. His response on one such occasion was: "I don't know what it means because I've never been out there." Thus, for him meaning was tied to specific location and he couldn't be expected to identify an image on a slide that he hadn't seen in reality, situated in its appropriate context. The importance of context was also revealed by those Zunis who came with me to rock art sites. They not only looked closely at the carved and painted figures on rock surfaces, but carefully observed the features of the landscape within which the rock art was located, paying particular attention to varieties of plants, sources of water when available, bird nests, and animal tracks. Sometimes they spent as much time instructing me in the uses of wild plants as they did talking to me about rock art—obviously, they consider all of these aspects of their environment to be significant.

As noted earlier, features in the landscape around the pueblo are perceived as powerful because of their relationship to mythical events and beings. In this situation, too, one might expect that the location of powerful rock art images at or near such areas would increase the power-invoking potential of both. Certainly pictographs and petroglyphs occur at areas such as Hanlhibinkya where, although the rock art is not necessarily responsible for the sacredness of the place, it may add to this sacredness, having supposedly been created by the ancestors. Hanlhibinkya derives its sacredness from its association with events that occurred in the myth time. It is identified as the place where the people stopped in their journey to find the Center and were given their clan names, and as the spot where the second pair of Twin War Gods was created. The rock art there serves as a sign of those events, for the clan symbols were carved on the rocks back in the time of the beginning and remain there today.

Although it includes rock art images associated with ritual activity, a site on Corn Mountain derives its importance primarily from mythic events said to be recorded in the distinctive geological formations there—the stone pillars described earlier as the boy and girl who were sacrificed to Kolowisi, the Horned Water Serpent (Figure 61). According to the accounts of some ethnographers, these pillars are shrines visited by parents seeking to ensure the gender of a future child.[21] Thus, couples who want a boy go the stone said to represent the boy; those who want a girl go to the shrine representing the girl. The latter, which received most of the early ethnographers' attention, seems also to function more generally as a fertility shrine for women who have been childless. I have little to add from personal observation because members of the Zuni Tribal Council told me that this shrine was still in use and warned me not to go near it. They did describe its general location, however, so that I could avoid it, since it was near a rock art site I was permitted to record. Both Stevenson and Fewkes describe the female fertility shrine as consisting of the large stone pillar, surrounded by boulders on which hundreds of female fertility symbols (vaginalike oblongs and triangles) have been carved.[22] The base of the stone pillar is also honeycombed with small holes, the creation of which mystified the geologists who accompanied Stevenson; they could not determine whether these holes had originally been created by humans. When Stevenson asked the Zunis who had led them to the site about the origin of the holes, she was told: "They belong to the old; they were made by the gods."[23] Zunis regard these excavations, then, as well as the stone pillar itself, as created in the time of the myth. Stevenson includes a photograph of this area, which she labels "mother rock," in her major work on Zuni.[24] Although I never saw them in such concentration in my fieldwork, I was able to recognize these symbols from Stevenson's photograph and found them to be common elements in much of the rock art of the region surrounding the pueblo.

There is evidence to suggest that Zunis do indeed regard some rock art sites as sacred *because* of the pictographs and petroglyphs there and not because of any other factors extrinsic or prior to the rock art. That is, the power of the site is derived solely from the image or cluster of images found there. The types of figures at such sites may include, of course, those described earlier as myth-evoking.

Another site that I was not allowed to see since it is regarded as sacred because of its rock art was described to me as consisting of a cave on the walls of which was painted a Kolowisi, the Plumed Water Serpent, mentioned earlier as a particularly dangerous and powerful being in Zuni mythology. When I asked to see the cave, the sheepherder who used that land said, "You shouldn't see that because Kolowisi is part of our religion."[25] On the other hand, although he did ask me not to take photographs, one religious leader had no apparent reservations about leading me to another site—a cavelike area containing a spring—and permitting me to see the six images of Kolowisi painted in the colors of the six directions. This site also contained pictographs of the most powerful kachinas in the Zuni pantheon, the six Shalakos and the Council of the Gods. As I discuss at the end of this chapter, power seems to accrue particularly to painted images of masks and kachina dancers in the rock art. Zunis must regard this site, then, as especially potent. Interestingly, such power seems to belong to the painted depictions but not particularly to carved images of the same figures, suggesting perhaps that there is efficacy in the paint itself.

Significance of Repetition

If rock carvings and paintings have power, a power that can be imparted to the places where they are created, then several images placed in close proximity to one another might make that place even more powerful. For example, published pictures of the "fertility shrine" mentioned above show a surface covered with hundreds of female fertility symbols. In the Zuni area, the repetition of figures on single panels or on several surfaces in a small area, often executed at different time periods, is not an uncommon phenomenon although rarely as extensive as in this example. Multiple handprints or footprints, rows of mountain sheep, deer, birds, animal tracks, geometric designs, or strikingly similar masks and kachina figures recur at single rock art sites or even throughout the entire region. This is perhaps another example of the Zuni aesthetic of accumulation—the tendency to repeat certain images over and over again so that their surroundings "echo" those concepts with which they are most concerned. Such sites seem to be characterized by specific dominant themes related to ritual activity and power or, in some cases, to the demarcation of areas where particular types of activity occur.

Handprints, footprints, and animal tracks (Figures 29 and 31) are of particular significance because they are often regarded as "signatures," both in the rock art of this region and in many other areas as well. For example, Schaafsma states that the handprint in rock art of the Southwestern Indians "served as a means of identification," dating from extremely early times (i.e., the Basketmaker period) up to the present.[26] Other scholars suggest that the early native peoples often used handprints to mark a sacred place, a practice (according to Ellis and Hammack) that is still carried on by modern Pueblo Indians:

Tracing one's hand on the wall of a sacred place brings a blessing into one's self, like "taking the breath" from any sacred object. Moreover, at completion of a ceremony, the leader may whiten his hand and press it against the kiva or other wall to signify that he has carried out his religious duty.[27]

Handprints (particularly those that are painted) are commonly located in what seems to be a rather circumscribed area—one or two rock art surfaces literally covered with handprints. If the handprint does serve as a signature, then this repetition may signify either many visits to a place by one individual or visits by many individuals, all of whom are impelled to leave their imprint on a particular part of the landscape. It is possible that thus leaving "a sign of oneself" at a sacred place facilitates or invites a personal experience of the sacred. Multiplying those signs by leaving many handprints (either at one particular time or over an extended period) may contribute to an intensification of that experience.

In the rock art of the Zuni-Cibola region handprints are most often executed in red paint, although one spectacular site includes such prints in unusual pastel colors such as lavender, pink, and light yellow. These prints are quite faded and do not appear to have been made with modern pastel paints.[28] As with pictographic images of masks, much of the power of painted handprints may derive from the very fact that they are painted.

Seemingly related is the practice, described in the ethnographic literature, of marking a house, room, or kiva with a handprint after plastering (plastering is a task traditionally performed by women). Matilda Stevenson describes similar markings at a site excavated near Santa Fe: "An impression of a hand and arm in color, probably of a maiden, was found on the wall. Such evidences of maidenly vanity are still to be seen in pueblo houses of the present time."[29] Although I would not describe such "signatures" in Stevenson's somewhat biased terms, I, too, have seen handprints on the ceilings of certain houses I visited in Zuni.

Human footprints occur repeatedly in the rock art of the Zuni-Cibola region with almost the same frequency as handprints (Figure 29), although rarely as pictographs.[30] Perhaps they too, like handprints, mark sacred areas or serve as individual signatures. In fact, as the following suggests, the footprint can even be used in certain contexts to embody the essence of an individual. In describing the Mudheads (Koyemshi) at Zuni, Parsons states that: "Into the knobs of the masks are put bits of soil from the people's tracks about the town. This device gives the *koyemshi* power over the people and it is probably the prime reason for the great reverence in which the *koyemshi* are held."[31] As discussed earlier in respect to handprints, the repetition of carved footprints at a site may involve leaving a sign (either of one self or many selves) on the landscape. It must be pointed out, however, that covering one's hand or foot with paint and pressing it against a rock surface is a different sort of activity than carefully pecking a representation of one's hand or foot on the rock. The pecking need not be personal (of one's own prints) but could be a more general symbol; further, even though they generally occur in sheltered areas, the images produced by painting are much more ephemeral than those that have been carved by some means. This differential technique might indicate differential function as well. The fact that pecked hand- and footprints do not occur in the same place or throughout a general area with as much frequency as painted prints also suggests a different purpose behind their production.

Rock art images of animal and bird tracks (Figure 31) often evidence repetition, either at one particular site or throughout a series of several sites. Those figures depicted most commonly are the tracks of the deer, the bear, the wolf, the turkey, and the crane. Most of these animals are conceived of either as predators or prey and, as with the carvings of full images of the same animals, these tracks may have been put on the rocks to ensure success in hunting. Nevertheless, birds and animals also embody other aspects of Zuni cultural symbolism, which may be represented by their tracks as well.[32] Zunis regard deer, for instance, as sacred animals, particularly since the kachinas may sometimes assume their form. Similarly, they associate eagles with the sky and the powers of the sun, they link badgers with healing, and they see turkeys as related to death. Repetition of the images of these animals or their tracks may involve the invoking of the particular power they embody. In addition, many Zunis also identified such tracks as symbols of the particular clans associated with these birds or animals. This identification of some images as clan symbols (including those of plants and of bird and animal figures and tracks) points to a very different kind of function for certain rock art sites than that related to hunting.[33] Zunis who suggested that some of these often repeated images were clan symbols or clan signatures based their opinion not only on oral traditions and scholarly writings associating clan symbols with particular sites[34] but also on their expressed opinion that "it is good to have pictures of your clan animal around you."[35] Not surprisingly, these people were delighted to receive photographs of rock art depictions of their clan animal that they could hang in their houses.

The carvings of clan symbols by Hopi participants in the extremely arduous annual salt-gathering pilgrimage has been described by Michaelis among others. This pilgrimage is a long journey (about seventy-five miles from the Hopi village of Oraibi to the Grand Canyon) undertaken on foot. Those who participate descend, sometimes using ropes, into the Grand Canyon to collect the salt from a deposit there. According to Michaelis:

On the way, [to the Grand Canyon] the participants stopped and engraved their clan emblems on a Rock Shrine they named Tuteveni (Writing). On subsequent trips, the same man would repeat his signature to the left of the original sign. This explains the series of identical signs carved one next to the other.[36]

Pilgrimages are central events in Zuni ceremonial life as well, and it is possible that the repeated symbols on some individual rocks or at specific sites are the clan emblems of participants in such pilgrimages produced in commemoration of these journeys.[37] Nevertheless, at this time I do not have concrete evidence of such activity—I have not found rock surfaces covered with carved or painted clan symbols along a recognized pilgrimage route in the Zuni area.

Some scholars have suggested that pictographs and petroglyphs of clans and similar symbols may have also served to mark tribe, family, and clan territories, especially those used for hunting, farming, and grazing.[38] Forde, for instance, has stated that Hopis delimited clan lands by placing numerous boundary stones, engraved with symbols of the appropriate clan, at the corners and junction points of the various sections of land. Some of these boundary stones are still standing.[39] At Zuni, too, single images recurring over and over again on one or more panels at given sites may have been created for this reason. Such reiteration is not, of course, always a signature marking a family or clan area. As already noted, repeated images may be related to ritual activity at that site, and their reduplication may have been intended to give power to the place or to augment its already existing power.

At Zuni, identical or similar motifs often reappear on single rock surfaces or at particular sites (sites 2, 5, 17) and even throughout several different sites (sites 10 and 11; sites 13, 21, 23, 25), especially when those sites are all relatively close together. Among the repeated motifs I found are nearly identical geometric designs, bird figures, and kachina masks. As mentioned in Chapter 2, at Hanlhibinkya, for example, there is a "circle-line-zigzag" mask or head complex consisting of thirteen strikingly similar images all located in the same enclosed and fairly inaccessible area at the head of the canyon (Figure 25).[40] They are located in close proximity to one another in this sheltered area, and hence have escaped the worst hazards of erosion. Within the canyon these masks/heads have a spatial as well as temporal definition: they are secluded in a chamber at the head of the canyon, separated from the rest of the canyon by a cavelike entrance where deep pools of rainwater collect. It is likely that this location near life-supporting water adds to the significance of these masks/heads. At another rock art site near the pueblo there are eleven almost identical birdlike figures, some placed at considerable distances from one another but all still within the same site (Figures 71a, 71b, 71d, 71e). Very similar images are also found at other sites near the pueblo and even at one site fifty-seven miles away in Arizona (Figures 71c, 71g). Like the "circle-line-zigzag" masks/heads at Hanlhibinkya, these birdlike figures are extremely abstract, but they are more recent, dating to circa A.D. 1400. Although most Zunis identified these images as birds, largely because of what seem to be feathers projecting from triangular or rectangular bodies, they added that they were "strange." One woman said: "Maybe birds like that lived here a long time ago." A Zuni man who is a well-known artist suggested that extensive repetition of a single element throughout some area or region may reflect the use of that land by certain clans and family groups who had developed "their own style and type of art." It is also possible that such a recurrent image may have been made by several unrelated individuals over a period of time, either because of its partic-

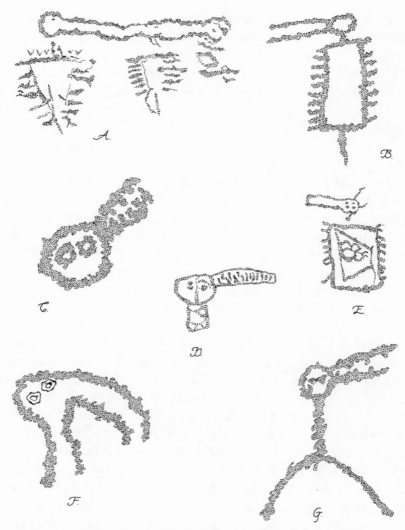

Figure 71. Bird figures (with fringelike projections, long beaks, and, sometimes, teeth), all pecked: (A) 50 cm × 120 cm, ZRAS site 5; (B) 60 cm × 50 cm, ZRAS site 5; (C) 20 cm × 35 cm, ZRAS site 20; (D) 40 cm × 50 cm, ZRAS site 5; (E) 50 cm × 50 cm, ZRAS site 5; (F) 50 cm × 45 cm, ZRAS site 25; (G) 35 cm × 25 cm, ZRAS site 20. Drawings by Murray Callahan.

ular meaning, known to them but not to us, or because individuals sometimes chose for whatever reason to echo and continue earlier, already-present themes. In any case, it is difficult to believe that the many similar images at some of the more extensive sites were all created by a single person.

Superimposition and Juxtaposition: Powerful Resonances

Of course, not all pictographs and petroglyphs appearing together were produced at the same time. There is, perhaps, an unsuspected dynamic aspect to rock art. Old figures erode with time or may be purposely altered or destroyed. New images may be created around them, thus changing the context in which they are viewed and, perhaps, their power as well. Older sites often contain depictions clearly made at several distinct time periods as well as particular carvings and paintings that have been subjected to later modifications. New images are sometimes even produced on top of older images (Figures 25b, 72, 82, 83). Superimposition is, in fact, relatively common in rock art throughout the Southwest and has often been of great value in establishing the relative dates of particular styles and techniques. The frequency with which such superimposition occurs, despite the availability of nearby unused surfaces that could support the creation of rock art and the often reduced clarity of the resulting figures, suggests that the decision to use such places is not random but quite purposeful. Perhaps this is because the superimposition of a second image over the first increases the power of the second image and, in addition, augments the efficacy of the place where it appears as well. It is also possible, of course, that putting one carving or painting on top of another is a means of taking power away from the first image, of capturing its potency. The reason for this action may be to establish dominion, particularly if more than one cultural group is involved, or to participate in the power of place.

Sometimes new depictions are placed not on top of older images, but next to these figures in a way that suggests a meaningful relationship. Two photographs, taken fifty years apart, of a panel containing several painted masks at the site called the Village of the Great Kivas clearly indicate this dynamic aspect while simultaneously demonstrating that rock art remains a continuing art form at Zuni. To see the changes that occurred during a fifty-year period, compare Figure 73, taken in 1930 by Frank H. H. Roberts, with Figure 74, taken from the same angle in the summer of 1980. Many of the older pictographs have partially worn away; a few have disappeared entirely. New paintings have been added, sometimes on top of the older, eroded images. Most of the kachina figures and masks created since the time of Roberts's photograph have been painted near those with which they have a ceremonial relationship. For example, the masks of the Council of the Gods are all placed as close to one another on this rock art panel as possible without obliterating the earlier painted masks.[41] The white-painted masks of *Sayatasha, Hututu* (Sayatasha's assistant), and one of the *Salimobia* have all been produced since Roberts's photograph was taken (see figure caption for identifications). Significantly, the masks of Hututu and the new Salimobia were both placed near the already-present Salimobia mask, the color of which was changed from white to red. There are now two Salimobia masks here, the red mask of the Salimobia of the south and the white mask of the Salimobia of the east.[42] Most of the other masks and figures on this panel are those that appear in the mixed kachina dance.[43]

The recent addition of an image to the other panel of kachina masks at this site (Figure 69) illustrates the juxtaposition of figures in a way that reflects their ceremonial relationships. Figure 75 is a photograph of the end of this panel taken in the summer of 1980; note the empty space next to the deer mask. Figure 76 was taken in the summer of 1981; note the new mask. Despite the differences in style and coloring, the artist evidently attempted to place the new pictograph on the rock face in such a way as to make it appear to have been done at the same time as the deer. Several Zunis identified this added kachina mask as that of a wild ram, an animal having a status

Figure 72. Overview of part of panel, numerous pecked elements, including animals with tails bent over their bodies and various animal tracks, 4 m × 3 m, ZRAS site 17. Photograph by Robert H. Leibman, 1980.

Figure 73. Painted masks and figures, 2.5 m × 6 m, ZRAS site 1 (Village of the Great Kivas). Photograph taken ca. 1930 by Frank H. H. Roberts, Jr. Courtesy of the Smithsonian Institution, National Anthropological Archives (Neg. No. 79-11643).

Figure 74. Same panel as in Figure 73, photographed from same angle by Robert H. Leibman, 1980. Images from left to right are: (A) Mask—unknown; (B) *Sayatasha*—Long Horn Kachina; (C) *Anshe*—Bear, or *Suski*—Coyote (note bullet holes); (D) *Kumance*—Comanche; (E) Mask—unknown, very faint; (F) *Hututu*—assistant of Sayatasha; (G) Red *Salimobia*—Warrior Kachina; (H) *Si:wolo*—Buffalo (note bullet holes); (I) White *Salimobia*—Warrior Kachina; (J) *Na'le*—Deer (note bullet holes).

Figure 75. End of panel depicted in Figure 69 showing *Na'le* (Deer) mask (note bullet holes on mask), 65 cm × 47 cm. Photograph taken by M. Jane Young, summer of 1980.

Figure 76. Same panel as in Figure 75 with new mask (*Mohakwe*—mountain sheep or wild ram) added next to deer mask. Photograph taken by M. Jane Young, summer of 1981.

similar to that of the deer. In the past, the two comprised the most important game animals for the Zunis. These are the animal figures that appear most commonly with spears or arrows through their bodies in early rock art. Their relationship is also made very clear in Zuni oral tradition. The deer and ram "go together" at the mixed kachina dance. They dance close to one another and are led away together from the other dancers when they are to be "fed" in one of the ceremonial rooms. The masks of these animals painted on the cliff walls at the Village of the Great Kivas are almost identical to those worn in the dance. All the participants in the mixed kachina dance are males who have been initiated into the Hunters' Society. In fact, Zunis believe that the impersonation of game animals by members of the Hunters' Society in the mixed dance gives these hunters the power to attract the animals when hunting; the imitation or acting out of the behavior of these animals in a ritual context serves to draw them to the hunters. The efficacy of this ritual thus hinges on establishing an iconic relationship—a relationship of similarity between hunter and hunted. This again emphasizes the importance attached to the visual depiction of game animals as a means by which to achieve success in the hunt and is, perhaps, another instance of the invocation of power; the hunters mask and costume themselves so that they look like the animals they are about to hunt.

I must add that my recent visits to this site have revealed that the wild ram mask is rapidly fading despite its location on a sheltered rock face; in the summer of 1984 it was barely visible. Unlike the other kachina masks and figures at this site, the wild ram was executed on the rock in pastels that lack the endurance of other kinds of paint. No one has attempted to refurbish the image. Whatever the original reason for its production, it is being permitted slowly to disappear.

Representation and Transformation

The site with the painted masks at the Village of the Great

Kivas is powerful not only because of the juxtaposition and superimposition of images through time but also because of the images themselves—the numerous painted kachina masks—represented there (Figures 69, 70, 73–76). The efficacy of the mask is so great that even the Zuni gods or kachinas wear such masks.[44] Zunis regard masks as having the power of transformation; when the dancers don their masks they become the kachinas, taking on their names and personalities.[45] In this way, the mask compels the presence of the god. Owing to their potency, masks may also be dangerous. A dancer who does not observe the proper taboos may, for example, be killed by his mask. Bunzel recounts a Zuni story in which the mask stuck to the face of a man who had ignored the taboos and suffocated him.[46]

Like a mask itself, the image of that mask may also be powerful, particularly when that image is painted; the masks at the Village of the Great Kivas are all painted primarily in those colors that are associated with the directions: yellow, blue, red, white, speckled, and black. It would appear, furthermore, that just as a real mask can be both powerful and dangerous, so too can the rock art depiction of such a mask if it is abused. I was told, for example, that a Zuni potter probably would not want to talk to me about rock art imagery because the death of her son the year before was attributed to his "copying" the Comanche mask at this site. It must be added, however, that the word "copied" was not explained, and that, further, the idea of accidental death is not accepted at Zuni—there must always be a reason and such reasons may not be truly intended as causal explanations.[47] Bunzel has suggested that the paint on the mask, more than its overall form, gives the mask its efficacy. She adds that when the dancers are inside the kiva and no masks are being used, the same magical power resides in the paint that is applied to their faces and bodies. This paint is always applied, even when a costume and mask are to be worn over it.[48] Some of the power inherent in the paint may relate to its connection to the myth time. For instance, in painting prayer sticks and kachina masks the

Zuni priests sometimes use special paint said to have been brought from the underworld at the time of the emergence. During the pilgrimage every four years, other sacred pigment is collected from the shores of the lake in which Kachina Village is located. The idea that power may be attributed to the paint itself is further supported by the comment one Zuni elder made to me. He said that when new images are to be painted on kiva walls, the old ones are scraped off and the paint fragments are buried in a sacred place outside the pueblo. Finally, it may be of some significance that the images at this site (with the exception of the one painted since the summer of 1980) are generally attributed by Zunis to one or another well-known mask painter of the 1920s and 1930s, for only special officers of the kiva are permitted to paint the masks. A number of Zunis suggested that the son of one of those earlier mask painters painted the new mask, the wild ram. This implies that all of the masks here were painted by men extremely knowledgeable of Zuni cultural symbolism—men who must have had some sort of special reason for originally painting and then adding to the series of masks.

Zuni behavior toward and commentary about certain rock art depictions in the landscape around the pueblo suggest that both the visual symbols and their particular locations embody power. Many of these images are too old to have been created by the Zunis or their immediate ancestors; nevertheless, contemporary tribal members incorporate these pictographs and petroglyphs in the network of symbolic associations by means of which they construct a meaningful environment. I do not, however, mean to imply that the images and sites I have discussed constitute those shrine areas which are central to the "official" Zuni religion. At the beginning of my fieldwork at Zuni and throughout its duration, both the Tribal Council and some of the religious leaders set up clear-cut guidelines concerning areas where I could photograph rock art as well as those I was to avoid. To my knowledge, with the exception perhaps of the site I was allowed to see but not to photograph, as well as the site called Hanlhibinkya that I was allowed to photograph, I never saw a site regarded as a shrine area. Still, I am aware from descriptions published in ethnographies that some shrine areas either incorporate or are located near rock art sites. Although it is impossible for me to speculate on what features contribute to the consensus that a particular site is a shrine area, I have formulated the hypothesis that sometimes the presence of rock art images may add to the efficacy of such places; conversely, the power inherent in some sites may increase the power of pictographs or petroglyphs that have been created there. Furthermore, despite the fact that Zunis designate special shrine areas as central to the execution of specific religious activities, one cannot claim that these are the only areas in the environs of the pueblo that are significant to the Zunis. They may at times single out certain phenomena for particular focus, but in a wider sense they view everything as alive and sacred; their religion is all-encompassing.

Whether or not Zunis regard them as officially sacred, then, they do perceive certain rock art images and sites to be powerful either because they evoke the myth time or because they depict beings that Zunis associate with vital aspects of the physical world; they regard these latter figures as efficacious in achieving various desired ends. Generally, such potent carvings and paintings are highly representational or iconic; they are powerful because of their similarity, both in form and function, to beings associated with the central theme of Zuni life—increase or fertility. Thus, because particular creatures live in or near the water, their depiction on rock surfaces near the village contribute to "making it rain." And, of course, the creatures themselves have this ability by virtue of their association with water; hence, on certain occasions, those who dance for rain carry living turtles in their hands. Sometimes this power derives not from association with life-supporting natural phenomena but from physical characteristics that make these creatures powerful. Certain insects and prey animals, for instance, possess desirable attributes that humans can accrue to themselves through ritual activities; such ritual activities seem sometimes to involve the depiction of these creatures as rock art images. Rock art elements in the Zuni area are thus integral to a complex symbolic system—a system that reflects concepts basic to Zuni life and definition of the world.

Powerful pictographs and petroglyphs are not always modeled on living creatures; sometimes they are representations of representations, part of a series of efficacious resonances that is characteristic of the Zuni aesthetic of accumulation. These images are repeated over and over again in various media; one cumulative effect of such reiteration is that the Zunis are surrounded by symbols of power, some of which refer to one another as well as to the underlying model of directionality. For example, the masks painted on the rock surfaces at the Village of the Great Kivas echo the masks worn by the kachina dancers; those masks have the ability to convert the dancers into the gods themselves. Each representation thus involves a transformation of power as well as a relation of similarity. Because certain of the kachina masks depicted in the rock art at this site represent kachinas associated with specific directions, and because the masks are rendered in the colors of those directions, they also refer to the directional symbolic system that extends to include "everything." Finally, whether specifically related to directionality or not, all such representations are part of the overarching framework of significance that characterizes the Zuni world.

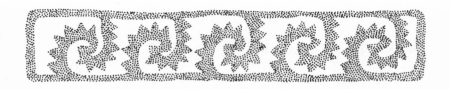

6

The Effect of Time:
New Images and New Meanings
for Old Images

Contemporary Images and Interpretation

I have focused on Zuni perceptions of particular rock art images as powerful, either because of their ability to evoke the myth time or because of their association with certain vital aspects of the physical world. Many of these depictions are quite old, some dating to a period before the Zuni tribe was formed in the Southwest, and most were created by the laborious technique of pecking. These include some of the petroglyphs Zunis refer to as "messages from the ancestors," frequently ambiguous in both form and meaning—an ambiguity that lends to them the same sort of multivocality characteristic of much Zuni traditional imagery, whether verbal or visual. I do not suggest that none of the images carved in more recent times in the Zuni environs is meaningful or relates directly to Zuni religious practice. The plethora of kachina masks and figures, for instance, some of which were created in recent times, obviously represents beings who are central to Zuni religion. Further, as mentioned earlier, I was not permitted to see most Zuni shrine areas. It is possible that some of them include or perhaps even focus on recently created rock carvings and paintings. In any event, Zuni commentary suggests that many of the newer images owe their existence to aesthetic rather than strictly religious motivations. Thus, Zunis do not regard all pictographs and petroglyphs surrounding the pueblo as powerful: they classify some as destructive graffiti, others as non-Zuni, and still others as beautiful but not necessarily efficacious.

One Zuni man, a recognized artist, looked through my photographs and picked out several figures (all from the same rock art site but not all together in my stack of photographs) that he had carved when he was a young sheepherder. He asked for copies of these photographs so that he could hang them in his store alongside his other artwork. He said he had only a penknife to work with then; he would find a smooth surface, visualize what he wanted to depict there, and then simply carve the petroglyphs. "The artist's mind works like a camera," he explained. The relatively soft Zuni sandstone, along with the use of metal tools, makes it possible to create small and detailed images in a fairly short period of time; this would not be the case if the artist were carving on basalt outcrops such as those found in other areas of the Southwest. Since one cannot "erase" in the creation of rock art figures, this preliminary visualization is quite important. None of the images this artist carved bears evidence of anything that might be construed as a mistake; they are small, finely detailed, and regarded by most Zunis as "beautiful." Next to one of these figures the artist carved his first name and last initial (Figure 78c). This is one of the few examples of rock art I have seen that has been signed by the artist. Other Zunis to whom I showed a photograph of this petroglyph readily identified the artist, perhaps because of his name but also, they said, because "he does paintings like that." When I asked this man his reason for creating the carving, he replied:

> Looking at other rock carvings
>   inspires you to do your own.
> I'd carve from memory things I'd seen.
> I carved that Plains Indian dancer

when I was fourteen or fifteen.
I'd seen him dancing at the Gallup Ceremonial.

He added, moreover, that in his opinion rock art is produced
today at Zuni "for the sake of art, not religious significance."
From a well-known artist, this comment illustrates a somewhat different perspective from that of the religious leaders
who tended to see certain rock art images as powerful and
linked to the time of the myth. Because this artist is in his
early forties it may also illustrate the differing attitudes of the
elders and the younger members of the tribe who have had
more contact with "mainstream" society.

Nevertheless, it must be pointed out that there are two
different sorts of rock art figures under discussion here. The
myth-evoking and power-invoking images are usually quite
old, and some are highly ambiguous in meaning as well as
amorphous in form. In contrast, the depictions described by
this artist as having been carved "for the sake of art" are generally recently produced, highly representational, and executed in great detail; few of them refer to explicitly religious
subject matter although, as noted earlier, it is difficult to divide the Zuni expressive realm into sacred and secular domains.

Interestingly, most of the men who said they had created
rock art when they were younger are today artists held in high
regard by Zunis and non-Zunis alike. Thus, although some
pictographs and petroglyphs may be similar to graffiti—consisting of names, dates, and initials or hastily executed figures—others evidence time and careful attention involved in
their production. One artist said that some of the creators of
rock art might not want to talk to me about it, hinting that
artistic ability is sometimes a private matter: "Just a certain
amount of people can draw, but some of them don't want to
mention it." Another Zuni artist said that he carved images
on the rocks because "time drags when you're a sheepherder";
yet he went on to add, "making rock art is sharing, just like

making music or painting a picture." He said that both he and
his father, also an artist, had carved and painted rock surfaces
while they were sheepherding, and stressed that placement
was not arbitrary but due to conscious choice:

> I would study the area first
> and choose an appropriate surface
> in a place with less weather, wind direction, and erosion.
> I would leave the sheep in good grazing land.

Precisely what is considered to be "appropriate" may in some
cases require, in addition to a particular sort of location, a
surface with a shape or contour suitable for the creation of
the particular type of figure the artist wishes to portray. An
example of such a carefully chosen placement is a rock art
panel at Kyaki:ma (site 2) that contains a single image—a
carved bird figure placed on the edge of a rock face that juts
out into space, so that the bird seems to be flying off the rock
face into the air (Figure 77). In other instances features of the
rock face, such as "natural" bumps and crevices, have been
incorporated into or have even initially prompted the design.
At site 13, the curved mouth of an incised mask is formed by
a natural break in the rock, as if this very feature of the rock
face had "suggested" the mouth of a mask to the artist who,
therefore, carved the mask around it. Sometimes Zunis ascribe
the production of rock art to certain features of a particular
site. As already mentioned, one man said that a spiral was
probably carved in one area because of the water there; another
man attributed the occurrence of snake figures in the rock art
at a specific place to the fact that the site itself was in a
location inhabited by many snakes. It is possible that sometimes other wildlife or natural features pictured at a rock art
site, such as deer, mountain sheep, or birds, may have been
seen nearby and formed an important factor in the initial choice
as a site.

Some of the more extensive rock art figures or panel groupings carved or painted within the last one hundred years in
the Zuni area are clearly the result of artistic endeavor, fre-

Figure 77. Incised bird figure near edge of cliff face, 25 cm × 25 cm, ZRAS site 2. Drawing by Murray Callahan.

quently an endeavor inspired by the desire to leave an enduring message in the landscape. The artist who discussed his efforts to find the appropriate surface said that his father had painted images of the participants in the Zuni Bear Dance on a canyon wall north of the pueblo so that they were "almost life size, because he wanted the people to remember." He added that in 1951 his father had also carved:

> . . . on a large flat rock nearby
>> an American flag with forty-eight stars.
> He carved it with flints and broken nails.
>> It took him six months to finish.
> He wanted it to be something.
>> that could be seen from the air.

In this case the rock art depiction of the American flag served as a patriotic statement from a man who had volunteered his services to the armed forces during World War II.

Some of the other men also remembered having created rock

art when they were younger as a way of passing time while
sheepherding. One of them said:

> . . . we were just young boys with nothing to do.
> We'd go up on the rocks after school and on weekends,
>   just go walking around and sometimes carve things
>   on the rocks.

He especially remembered having carved from memory a map
of the pueblo that he now wished he could find in order to
see how things had changed. When I asked him for his thoughts
on why rock art was done in the past, he responded:

> They've seen something like this—strange figures;
> They carved this to remember what it was like,
>   just to remember . . .
> They carved kachinas and stuff like that because
> they were always thinking about them
>   and didn't want to forget how they were dressed.

But as he was sorting through drawings and photographs of
rock art and came to some of those images of anthropomorphs
that seemed so perplexing to most of the Zunis—figures that
I ended up categorizing as "unknown"—he suggested that they
might have some kind of hidden meaning and mused: "I wonder what these really represent."

The kachinas are central to Zuni life, and it is by no means
surprising to find that a large proportion of the rock art produced since A.D. 1325 is made up of painted or carved images
of kachina masks and full figures of kachinas. Because these
depictions are very representational and often characterized
by distinguishing features, Zunis easily identified many of
them as representing specific kachinas. Some of the most
recently created pictographs and petroglyphs in the Zuni area
include kachina masks—the mask of the wild ram painted
during 1980–81 at the Village of the Great Kivas site, for example. Kachina images are often repeated in other Zuni graphic
media as well, constituting a predominant visual theme, their

very redundancy revealing their significance; it does, indeed, seem that Zunis are "always thinking about them." As I spent more time with Zuni families I noticed that a considerable amount of the play of young children revolved around enactments of kachina dancing. Later, the girls discontinue this activity while the boys who are initiated into the Kachina Society learn to perform the parts "for real." In addition, the predominance of kachina figures in visual media is illustrated by this comment from one of the Zuni high school art teachers: "When the students are given a choice to draw anything at all, they generally draw kachinas." I found this to be true of younger children as well; several of them who lived near where I was staying made a habit of visiting me during the summer afternoons and evenings. When I gave them crayons and paper in an attempt to amuse them, they tended to draw pictures of the mesas surrounding the pueblo and of the kachinas.[1] Thus, as these various examples illustrate, representations of the kachinas are a primary focus of attention in Zuni forms of expressive behavior, including rock art depictions.

While Zuni women are certainly aware of the rock art surrounding the pueblo, none of the ones I talked with had ever carved or painted images on the rocks, nor did they know of any other Zuni women who had done so. The older women in particular were most familiar with rock art located at sites near places where they gathered clay for making pottery, and it was these women who most often associated rock art imagery with traditional narratives. The interpretations of particular rock art figures offered by female potters and fetish makers frequently included discussions of which of these images they might paint on pots or use in making fetishes. Such cross-media depictions consisted of figures identified as Beast Gods, creatures that live near water such as frogs and dragonflies, geometric designs, deer, and birds. A number of women suggested that these images were created on rock surfaces for the same reasons that they are painted on pots or used in making fetishes: so that there would be rain for the crops, good luck in the hunt, long life. It is of note that these women, although not formal members of the Kachina Society, were as able to identify particular kachina figures or masks in the rock art as were the men; obviously their informal knowledge of religious matters is more extensive than most non-Zunis realize. Most commonly such identifications were made on the basis of distinguishing features such as Sayatasha's one long horn, Shalako's clothespin-like beak and bulging eyes, the *hepakinne* design on the cheeks of the Salimobia, and so on.

Some pictographs and petroglyphs were interpreted by Zunis in a way that reflected the concerns of day-to-day life rather than their inclusion in a framework of symbolic associations. Concentric circles in the rock art of the Southwest have often been identified as sun symbols by other Puebloans, and I initially expected similar interpretations from Zunis, but never once were such expectations fulfilled.[2] This leads me to suggest that concentric circle figures may not *always* be regarded as sun symbols by members of other present-day Pueblo tribes, either; nor may they always have been perceived as such in the past. Of course, it is also possible that the Zunis simply differ from other Puebloan groups in the way in which they regard concentric circle symbols; because of the high degree of multivocality of Zuni symbols, however, it is more likely that there are simply a number of interpretations for concentric circles, some of which may relate to the everyday world. For instance, a religious leader who was quite interested in rock art and offered some very traditional interpretations for some images once identified one of the most impressive concentric circle figures in the Zuni area as "a big old car tire" (Figure 57). It should be added that this petroglyph is located at a site that is of great importance in Zuni mythology and present-day ceremonialism. On the other hand, this man had become a good friend of mine, well aware of my enthusiasm for rock art, which matched his own. He was also endowed with a marvelous sense of humor and may simply have been teasing me, particularly since he knew of my interest in "traditional" interpretations. The same man sometimes took me to sites he thought I would like to photograph. At one site he said: "Watch out for snakes. There are lots of snakes in this area. That's why there are so many snakes carved on the rocks here." Zunis identified many of the square and rectangular fringed designs carved or pecked on the rocks as rug, blanket, or pottery designs put there for "practice" (see Figure 39). One woman added: "the rug designs must have been put there by the Navajos. Zunis don't make rugs." Sometimes the association of rock art images with aspects of the ordinary and modern world took on a playful aspect. At one site where the rock art consistently fell within a time period prior to A.D. 1325, a Zuni colleague identified particular geometric figures as "coat hangers" and "table lamps," laughing when he observed the disappointment that I was trying to hide. Yet, in a more serious mood he identified certain anthropomorphic images at the same site as "Zunis at the time of the beginning," reciting the part of the origin myth that describes these people. As a way of making sense out of unknown or difficult-to-identify depictions, other Zunis suggested that they were "put on the rocks by Martians"—an identification that reveals the Zuni propensity, at least in some cases, to mystify some of the more amorphous figures. Attributing the creation of specific images to beings from outer space accounts for their strangeness and, at the same time, distances them from contemporary Zunis and from "the ancestors" as well.

Some Zunis also discussed the aesthetic qualities of individual carvings and paintings. For example, they described many of the most recent figures as beautiful because of their bright colors or excellent form. Most of these images are small, quite detailed, carved with a metal tool such as a penknife, and highly representational; they include carvings and, less frequently, paintings of animals such as deer, bear, elk, cattle (some complete with brands), horses, and birds (Figures 78 and 79, for example), as well as of kachina masks and kachina figures. I was often asked for copies of my photographs of these pictographs and petroglyphs. Some of these photographs

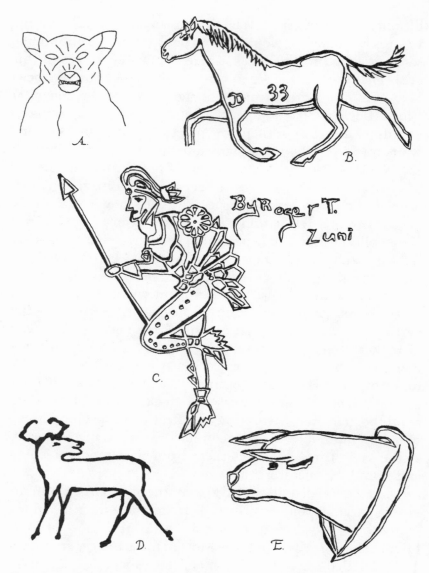

Figure 78. Contemporary designs: (A) incised and painted bear head, 40 cm × 30 cm, ZRAS site 1; (B) incised horse with brand, 17 cm × 25 cm, ZRAS site 10; (C) incised Plains Indian dancer, 30 cm × 17 cm, ZRAS site 7; (D) incised elk, 15 cm × 20 cm, ZRAS site 10; (E) incised head of bull, 17 cm × 20 cm, ZRAS site 11. Drawings by Murray Callahan.

Figure 79. Incised deer, 15 cm × 15 cm, ZRAS site 7. Photograph by Nancy L. Bartman, 1979.

now adorn the walls of a number of Zuni homes; others have served as design patterns for pottery. Among the older depictions, those they regarded as beautiful were the "designs," the same geometric or extremely nonrepresentational figures that some Zunis thought embodied undecipherable messages (see Figure 23, design to far right, and Figure 39). One man who made a practice of guiding me to rock art sites he had discovered during many years of hiking had his favorites among images at such sites. Some figures he virtually ignored, but when he came to others, obviously important to him for various reasons, he said: "You should take a picture of this one."

Many of the rock carvings and paintings created within the last seventy years or so are characterized by techniques that give the illusion of three-dimensional, dynamic form (see Figures 69, especially 69d, and 78); this is perhaps due to the influence of "Western" graphic-art styles. Several Zuni paint-

Figure 80. Pecked Shalako, 60 cm × 25 cm, ZRAS site 27.
Photograph by M. Jane Young, 1981.

ers told me that they and their parents had learned "Western" techniques of painting in art classes at boarding schools. One painter had attended the Institute of American Indian Arts in Santa Fe and attributed to that institute a substantial impact on Pueblo and Navajo artistry, an impact that may extend to rock art as well. For instance, rock art figures in the Zuni area that reveal three-dimensional perspective are relatively contemporary productions. Also evident in the more recent rock art is an interest in portraying fluidity of form and, in some cases, motion. (See, for example, Figure 80, a pecked Shalako figure whose partially raised legs suggest the motion of the dance—a style of depiction not characteristic of the period prior to A.D. 1325.)[3] The Plains Indian dancer discussed earlier (Figure 78c) also illustrates the action of dancing. It is further possible that the creation of a two-headed bird (Figure 38d) and a horse with two tails alludes to motion. In sum, this contemporary Zuni style is characterized by images that are fluid, dynamic, and representational and, in the case of pictographs, by the use of bright and distinct colors. This delineation of a Zuni style in recently executed pictographs and petroglyphs fits well with Barbara Tedlock's description of the Zuni aesthetic of "the beautiful": dynamic, multicolored, varied, and clear.

Some of these newly created and highly detailed carvings portray subjects that are not related to traditional Zuni themes, although this by no means implies that they could not have been produced by contemporary Zunis. At one site, for instance, there is a finely carved train complete with numerous railroad cars, an engine from which steam curls into the air, and a caboose. At another site is a carving of a man in plaid deerstalker cap and cape, which Zunis and non-Zunis alike described as Sherlock Holmes. Airplanes, cars, women in bikinis, and other such "modern" carvings and paintings occur at a number of sites, especially those near a roadway. Such non-Zuni imagery includes elements that are traditional to other nearby peoples: Navajos, Hispanics, Hopis, and Anglos, for instance. Zunis identified various images as Hopi or Navajo because of their distinctive subject matter: they called female figures with hair whorls "Hopi maidens," humpbacked fluteplayers "Hopi rain priests," and fringed designs "Navajo rugs." Additionally, at one site, amid images that generally depict Zuni themes is a cluster of figures that are strikingly different. Historic in style and incised, they are dominated by a large rendition of a Mexican soldier. To the left of the soldier is a Mexican eagle holding a snake; above the eagle is the inscription, "Pedro Madrigal" (Figure 81). Obviously Anglo-produced depictions are rare in the immediate area surrounding the pueblo, or at least difficult to definitely label as such; but Inscription Rock, a site east of the pueblo at El Morro, contains Anglo and Spanish carvings identifiable because they consist largely of signatures and dates (Figures 11, 12). Indian pictographs and petroglyphs that occur here are similar in style and content to those in the Zuni environs dating to the thirteenth and fourteenth centuries.

Zuni Attitudes Toward Vandalism, Graffiti, and Preservation

Although many of my older Zuni colleagues showed no great interest in carvings and paintings that depicted "modern" themes, they seemed undisturbed by their appearance except when these newer images had been superimposed on older figures or created at "special" sites. Tribal leaders concerned about vandalism worried most about those sites where older rock art was being altered by graffiti, such as spray-painted or chalked names, dates, and initials (Figures 82, 83). At one site Zuni policemen were able to identify the producers of graffiti as members of a Zuni junior high school class who had been picnicking in the area. Since the graffiti in this case consisted of names and other images chalked near and sometimes on top of older carved figures, the policemen required the students to go to the area and "erase" their names using water and hard sponges—by no means a task as simple as erasing writing from a blackboard. The Zuni man who supervised the procedure was very interested in the preservation of rock art

Figure 81. Incised Mexican soldier and eagle, 1 m × 2 m, ZRAS site 11. Photograph by M. Jane Young, 1979.

and took care that none of the older images were further damaged by this process. Of course, in areas where the graffiti have been painted or carved over older pictographs and petroglyphs there is no effective means of removal. That some rock art depictions have an affecting presence is clearly illustrated by the distress occasioned among older tribal members when sites that they have long been familiar with are suddenly subjected to this superimposition of graffiti.

The elder Zunis generally described those responsible for graffiti such as chalked or spray-painted names, dates, and initials as "young kids who don't know any better." They hoped that the materials I produced—the exhibit of photographs, the explanatory brochure, and the detailed fieldnotes along with their own statements about their cultural heritage—would contribute to teaching their children the value of the rock art surrounding the pueblo. Thus, if they were still

Figure 82. Chalked elements (on top of pecked elements), 1 m ×
2 m, ZRAS site 11. Photograph by Robert H. Leibman, 1980.

impelled to carve or paint their names somewhere, they would
choose, as one man said, "a clean page": a surface on which
no images had been created previously. Although a number of
the tribal leaders most concerned about the problems of graffiti and vandalism at rock art sites credit my project with
lessening their occurrence, the problem still exists. It is indicative, perhaps, of the tension between older and younger
members of the Zuni tribe—a tension strongly related to other
problems wrought by contact with mainstream society. It seems
to be a truism that the elder members of any group "wonder
what the younger generation is coming to," but any sort of
generation gap at Zuni is aggravated by the pervasive impact
of "Western" society on the younger members of the tribe as
well as the conflicting values of tribal factions concerning the
degree to which one should interact with Anglo society.

Figure 83. Spray-painted elements, 180 cm × 270 cm, ZRAS site 7. Photograph by Nancy L. Bartman, 1979.

Like other American Indian groups, Zuni has its conservatives and progressives and the friction between the two is frequently a cause for anxiety. Fundamental to this anxiety is the fear, most often articulated by the older members of the tribe, that "the old ways will be lost," that "the young people will turn away from the old religion" in their eagerness to pursue "Western" life-styles. Certainly, anyone who visits the pueblo today cannot help but notice the widespread use of technological items from mainstream society; these include videogames, electric guitars, "boom boxes," VCRs, and, of course, computers. Yet, although some of the young people may spurn tribal ways, others are experiencing a resurgence of pride, contributing to the preservation and revitalization of the old ways and using technical advancements such as cameras, tape recorders, and videotapes as a means of documenting

tribal traditions. It is impossible to judge the eventual outcome of these conflicting attitudes and experiences; even the
opinions of the elders about the young people are at times
contradictory. For instance, a man in his mid-sixties who worked
extensively with the younger members of the tribe, had this
to say about their search for identity:

> The young people are interested
>> in the kivas and the priesthoods.
> It makes a Zuni feel good
>> to know that there will be
>>> a continuation of the religion . . .
> If we lose the religion
>> that will be the end of this time.

In contrast, a middle-aged Zuni man who is quite active in
the tribal religion was prompted by a cluster of rock art images
to discuss the initiation of young boys into the Kachina Society in rather pessimistic terms.[4] Looking at a group of kachina figures that he identified as "whippers," those kachinas
who play a central role in the initiation, he said:

> This last initiation they relied on something
>> that was recorded eight years ago.
> There was a big argument about how to do it.
>> People forget . . .
> In the next five, ten years we may not have it
>> because the young people don't care:
>>> they don't ask questions,
>>> they don't take part,
>>> they don't know why . . .

The phrase "they don't ask questions" is an exceptionally
important one in understanding the way Zunis rear their children and induct them into religious life. Coercion of any form
is rare; I never saw a Zuni parent hit a child and seldom heard
a parent respond to a child's disobedience by shouting. A firm
statement was frequently enough to get the point across; yet

Zuni children are generally well-behaved. They are treated as individuals who have a right to their own choices; not the choice to misbehave openly, but the choice to take their own direction in life even if the exercise of that option takes them away from the traditional religion. A religious leader once told me that one of the healing societies had died out with the decease of the last old man who knew its secrets. When I expressed surprise that the old man hadn't recruited some young men to learn the secrets, I was told:

> He was waiting
> for someone to come to him.
> If they really wanted to learn,
> they would have asked.
> Otherwise the right spirit isn't there
> and it's better that the secrets die.

Sometimes vital information is lost because of the lack of young people to serve as "apprentices," but this is not always the case. Despite the lament that the old ways are disappearing, it often happens that when a person knowledgeable in the traditional ways dies, someone else has learned the secrets and is able to carry on.

These comments by tribal members illustrate some of the conflicting pressures experienced by young Zunis. It seems that sometimes they respond to that stress and give vent to their frustrations by creating graffiti; perhaps this is their way of marking the landscape as their own, making a public claim to particular territory. Certainly, many Native American children need some means by which to cope with the fact that their access to mainstream culture is blocked. This is not to condone the defacement of rock art but rather an attempt to point to some of the social pressures that give rise to this sort of behavior. My discussion of the reasons for the production of graffiti must remain speculative however, because it was not a subject I could pursue directly. Although I became acquainted with a number of young people during my fieldwork at Zuni, my position as director of the Zuni Rock Art Survey made it extremely unlikely that any of them would tell me about defacing rock art. Indeed, the young people I worked with seemed to share my enthusiasm for preserving and recording pictographs and petroglyphs.

Although one can draw some parallels between the Zuni situation and the production of graffiti and subsequent defacement of buildings and subway cars in urban environments, there are limits to the analogy. I would hesitate to use the term "graffiti artist" to describe any of the young Zunis: they do chalk, paint, and carve abundant graffiti in certain areas, but their graffiti are much less elaborate and, probably, less self-conscious than those created by street gangs in New York or Philadelphia. The Zuni graffiti rarely include more than a person's name and a date or the name of a boy and girl surrounded by a heart. Nevertheless, the motivations may be similar; urban graffiti are often attributed to "the need for spatial mastery," a way of "ascribing a proprietary meaning to space."[5] In this respect it is important to consider the meaning of the locations chosen for the manufacture of graffiti. Often it seems that the very inaccessibility or special nature of a place makes it a likely target for the creation of signatures or statements to the effect that "——— was here." Furthermore, in urban and other environments, graffiti are generally produced in areas that are already bounded by some means; frequently new graffiti are superimposed on statements already made by others, whether they be billboards or other graffiti, thus effectively obliterating the older statements. Putting one's signature or statement on top of that composed by someone else is an assertion of power, which could be the reason that those who do graffiti don't choose a "blank page." Finally, it must be reiterated that carving or painting new elements or even graffiti over old rock art is not an exclusively recent phenomenon. Extensive superimposition is characteristic of Southwestern rock art; often many images created at different time periods occur on one rock face even when "blank" rocks are located nearby.

Creating graffiti on top of or otherwise destroying rock art images isn't solely attributable to the young members of the Zuni tribe; much of it is done by non-Zunis, perhaps as a statement of hostility or from thoughtlessness. During a visit to Zuni Pueblo in the summer of 1984, I was told that Anglo visitors had vandalized a number of rock art sites near the pueblo; many of these places have now been declared off limits to tourists. Furthermore, occasionally scholars who study rock art are responsible for the destruction of certain images in their attempts to take good photographs. As I photographed rock art in the Zuni area, I found that a number of figures had been previously "chalked" (Figures 59, 84), a practice unfortunately common among certain rock art enthusiasts and particularly harmful in an area such as the Zuni-Cibola region where petroglyphs are predominantly carved on soft sandstone.[6] Nor do vandalism and destruction of rock art occur only in the Zuni area; for a variety of reasons, defacement of rock art sites is a problem faced by preservationists throughout the country and even the world. It is difficult to curb the human impulse to leave a signature, to quell the temptation to make a tangible mark on the landscape.

Zunis also object to the appearance of non-Zuni carvings at sites that are of special importance to them either because of the meanings associated with other depictions located there or because of the importance of the place itself. Sometimes these objections result in action. In the summer of 1984 I discovered that an incised rock art figure I had seen in previous summers during my visits to the Village of the Great Kivas site had been almost completely scratched out. This petroglyph had depicted the head of a man in profile inside a circle that contained a crescent at the top (my private way of describing it was "the man in the moon"). The style, technique, and degree of patination of the carving indicated that it was created in the past twenty to thirty years. A Zuni man who frequents the site said he had scratched out the image: "I picked up a rock and tried to erase it because it doesn't belong here." One can no longer see the earlier elements, but the scratch markings on the rock face are now very apparent. As

Figure 84. Pecked and chalked human figure, with oversized hands and feet, spur on left ankle and vaquero's hat, 40 cm × 27 cm, ZRAS site 17. Photograph by Robert H. Leibman, 1980.

I mentioned earlier, this particular location is of importance to the Zunis because of the painted kachina masks as well as the figures carved there to bring rain, success in the hunt, or power over traditional enemies, and perhaps there are other factors that also contribute to the "specialness" of this area. This Zuni man's actions illustrate the fact that sometimes the attempt to preserve rock art, or even to destroy it, relates to an aesthetic choice made on the basis of what is perceived to be appropriate subject matter at specific places. Yet, one wonders why a depiction that had existed alongside the others for twenty or thirty years was suddenly undesirable to a man who had visited the site often in the past ten years. Certainly, the petroglyph did not fit with the others at this location, but there seem to have been other reasons for its removal, among which were the reactions of non-Zunis to the image. Important visitors to the pueblo as well as casual tourists are frequently taken to this site; my conversations with Zunis who are familiar with the place reveal their awareness that some of these visitors have commented on the non-Indian appearance of this particular petroglyph. Thus, its removal may have been due not only to a Zuni consensus of its inappropriateness but to the impact of the opinion of non-Zunis as well.

Despite the opinion that some rock art depictions in the Zuni environs "don't belong," most Zunis regard both the older and the more recent images as an important part of their cultural heritage that ought to be documented and preserved. My invitation from the Tribal Council to record the rock art and produce a brochure that would reduce vandalism illustrates that such documentation had official sanction, but private individuals also agreed wholeheartedly with this stance, as the following examples make clear. Looking at the most extensive site I had recorded, one religious leader said: "This is our history book." Indeed, pictographs and petroglyphs can serve as a record of the past for a people who until recently had no written language. I must point out, however, that the Zunis regard their myths as history, for this is the place where the Zunis say the second set of Twin War Gods originated and the clans were given their names. Whether or not the petro-glyphs at this location actually depict such events, the Zunis believe that many of them refer in some way to these and other incidents that happened at "the time of the beginning." It is significant, then, that under the aegis of the Zuni School Board the rock art at this entire site was recently videotaped so that the films could be shown in Zuni classrooms. Video-tapes are, in fact, becoming an important means of preserving certain Zuni traditions. Recently a Zuni man videotaped the process of prayer stick making, "so that the knowledge wouldn't be lost." One tribal leader who has for years supported projects to create a Zuni Tribal Museum said of rock art documentation as well as record keeping in general: "The only way to preserve things is through documentation. If we don't do that, the whole thing dies out." Referring to Zuni artifacts in museums throughout the country, he added: "These things should be here with the Indians, not somewhere else."

An elderly potter spent hours pouring through my photo-graphs and drawings, explaining the meaning of a wide range of images and narrating the traditional stories to which some of them referred. Interestingly, she had an excellent grasp of information that until that time I thought was exclusive to the male domain. She was able to name all of the individual kachina figures and animal and bird tracks, and her interpre-tations corresponded with those of the most knowledgeable men who also identified these images. As I made painstaking notes and tape recorded her comments, she remarked on how important it was to keep such records. She added that she had learned to write in English but didn't make use of her knowl-edge: "My grandmother told me these things, but I was too stupid to write them down the way you're doing now." As we discussed rock art designs that were similar to those that might be used on pottery, she said: "I'll show you where I get my designs. I have some books." I had anticipated personal scrap-books of various patterns and figures, but, instead, she brought out a reprint of Bunzel's *The Pueblo Potter*, published in 1929, and Mera's *Pueblo Designs*, published in 1938.[7] She showed me her favorite illustrations, stressing that she had taught her daughter and granddaughter to use such books too: "It's important to have things written down somewhere, it's a way of keeping to tradition." When I gave her a copy of the rock art brochure I had produced for the tribe she said she'd use some of the rock art figures on her pots.

Finally, it is of note that most Zunis were quite concerned with knowing the particular time period within which various pictographs and petroglyphs had been created. "How old is this?" was a constant question, and for some Zunis the great age of certain images seemed to be a way of validating the "ancientness" of the tribe itself. Although most Zunis would agree with the literal statement of archaeologists that the tribe came into existence somewhere around A.D. 1200 as an amalgamation of Anasazi and Mogollon groups, many Zunis also believe, in a metaphoric or symbolic sense, that the tribe has been in the Southwest since "the time of the beginning." As I discussed the difficulty in trying to establish time periods for some of the oldest images with the tribal historian, he said:

> It's too bad we didn't have a written language
> > back then,
> because we would have included the dates
> > with the pictures
> > > the way artists sometimes do today.
> Then your job would be a lot easier.

The Process of Reinterpretation

The influence of outsiders on Zuni interpretations of particular rock art figures is illustrated by reinterpretations of images at a number of sites in the Zuni environs, particularly those most accessible to tourists. Some of these changes in meaning have been occasioned by the recent scholarly and popular interest in American Indian astronomical practices. It must also be noted that the various scholars—ethnographers, archaeologists, linguists, and folklorists among them— who have conducted research at Zuni Pueblo in the last one hundred years or so have had an undeniable effect on Zuni culture. For instance, contemporary Zuni explanations of a variety of forms of expressive behavior have been subjected to the influence of "distorting feedback" from sources outside the culture. Scholars who have studied Zuni culture have influenced it not only by their presence in the field, but also by their creation of written records of interpretations by certain individuals, giving these greater status and broader distribution than they might otherwise have had. For such reasons, contemporary identifications must be projected onto prehistory or even recent history with only the greatest caution and a full recognition of the dynamic aspects of tradition—the change as well as the continuity.

Many Zunis are familiar with the published books, articles, and monographs about various aspects of their culture. Despite the fact that they often describe such works as "containing many lies," the Zunis seem to incorporate much of this material into their own oral tradition. For example, in the summer of 1979 a Zuni man interpreted a number of petroglyph panels at the Village of the Great Kivas site in words that were almost identical to the identifications recorded by Frank H. H. Roberts, Jr., from his Zuni workmen while excavating the site in 1930.[8] According to both accounts, Figure 85 is a depiction of poisonous insects that the war chief carved on the rocks as he sang a song requesting the insects to sting the Navajo, the traditional enemies of the Zuni. Figure 86 was said to consist of a humpbacked fluteplayer (referred to as a rain priest), a horned toad, and an insect, all of which were "pictured on the rocks for the purpose of attracting clouds and moisture" to this area. The spirals in Figure 87 were described as representing the period in the Zuni emergence myth when the people were traveling about looking for the Center, where they would build their permanent home. The deer with elongated antlers was "a record . . . of an unusually successful hunt . . . placed there in order to propitiate the spirits of the slaughtered animals and to attract others to the region." The turtle,

Figure 85. Pecked insect figures (red ants and other stinging insects), 50 cm × 120 cm, ZRAS site 1. Photograph by M. Jane Young, 1979.

also called a "horned toad," is an important water creature; it was carved in order to bring rain to the Zuni area.

Although the Zuni man I talked with in 1979 had read Roberts's written account and thought it to be correct, it is unclear whether his interpretations were based on accounts in Roberts or flowed directly from a stable and widespread oral tradition about this site, of which his recent explanations of these images to me were but one performance and the telling by Roberts's workmen another.

A second, perhaps clearer example of the adoption by Zunis of interpretations made and promulgated by outsiders con-

Figure 86. Pecked fluteplayer, toad, animal, or insect, 1 m × 60 cm, ZRAS site 1. Photograph by M. Jane Young, 1979.

Figure 87. Pecked spirals, deer, horned toad, 1 m × 80 cm, ZRAS site 1. Photograph by M. Jane Young, 1979.

cerns another panel at the same site (Figure 88). In the summer of 1979, my Zuni colleague explained the meaning of some of the rock art elements on this panel (as had Roberts's workmen) by referring to a common Zuni folktale: "The zigzag from the moon and star to the owl is the owl's flight during the night—when it would spy on the Navajo and then return to Zuni to report the number and location of the enemy to the Zuni war chief."[9]

A year later, the same Zuni colleague said that the same petroglyphs represented the "supernova explosion a long time ago." In the summer of 1981, the tribal historian also gave this interpretation of the panel, saying that someone who had visited the pueblo had told him about the "Crab Nebula" and the suggestion of some astronomers that this panel and several other similar ones in the Southwest recorded the supernova explosion of A.D. 1054, which resulted in the formation of the Crab Nebula. This was a striking event, especially visible in the Southwestern United States, which would have initially appeared as an extremely bright star close to the crescent moon in the morning sky, then in the night sky, for approximately 650 days. Some astronomers have consequently argued that, because of "the propensity in men to notice and record unusual sky events, particularly if they correspond with a terrestrial event of great importance,"[10] an event of this magnitude and visibility might well have been recorded in the rock art of the area. Rock art configurations such as this one, which depict a star in close association with the crescent moon, are used to support this hypothesis. Whether or not this might actually be the original meaning of these images may be argued, but the comment of the tribal historian indicates that the idea did not begin with the Zunis. Rather, he and other Zunis learned of and adopted the recent theory of these astronomers that this panel is a record of the supernova explosion. Apparently, then, a story about this site told by non-Zunis has influenced the interpretations of some Zunis. Interestingly, although the identification of individual figures at this site was generally straightforward—owl, star, crescent

Figure 88. Pecked crescent moon, star, zigzag line, owl, brand, and corn plant, 2 m × 180 cm, ZRAS site 1. Photograph by M. Jane Young, 1980.

moon, owl's path at night, the meaning conveyed by the cluster of images as a whole was somewhat ambiguous, in some cases adding up to a whole that is more than just the sum of the parts. Thus, in addition to referring to the Zuni folktale described above, the cluster can take on a completely different meaning under the influence of assertions made by non-Zunis.

An interesting final irony to this particular example of the process of reinterpretation is that some Zunis seem to have associated the entire panel of rock art elements rather than just the star and crescent with the supernova so that, subsequently, they could associate it with the zigzag alone. I was surprised recently to find that several Zunis identified a zigzag figure as "Crab Nebula" that others described only as a "snake with a zigzag body" (Figure 89).

The discoveries at Fajada Butte in Chaco Canyon and their ensuing wide promulgation in the media have led to another similar instance of reinterpretation at Zuni.[11] Because at the Fajada Butte site so-called "daggers of light" interacted with spiral petroglyphs, several individuals went to Zuni to inquire about the meaning and use of spiral symbols for contemporary Zunis. As a result, however, one of my Zuni colleagues now believes that the spirals at the Village of the Great Kivas (Figure 87) are bisected by streaks of light at the winter solstice—an impossibility since the necessary special configuration of nearby boulders, or any other physical feature that might produce such phenomena, is completely missing. Thus, this man, the same one who reinterpreted other petroglyphs at this site as symbolizing the "Crab Nebula," has once again changed his identification of a panel since 1979; at that time he had told me that the spirals represented "the journey of the ancestors in search of the Center." This change in meaning seems to have been sparked directly by a visitor who told him about the site at Chaco Canyon and suggested that he might find something similar in the rock art near Zuni. The visitor must have been quite convincing, for my colleague was prepared to go to some lengths to observe this phenomenon. He said: "In the winter near the solstice I want to spend the night up there

Figure 89. Pecked snake figure, 10 cm × 60 cm, ZRAS site 16.
Drawing by Murray Callahan.

at the Village of the Great Kivas. I'll look at the spirals just
before the sun comes up. I bet the same thing might happen."
Furthermore, because it has been implied that the spirals at
Fajada Butte represent "time" (i.e., the motion of the sun during the year), this Zuni colleague wonders if the same might
be true for the spirals at the Village of the Great Kivas. When
I visited Zuni in 1984 he said: "Maybe those spirals are supposed to be the travels of the sun during the year. There are
two of them—maybe they're the two halves of the year." Yet,
when I reminded him that three years earlier he had said that
these same spirals depicted the "journey in search of the Center," he replied, "They mean that too."

I suggest that at least part of the reason some Zunis are so
willing to accept and incorporate these "astronomical interpretations" of rock art into their contemporary tradition is
that it provides a way of emphasizing that science is not the
sole property of the Euro-American. They are saying, "we knew
about that back then," thus validating the knowledge of their
ancestors and the credibility of traditional accounts.[12] It is
certainly the belief of many ethnoastronomers, myself among
them, that the ancestors of the contemporary Pueblo Indians

had an extremely sophisticated knowledge of astronomy that had been transmitted orally for hundreds of years, and it is not unlikely that some of it *was* recorded in material forms such as rock art. Because of this depth of tradition, however, one cannot simply "decode" astronomical motifs in rock art solely on the basis of present-day interpretations, or the "well, it looks that way to me" stance of the outside observer.

Although I have used the term "reinterpretation" to describe this process of change in identification, my Zuni colleague's comment that, despite the new meaning, the spirals also represent "journey in search of the Center" indicates that the fundamental import of the symbol has not changed; instead, he has simply added a new meaning to those already attributed to this symbol. This illustrates a characteristic Zuni response to cultural contact with mainstream society: they add on to what they already have so that if one looks beyond the superficial trappings of Western society, one finds a stable Zuni cultural core.[13] As I mentioned earlier, the spiral is a multivocal symbol; it can stand for many things at the same time. Now, in addition to its earlier meanings, it can also signify (at least for this man, and, perhaps, for others) the motion of the sun during the year, particularly if there are two spirals to represent the two major divisions of the year. Presumably the cluster of symbols that depicted the owl's journey during the night may also, for some Zunis at least, serve as a record of the appearance of the sky at the time of the supernova explosion that resulted in the Crab Nebula; perhaps the zigzag figure as well now denotes both snake and Crab Nebula for some Zunis. One wonders, then, what explanations are used in which contexts; it seems highly likely that the supposedly scientific Anglo-influenced meanings are reserved for use when speaking to or interpreting symbols for Anglos.

Zunis explain some images not on the basis of personal familiarity with a given rock art site, but on the basis of tribal tradition about such areas. Whether because of Matilda Stevenson's description of the place in these terms[14] or the pervasiveness of oral tradition about it, the canyon off the reservation in Arizona called Hanlhibinkya was consistently referred to as the place of origin of the second pair of Twin War Gods and the location where the clans were given their names. Consequently, some Zunis who went to this site with me for the first time identified some of the petroglyphs there as clan symbols (see Figure 72) even when they could not tell what symbol belonged to which clan. The interpretations of rock art by these tribal members seemed predetermined; even if the symbols weren't familiar to them, they knew what they *should* find at that site. One man, perplexed that the rock art there included many more kinds of images than those that might be described as clan symbols, said in some confusion: "They say these are supposed to be clan symbols." Another man, who also referred to the tribal tradition that Zunis were divided into clans at that particular place, spent hours examining the hundreds of rock art depictions there trying to find some cluster of images that might represent the origin of the second pair of Twin War Gods. He was unsuccessful but concluded that the images he sought might have been covered up by the mud that had accumulated on the canyon floor over the years and definitely obscured some of the early petroglyphs. This is not, of course, an instance of reinterpretation so much as an example of interpreting images in a certain way because of the pervasive tradition that has developed concerning the place where they occur—a tradition that might be reinforced by its incorporation in published ethnographies. For some tribal members, it is not knowledge of the symbols found there that determines their significance but rather knowledge of events that happened there "at the time of the beginning." They focus primarily on the meaning of the canyon, which in turn shapes the meaning of the particular visual symbols that have been carved and painted on its rock walls.

These examples illustrate the difficulty in attempting to discover original meaning on the basis of contemporary interpretations; meanings have changed through time, sometimes because of outside influence. Even though many Zunis felt that the older rock carvings and paintings had been made by their ancestors and were somehow related to the corpus of myths underlying Zuni ceremonial activities, they were not precisely sure what these figures depicted; they often hoped that I could tell them. It is frequently not the exact explanation of such images that is important to Zunis but rather the knowledge that they are signs from the ancestors. Looking at one such cluster of petroglyphs, an elderly religious leader asked me: "Do you know what this means? I think it must mean something."

7

Conclusion

Zuni interpretations of rock art reveal that some images are part of a graphic system that is linked to an underlying organizing principle of directionality. This principle is based on the apparent daily and annual motion of the sun together with the rain- and snow-bearing winds that emanate from the solstice positions plus the zenith and nadir. Implicit in this six-directional model is the Center—a condensed symbol that embodies both time and space. Pictographs and petroglyphs, kiva murals, sand paintings, pottery, kachina masks and costumes, all depict certain figures, repeated over and over again, that are integral to this paradigm. Not only does this cosmological model serve to structure visual art, however, it structures verbal art as well. Zuni ritual poetry, for instance, is sometimes patterned on the basis of lines that describe the apparent motion of the sun and the moon, particularly at crucial times of the year, such as the winter solstice. Significantly, the Zuni name for the winter solstice translates as "the Center." Both verbal and visual artistic systems are thus bound together in a network of symbolic associations ideologically oriented towards the Center and the people of the Center Place.

Rock carvings and paintings and other features of the landscape are especially important elements of Zuni cultural symbolism because they are visual records, constant and immediate reminders, of the past; certain boulders and pinnacles projecting from mesas, for instance, encapsulate beings from the myth time in stone, others reflect actions undertaken by powerful personages such as Salt Old Woman or the Twin War Gods. But not only may rock art images serve as records of certain events—such as the petroglyphic clan symbols at Hanlhibinkya that, according to Zuni tradition, were carved at the time the clans were created; in some cases they are a "message from the ancestors," rarely explicitly understood but signs of the ancestors' involvement with and concern for contemporary Zunis. Such pictographs and petroglyphs are frequently somewhat abstract in form and ambiguous in meaning, allowing for interpretations based on features that are not necessarily explicitly represented. Other rock art figures serve to evoke the past so that it becomes, for a brief period at least, cotemporal with the present. These are the images I have termed "metonyms of narrative," those affecting presences imbued with the power of evocation, the visual depictions of which call forth recitations of traditional narratives. Some of these images are quite old and characterized by a certain ambiguity of both form and meaning. I do not mean to suggest, however, that they are like inkblots onto which Zunis project their own culturally significant meanings; indeed, these particular rock carvings and paintings are generally representational to the degree that someone outside the Zuni culture can grasp the reasons for their identifications. The lizardlike figures described as "Zunis at the time of the beginning," for instance, have certain distinguishing features that the Zunis pointed out; especially important were a tail and webbed feet and/or hands, although both did not have to occur together. Nevertheless, these figures are ambiguous to the extent that they can depict "Zunis at the time of the beginning" or "things that go on pottery (lizards)" or both simultaneously. Similarly, the multivalent spiral figures represent not only wind, water, snails, and other related elements but also "the journey in search of the Center." Thus, the very ambiguity of form and meaning of a number of rock art figures, especially those that were created some time ago, allows for a fluidity of meaning and the creative use of the imagination in constructing cultural interpretations that probably differ from the "original" meanings of such images.

It is likely that the ability of certain rock art depictions to evoke the past is related to their location in a landscape that *was* the scene of events of the myth time and *is* now the setting for contemporary Zuni life and stories that describe those past events. The landscape in itself is an affecting presence for the Zunis; various features of that landscape are emotionally charged symbols that stand for significant events in Zuni myth and history. Although this claim might be made for any location that contains visual reminders of the past, such as old buildings or ruins partly buried in the ground, the Zunis' association of the landscape surrounding the pueblo with the past is especially potent because they believe that their ancestors have resided in this particular locale since the finding of the Center Place. Certainly, any group of people who have remained in the same place for a long period of time are reminded of past events by visual markers in the landscape—sometimes these memories are even preserved in print, but for the Zunis such markers are generally signs not of events in the recent past or those that occurred several hundred years ago, but rather of the myth time. It is this time they are most concerned with, "always thinking about," and it is the beings from this time period who are still involved with contemporary Zuni life. Not only did they leave messages on the rocks for their descendants, but they actually return in certain ceremonial contexts as, for instance, the kachinas who dance in the plazas to bring summer rains. Such occurrences are possible because the Zuni concept of time is circular and fluid; the permeable boundaries between past and present permit a dialectic relationship, a movement back and forth between the beings of the myth time and those of today. Thus, for the Zunis, markers in the landscape evoke not so much one's personal past—idiosyncratic events known to only a few, but those events that make up the past of the entire tribe—the time of the beginning when various events happened that now influence the shape of the present. The constant referral to the past is a validation not only of events in the past that formed the basis for contemporary Zuni socioreligious life but a validation of events in the present that continue to be informed by that past.

The older pictographs and petroglyphs in the Zuni environs (for instance, those that date to A.D. 1100 or earlier) were not necessarily made by the direct ancestors of the present-day Zunis. Nevertheless, Zunis today interpret many of these depictions as relating to Zuni tribal history. One might even say that they appropriate these images in the landscape, characterizing them as distinctively Zuni even though they may not have been of Zuni creation originally. Although this appropriation may be facilitated by the fact that such rock art figures occur in a setting that the Zunis claim as their particular homeland, it may also relate to the characteristic Zuni tendency to regard everything in their environment as meaningful and significant. An extension of this Zuni view of reality is the belief that nothing happens accidentally, that there must be a reason for everything. This includes very serious occurrences such as individual death or "natural" disasters, but it extends to somewhat casual events as well. I am reminded of a time when I was walking with one of my closest Zuni friends in a grassy area near a rock art site. We were discussing a recent event in the pueblo and I was not paying much attention to our surroundings. But I did note that, in the course of a forty-minute walk our path was crossed a number of times by a rabbit—or it may have been several rabbits—that seemed oddly unafraid of us. Near the end of our walk my Zuni friend said: "That's the fourth time that rabbit has hopped in front of us, it must want to lead us somewhere." We went in the direction that the rabbit had gone and came to some tiny petroglyphs located on a rock face that I had missed when I first documented the nearby rock art site. Of course, that the event happened four times was in itself important to this Zuni man, but this example also reveals his tendency to see what I might call chance incidents as meaningful and purposeful. During my various periods of residence among the Zunis I often discovered that things I took for granted were regarded by them as omens, phenomena that had taken place for some reason or were harbingers of other events. By analogy, then, present-day Zunis think that certain undecipherable rock carvings and paintings are purposeful communications from the ancestors rather than the creations of strangers who lived in the area many years ago or who were just passing through.

I link the Zuni tendency to perceive everything around them as meaningful to their ability to take on alien concepts and material items without greatly changing their own cultural stance. Once they have willingly brought something new into their world it becomes their own. That may be related to what I have described as the Zuni aesthetic of accumulation, their delight in things that are various, dynamic, and plentiful. Just as in the past their early contact with other cultural groups led Zunis to be particularly receptive to new ideas while continuing in their own basic beliefs, so Zunis today respond to the pressures of culture contact by adopting new ideas and material goods while utilizing them in a "Zuni" manner, adding them on to a stable cultural core. Through time, these ideas and materials take on Zuni attributes. For instance, the brightly colored Czechoslovakian shawls worn by the matrons of the tribe are now a sign of "Zuni-ness" to Zunis and non-Zunis alike. Similarly, certain rock art images, some so amorphous that they could mean anything at all, become messages from the ancestors for the Zunis. Those visual depictions thus add to and reinforce the Zuni vision of reality, the cosmological scheme that combines nature and the human creative world in an elaborate system of significant relationships mediated by their concept of the Center. Thus, rock art that may not have been originally created by Zunis is drawn into the Zuni network of symbolic associations so that it becomes part of the meaningful environment that surrounds them, even serving to evoke events from the mythic past. Some of those rock art figures differ from other images in Zuni visual art forms such as fetishes, pottery, and kiva murals precisely because of their great antiquity; they are so old that they must have been made by people other than contemporary Zunis. But because they are carved and painted on rock surfaces surrounding the Center Place, the place where the Zunis and their ancestors have lived ever since the Water Skate stretched out his legs to the solstice points and marked the Center with his heart, those people can be none other than "the ancestors." An analysis of Zuni interpretations of these images, then, reveals much about the Zuni vision of reality and the way that they extend that vision to include "everything." The Zuni concept of the Center is emblematic of this world view in which everything becomes significant; the pueblo itself is the center of various phenomena that surround it in a series of concentric circles all oriented inward towards the Center Place. The people who live at the Center are accustomed to being surrounded by layers of significance.

Of course, Zunis do not associate all pictographs and petroglyphs with the myth time. They regard some images as efficacious because they typify powerful beings in nature such as mountain lions, eagles, and poisonous insects or because they are associated with vital aspects of the natural world—toads and serpents that live near bodies of water, for example. In either case, Zunis portray those powerful beings in various graphic media so that certain outcomes will be realized. The potency of those depictions is invocative and iconic; it lies in their similarity to, or their ability to represent actual living beings. Even though some of those figures are so old that they were probably not created by direct ancestors of the Zunis, they are generally so representational that one can identify them as depicting certain species of animals, birds, and so on. Furthermore, the images are *functionally* similar to the beings they portray; the petroglyph of a turtle carved on a rock surface serves the same rain-making functions as does the living turtle carried in the hands of the kachina dancers. Because the Zunis see themselves and all humans as somewhat impotent ("fin-ished" rather than "raw"), they find it necessary to engage in activities that will bring them the aid of more powerful beings. They believe that if those activities are conducted in the proper ritual manner, with "a good heart," the desired result will come about. Thus, there is no room for chance or accident in the Zuni world—the gods are not capricious. If the Zunis per-form their ritual obligations, the gods will surely respond by giving them those things that they request.

The creation of representations of powerful animals on the rocks and in other visual art forms is an instance of ritual activity in the context of which the relatively powerless Zunis accrue to themselves the potency of those beings—whether it be for success in the hunt, rain for the crops, or some other means of obtaining increase and well-being. The creation of that imagery is an act of concentration involving both the eyes and the mind, a focusing of energies so that the desired event will follow. At the same time, however, Zunis recognize that none of those procedures will be efficacious if one engages in them with an impure heart. Moreover, in some cases the power of the place where figures are carved or painted adds to the efficacy of the visual depiction. Those places that were the scene of events in the myth time, for instance, are fre-quently locations of rock art imagery and usually are shrine areas. Nevertheless, at times a place is regarded as powerful primarily because of the rock art located there.

Although power, either of evocation or invocation, is an important attribute of many pictographs and petroglyphs lo-cated in the area of Zuni Pueblo, a number of other images are important to the Zunis because they are beautiful. Thus rock art images illustrate the two primary, though not always exclusive, categories of Zuni aesthetics: "the powerful or dan-gerous" and "the beautiful." Those figures belonging to the latter category (with the exception of certain geometric de-signs described by Zunis as "pottery and rug designs") are highly representational and usually date to within the last fifty years or so; they are not signs of anything and refer only to the things they explicitly depict. As one Zuni man implied, they are "art for art's sake." Despite instances of their execution merely to pass the time while sheepherding, the commentary of Zuni men who made a number of those images indicates that some of them were undertaken with the intent to produce something "artistic" or "beautiful." In either case, contemporary Zunis may have carved and painted rock surfaces at least partly so that they might leave their own mark on the landscape, claiming that particular territory as their own; some may even wish to leave messages for the Zunis who will come after them, taking on the role of "the ancestors" who leave signs in the landscape. Whatever the reason for the production of any of those pictographs and petroglyphs, the sorrow with which Zunis respond to a vandalized site is one indication of the importance those images have for them. They recognize certain figures as the creative endeavors of their fathers, grandfathers, and even their sons, while they regard others as powerful, meaningful, and significant, whether or not they can decipher any of these attributes.

Rock art images, whether old or recent, have another kind of power as well—a power that is related to Zuni ethnic identity. The mere presence of carvings and paintings on the rocks heightens the sense of place for the Zunis; it reinforces their perception of themselves as a people intimately linked to their particular landscape, a landscape where powerful beings dwell and where significant events of the past took place. Rock art thus intensifies the Zunis' sense of relationship with the universe, augmenting their social cohesiveness and social identity. Petroglyphs and pictographs constitute affecting presences because they are *immediate* reminders not only of the dialectic interaction between past and present but also of the interrelatedness of all things in the Zuni cosmological scheme. Like other artistic imagery, rock art figures serve to focus ideas, concepts, and cultural values, thus contributing to the way in which the Zunis define the world. In this very process they not only define, but confirm and validate Zuni existence.

Rock art elements in the area surrounding Zuni Pueblo are

integral to the complex system of symbols that constitutes the Zuni world view. Even those images that were created prior to the formation of the Zuni tribe in the Southwest have become imbued by the Zunis with meanings that link them to concepts basic to Zuni life and perception of the cosmos. Pictographs and petroglyphs and Zuni commentary about those figures are thus important expressions of Zuni ideology. Yet this by no means points to a neat network of common cultural meanings; the diversity of interpretations of imagery and reasons for the production of rock art reveal considerable individual variability of meaning as well. The generation of those depictions is not a community endeavor, nor is it akin to a ritual of the Kachina Society during which the identity of the impersonator becomes one with the god; rather, in carving or painting rock surfaces, a man can inscribe himself on the world—he can contribute something of his own while feeling part of, continuous with, something traditional. He joins his artistry to a landscape in which both older rock art figures and certain geological formations constitute a lasting record of ancestral activities. The individual who makes such figures is engaging in an activity that is both personal and cultural— though he may leave a mark of individual expression on the landscape, he is leaving that mark in a place that is perceived as the focus of significant events of the Zuni past. His work does not stand alone, then, but is encompassed by a landscape that is in itself a sign of Zuni tribal identity and a manifestation of that mythic reality in which the Zuni continue to live.

Appendix
Field Procedures
and Documentation

During the summers of 1979, 1980, and 1981, the members of the Zuni Rock Art Survey, under my direction and with the permission and support of the Zuni Tribal Council and the private landowners involved, began the first systematic attempt to document the rock art of the Zuni-Cibola region. We undertook this project, initially suggested by the Zuni Archaeology Program, for the following reasons.

(1) Rock art is an integral part of the Zuni cultural heritage and, therefore, its documentation is an important step towards cultural preservation, including preservation of rock art images themselves. Because pictographs and petroglyphs erode through time and also are subject to vandalism, written and photographic records are necessary. One goal of the project was to set up a system of recording that could be continued by tribal members. With this end in mind, I gave copies of all photographs, written records, and sketches to the Laboratory of Anthropology of the Museum of New Mexico and the tribal archives of the Pueblo of Zuni.

(2) Because of the high incidence of vandalism of rock art depictions in the Zuni-Cibola region (Figures 82, 83, 84),[1] those involved in the project hoped that its products, such as the photographic exhibit, brochure, slide show, pamphlet, and informal discussions, would increase Zuni and non-Zuni appreciation of the rock art, emphasizing its artistic quality and cultural-historic importance, and, as a by-product, would reduce vandalism.

(3) In addition to decreasing the incidence of vandalism, I designed this project to lead to a wider acquaintance with, and knowledge of, the figures that the Zuni people and their ancestors have been painting or carving on the sandstone cliffs of mesas surrounding Zuni Pueblo. I produced some project materials that could be used in the schools to stimulate broader interest in Zuni cultural heritage among the young people of the tribe.

(4) Although Pueblo rock art in the Southwest has been described generally, the carvings and paintings of the Zuni region have received little specific attention. One goal of the project, therefore, was to study the rock art of Zuni and the surrounding area with the intention of defining it within the overall Pueblo context. More specifically, this would entail tracing similarities to surrounding style regions and delineating particular aspects or design elements that manifest this interrelationship. At the same time, characteristics that distinguish the pictographs and petroglyphs of the Zuni and their ancestors from those of neighboring groups would be isolated, establishing a Zuni-Cibola rock art style. Thus, a further objective was to add to the data on southwestern rock art already assembled by academics. Such a study of rock art of the Zuni-Cibola region has far-reaching implications for other similar studies in the Southwest, particularly in establishing a pattern of relative dating and stylistic analysis.

(5) Rock art is a valuable component of the archaeological record, adding a significant dimension to our knowledge of prehistoric peoples. The various stylistic manifestations of rock art can serve to identify cultural relationships, patterns of communication, evidence of trade, and other spheres of interaction.

In the course of the three summers' work, the Zuni Rock Art Survey team documented a total of thirty-four sites on and about the Pueblo of Zuni (see Map 2). We recorded sites beyond the boundaries of the Zuni Reservation at Lyman Lake, Petrified Forest, Hardscrabble Wash, and El Morro, all places for which archaeologists have posited relationships to Zuni. The similarity of style and content between the rock art found in those places (all within a sixty-mile radius of the reservation) and that located on the Zuni reservation proper supports those hypotheses.

We divided each site into panels, expanses of image-bearing rock treated as a unit, and recorded pertinent information about each—

such as its location, degree of patination (discoloration of rock surface due to weathering), and condition. The team documented specific designs, their position on the rock and relative to one another, and the relationship of the given panel to surrounding panels or rock formations in a series of black-and-white and color photographs.

Although previous researchers had chalked some of the rock art (Figures 59, 84), the Zuni Rock Art Survey team limited its recording methods to photographs and freehand drawings in order to affect the rock art depictions as little as possible. Only these latter methods should continue to be used in recording rock art in this area, because the soft sandstone is easily worn away by documenting techniques that require surface pressure, such as painting with aluminum powder, tracing, rubbing, spraying with water, and chalking. Although some of these practices have been used by other researchers in areas where the rock surface is hard (for example, on basalt) without causing great damage, their use in the Zuni-Cibola region would most certainly result in considerable damage to the rock art images.

I included the following items in the materials that I filed with both archives; they constitute the "record" of the thirty-four rock art sites.[2] (a) Contact sheets of black-and-white photographs of each rock art panel. This black-and-white record included at least one shot of the full panel against a meter stick to indicate size, site, and panel number. To simplify the process of matching written reports with actual photographs, I added an explanatory overlay indicating site, panel number, and design element (or elements) to each contact sheet. (b) Color slides of selected panels and individual design elements. (c) Enlargements of sections of U.S. Geological Survey maps showing relative positions of rock art panels and detailed information concerning the location of the site. (d) A carefully drawn freehand map that complemented the information on the U.S.G.S. enlargement but allowed more detail. (e) Sketches of design elements and often entire panels, particularly those too eroded to photograph well. Such drawings often served to bring to my attention images or entire portions of panels, and relationships among images, that I might otherwise have missed. These are an important addition to the site record, for the artist is forced to focus on minute details and relationships in producing sketches. Of course, the drawback to such freehand renderings is that scale and proportion are often not very accurate, but those black-and-white photographs that include a meter stick in juxtaposition to the images provide the necessary corrective. (f) Written reports (Museum of New Mexico Rock Art Site Report forms and individual reports for each rock art panel at the site) containing information regarding the organization doing the recording, site number, map source and section, accessibility, location, physical situation, type of rock, orientation, technique of work, dimensions, exposure, design elements, superimposition, patination, natural deterioration, vandalism, associated cultural features, proximity to dated archaeological sites, natural resources, number of photographs taken, pertinent ethnographic references, and remarks.[3] These records have laid the groundwork for an ongoing rock art recording project that can be carried out by the Zuni Archaeology Program or interested tribal members.

Although the survey sites admittedly represent only a small percentage of the abundance of the pictographs and petroglyphs in this region, we documented sufficient examples to permit us to make some temporal distinctions with respect to the style and content of different examples of this rock art.

Site Descriptions

Individual rock art sites in the Zuni-Cibola region often exhibit distinctive variations within the overall rock art style of a particular period. This may indicate differential use of sites. Furthermore, cotemporal elements, especially those of late historic times at sites found in the same general area, often appear to be thematically related—evidence of a kind of substyle within the Zuni-Cibola style that might relate to the use of certain locations by particular social groups. Although I am unable at present to attribute the creation of such rock art images to any particular social group, I can, for example, discern a similarity of style, content, and technique in many of the fairly recent pictographs found at sites 1, 6, 22, and 29—all located in fairly close proximity to one another. There are also distinct similarities to be seen in the deeply incised kachina figures and masks found at sites 13, 21, 23–25, 28, and 31–34 (see Map 2 for the geographical clusterings of these sites). It is impossible, within the scope of this book, to give more than a very general overview of each site. Detailed descriptions for each site and panel (numbering well over one thousand panels in all) are on record in the archives of the Zuni Archaeology Program and the Laboratory of Anthropology of the Museum of New Mexico.

Although by no means constituting an all-inclusive document of the pictographs and petroglyphs of the Zuni-Cibola region, the thirty-four recorded sites serve as representative both because they contain depictions from the entire range of time periods in this region and also because they illustrate style change, including a diversity of technique and content, through time. Of further importance is the fact that Zunis sometimes categorized figures from the same site (site numbers were not included with the images on the cards) as those that "go together." This may point to the kind of site-specific theme that I mentioned earlier.

The site numbers indicate the chronological sequence in which sites were recorded. For example, site 1 was recorded first and site 34 last. The survey team did not fully record every site before beginning a new one, however. This apparent randomness in recording was due in part to the fact that during the heavy summer rains, places at a distance from the pueblo on dirt roads became virtually inaccessible. At such times the recording team turned to more accessible locations, completing the other sites when weather permitted. The first sites recorded had been located previously by the Zuni Archaeology Program during archaeological surveys of the area, but as our project became known better throughout the pueblo, tribal members would tell us about other sites, sometimes guiding us there as well. I have included site numbers with all the illustrations throughout the book. Map 2 shows the general locations of all the sites recorded; of course, this figure cannot actually be used to find particular places since sufficient detail is not included. The vagueness is intentional—no one should visit any of the sites on the Zuni reservation without tribal permission; to visit sites off the reservation on private property, one should have the permission of the landowners.

Site 1 (Village of the Great Kivas)

Occupied during the early part of the eleventh century, this area contains the ruins of a large, multiroomed living complex that included two large and several smaller circular kivas. Pictographs and petroglyphs occur on mesa ledges about the site as well as on boulders near the ruin. Most of the rock art is prehistoric (i.e., contemporaneous with the ruin), made up of solidly pecked elements that are similar in style to those of the Chaco Canyon area, but there are also historic petroglyphs and several groups of pictographs. The most vivid of these paintings depict masks of kachina dancers. Many tribal members were familiar with this site and, as I discuss in Chapters 4 and 5, with the rock art located there, especially that dating to the same time period as the ruins. The various carved figures frequently evoked stories and interpretations. Zunis were also well-acquainted with the modern, painted kachina masks and they generally attributed them to men who had painted the actual masks worn during kachina dances. This is the site of the "new" figure painted between 1980 and 1981, that of the wild ram (see Figures 13, 23, 32f, 33a, 33f, 69, 70, 73–76, 78a, 85–88).

Site 2 (Kyaki:ma)

Located at the southeast base of Dowa Yalanne, Kyaki:ma was one of the six villages occupied when the Spaniards arrived in 1540. Nearby sites were inhabited sporadically from the tenth to the beginning of the eighteenth century. Most of the rock art appears to date from the late seventeenth-century period of occupation ("Refuge Period"), although earlier and later examples are also present. The site contains mostly petroglyphs of large masks or shields, anthropomorphic figures, and elaborate geometric designs. Many of these have been executed with a relatively unusual technique—deep gouging, perhaps due to the extremely soft sandstone of the area. The images labelled "kachinas or dancers" in the card-sorting experiment are almost all from this site. Although there are many other images here, the incised figures of individual kachinas and groups of kachinas constitute a definite "theme" (see Figures 1, 14, 15, 16, 20, 26b, 26c, 26e, 29b, 35d, 37a, 38b, 38c, 40, 54, 65, 66, 77).

Site 3 (Dowa Yalanne)

The same mesa that Kyaki:ma is set against has rock art in several other locations. One panel is situated along the northeast trail up to the mesa top and contains both prehistoric and modern rock art. The prehistoric design elements include both pictographs and petroglyphs. Especially striking elements are a human figure with oversized hands and feet (Figure 22) and a number of large shields with interior designs (Figure 36). Most of the more recent rock art, superimposed over the earlier elements, consists of incised names and dates. The rock art at both Kyaki:ma and this site at Dowa Yalanne provides examples from the late prehistoric and early historic periods at locations close to modern Zuni Pueblo.

Site 4

Located along the road to Black Rock, this site consists of dimly pecked images on basalt boulders. There are no architectural features directly associated with the site. Style and content suggest that the rock art here predates A.D. 1325. There is a fluteplayer, a stick figure, an animal in profile, a geometric design, and a lizardlike figure, in addition to other, more difficult to distinguish elements.

Site 5 (Heshoda Ts'in'a)

This is a district that was occupied in the late prehistoric period and reoccupied in the historic period as a satellite farming village (Pescado); it lies along a well-used trail between Zuni and Acoma. The place name here literally translates in English to "Place of Writing"—a reference to the abundance of rock art. Pictographs (mostly handprints painted in a variety of colors) and petroglyphs (many of which are highly unusual geometric designs) occur both on large boulders on the valley bottom and along the side of a mesa. Perhaps the most striking elements at this site are the fringed and toothed bird figures (showing evidence of the Rio Grande style), which are similar to those found at sites 20, 21, and 25 (Figure 71) (see Figures 26d, 32e, 39c, 39e, 39f, 71a, 71b, 71d, 71e).

Site 6

Just slightly northeast of site 1, this site can be seen from the road that skirts the nearby reservoir. The images, including a woman in a bikini, are almost all recently executed pictographs.

Site 7 (along Highway 53)

Several recently made, carefully executed petroglyphs are found here near an archaeological site with a prehistoric artifact scatter. The motifs include a small deer (Figure 79) and a dancer (Figure 78c) as well as names spray-painted in white (Figure 83).

Site 8

This is a small site near the Zuni rifle range, consisting of scattered petroglyphs. There is an animal figure with five legs and a pecked Shalako mask, the latter indicating that the images were produced after A.D. 1325 (see Figure 35e).

Site 9

On a series of boulders beyond a farming area and at the verge of a small pine forest are pecked images consisting of many spirals, several fluteplayers (without humpbacks), insect figures, figures with clawlike appendages, quadrupeds, and geometric designs. This site probably predates A.D. 1325 (see Figure 32b).

Site 10 (near Kwili Yalanne)

This site was occupied as a temporary sheep camp, probably during the 1700s. The pictographs and petroglyphs, including some very intricate geometric motifs, kachina figures, and representational depictions of horses and deer, most likely date from that period. Other elements found here are lizard men, deeply gouged slashes, plant figures, stars, bird tracks, painted handprints, and cattle or horse brands (see Figures 33e, 35f, 37d, 78b, 78d).

Site 11 (Petroglyph Canyon)

Several women potters said this area was a good source for the clay used in making pottery and remembered having noticed the rock art images while collecting clay here. This site contains many panels of petroglyphs, some of which consist of design elements similar to those at Site 10, which is nearby and was inhabited at about the same time. The rock carvings at this site include a large number of anthropomorphs that show the influence of the Rio Grande style—that is, their bodies are rounded and representational, often including projections from heads that may denote horns on masks. These are the figures that made up the major part of the group labelled "round bodies, clowns, Mudheads" in the card-sorting. Other rock carvings here are strikingly different from anything else found at Zuni to date. Those images, historic in style, depict a fish, a cat, an unusual upside-down figure, and a Mexican soldier (Figure 81). In addition, there are some recently incised petroglyphs, including a train with several cars and a very detailed depiction of Sherlock Holmes. Extensive vandalism occurred in this area between the summers of 1979 and 1980 (see Figures 10, 17, 21, 26f, 32g, 33b, 33c, 33d, 35b, 35g, 37b, 38a, 38d, 39b, 41, 59, 60, 64, 78e, 81, 82).

Site 12 (parts of El Morro National Monument)

This site is famous for its Inscription Rock, where early Spanish and Anglo explorers marked their passage with carved signatures, dates, and travel records (Figures 11 and 12). It is also the location of earlier petroglyphs and pictographs carved and painted by Indians on outlying boulders as well as on the rock itself. Atsinna, a thirteenth- to mid-fourteenth-century archaeological site situated on the top of the mesa, was so named during its excavation by Zuni workmen because of the nearby "pictures on the rock." Much of this rock art appears to have been contemporaneous with this habitation site (see Figures 11, 12, 29a).

Site 13

Located in a sheep-grazing area in close proximity to sites 21, 23, 24, 25, 28, 31, 32, 33, and 34, this site also shows a strong thematic relationship to those other sites. There is evidence of prehistoric and historic structures in the area. Most of the rock art figures are finely incised and appear quite modern in content. For example, there is a warrior kachina mask, a horse's head in profile, a frog, and a mouth with full lips carved around a natural crack in the rock.

Site 14

This cavelike spring area is made up almost entirely of faded paintings that appear to be historic. There are a number of kachina figures: Mudheads, eight Shalako figures, and figures of the Council of the Gods. Deer with heart lines and paintings of Kolowisi also occur at this site. One of the cave walls contains human figures with clubs who seem to be fighting one another. On the roof of the cave are a concentric circle and a number of black-painted stars. The cave is located near a Refuge Period site. Although I visited this site with a tribal religious leader and a member of the Zuni Archaeology Program, I did not photograph any of the images because the spring area was described as a shrine.

Site 15

Distinctive because of its white-painted geometrical human and animal forms, this rock art site is located in the general area of Kwili Yalanne (see Figures 37c, 48).

Site 16

This is a small site with three distinct styles of petroglyphs. The earliest style is associated with the prehistoric occupation of the vicinity (ca. A.D. 950–1075) and consists mainly of pecked anthropomorphs, quadrupeds, spirals, and geometric designs. The second style corresponds with historic occupation (ca. A.D. 1680–1750), as evidenced by nearby ruins and pottery sherds. It includes a pecked three-dimensional (corner) mask, pecked and incised plant figures, an incised horse with two tails (possibly indicative of motion), incised and abraded cloud-altar shapes, and pecked and incised geometric designs. The third style, predominantly incised masks, is fairly modern (see Figures 19, 35c, 89).

Site 17 (Hanlhibinkya)

Located in the Hardscrabble Wash region of Arizona, this site has long been linked with Zuni both in Zuni mythology and by archaeological studies of the Zuni-Cibola region. In the Zuni origin myth this is said to be the place of creation of the diminutive Twin War Gods as well as the place where the clans were given their names; hence, some of the rock art is considered to be comprised of clan totems. Rock art dating from Basketmaker II to the present time is found in abundance in part of this mile-long canyon. Although much of the rock art there is closely related in style and content to that surrounding Zuni Pueblo, this site also contains rock art that is probably the earliest in the area (a cluster of circle-line-zigzag masks/heads). Predominant elements are deer, mountain sheep, animal tracks, bird tracks, meanders, concentric circles, spirals, anthropomorphs (especially lizard men), fluteplayers, geometric designs, and patterned handprints and sandal tracks (see Figures 9, 24, 25, 26a, 27, 28, 29c, 29d, 29e, 29f, 29g, 30c, 31, 32a, 32c, 35a, 38f, 39d, 47, 57, 67, 72, 84).

Site 18

Located in an area currently in use for obtaining the clay and pigments used in pottery manufacture, this is an almost exclusively pictographic site. In addition to other functions, it is possible that the pictographs were produced by potters as a means of "experimenting" with the various colors. Archaeological data suggest that the area was temporarily occupied during the 1800s–1900s. The painted elements include handprints, human figures, a cross, masks, names, geometric designs, deer, and a plumed serpent.

Site 19 (Lyman Lake)

Only parts of this site were recorded. It is an area of abundant rock art that was investigated because of postulated archaeological relationships with the Zuni region. The rock art of this area is almost entirely pecked and appears "Anasazi," or pre-A.D. 1325 in style and content. There are many elaborate geometric designs, mountain sheep, birds with fringe-like wing and tail feathers, and human stick figures, all somewhat similar in style to those found in the area surrounding Zuni Pueblo (see Figures 30a, 30b, 32d, 39a, 68).

Site 20 (Petrified Forest)

The focus of recording here was in the area of Puerco Ruin, which was occupied prior to A.D. 1400. Nevertheless, much of the rock art here clearly shows the impact of the Rio Grande style, an indication of its rapid spread throughout the Pueblo area. The most frequent images are pecked and include elaborate geometric designs, rounded masks, animals, and birds with long, possibly toothed beaks, similar to those found at sites near Zuni (Figure 71) (see Figures 30d, 38e, 39g, 39h, 71c, 71g).

Site 21

Located in an area that shows evidence of several periods of occupation ranging from prehistoric to historic, the most frequent design elements at this site are deeply incised kachina figures and masks, anthropomorphs, serpents, and a bird figure with toothed beak similar to those found at sites 5 and 20.The majority of these elements appear to have been made after A.D. 1325 (see Figures 34, 56).

Site 22

This is a small site located across the arroyo from site 1. It is comprised of only one pictograph panel consisting of eight pairs of handprints, an anthropomorph with hair whorls, and a zigzag, all painted reddish brown.

Site 23

This site is located in the same sheep-grazing area as sites 13 and 21 (see Map 2 for grouping). The rock art depictions from all the sites in this area are similar in style, technique, and content and probably all date to post-A.D. 1325. Images here are mostly incised and include a deer figure, spiral, slashes and gouges, masks, geometric designs, a bird figure in profile, and an anthropomorph whose entire body is formed by drill holes.

Site 24

Found in the cliff area above site 23, this is a single boulder containing an incised date, a name, and an extremely representational human figure.

Site 25

Also located in the cliff area above site 23, this site appears to be post-A.D. 1325. There is some pecking but most images are incised. Included are pecked and painted (red) handprints, masks, altars, plant figures, geometric designs, gouges, quadrupeds, faces, an outlined cross, a bird figure with an extremely long beak, and names and dates (see Figure 71f).

Site 26

This site is located in the mound area west of Dowa Yalanne. There are many deeply incised snake figures, pecked anthropomorphs, abraded fluteplayers, an abraded anthropomorph with a headdress, and an abraded animal figure with five legs, its tail bent over its body, and prominent teeth. The site probably dates to post-A.D. 1325 (see Figures 58, 62).

Site 27

Located in the main canyon of Horsehead Canyon, this is an extensive site encompassing pottery and habitation areas that date from ca. A.D. 800–1375.[4] The rock art seems to fall within a temporal framework similar to that postulated for the habitation sites, but there are also some very recent images, especially finely incised and highly representational kachina figures. Many of the painted images, Anasazi in style, appear to have been executed from the tops of room blocks and are mural-like in appearance (Figure 18). Handprints appear in abundance, colored mostly red, yellow, and white. There is a wide range of deeply pecked anthropomorphs, stick figures, quadrupeds, geometric designs, animal tracks, masks with horns, turtles, and insect figures. Two different styles of pecking are found throughout this area—exhibited by those figures just mentioned, which are solidly pecked, and those that are pecked only in outline, almost with the appearance of being incised but with the dint marks visible (Figure 80). Finally, there are instances of designs made with drill holes.

Site 28

Located in the general vicinity of sites 13, 21, 23, 24, and 25, this is one panel only, comprised of a lightly scratched and very recent-looking mask.

Site 29

East of site 1 and near sites 6 and 22, this is a predominantly pictographic site consisting of several masks painted in red, a black-and red-painted anthropomorph, and incised words and dates. The rock art appears to have been done within the past fifty years or so.

Site 30

This site consists of scattered panels in Knife Hill Canyon. Elements include a pecked anthropomorph, a lizard figure with horns, a spiral, cattle brands, several finely incised and extremely small masks depicting Shalako and the Council of the Gods, and a panel of yellowish-white painted elements consisting of a deer, mountain lion, horned toad, and splatter handprint. The elements are probably all post-A.D. 1700 (Figure 52).

Site 31

Sites 31 through 34 are all located close to one another in a sheep-grazing area and were probably carved in the last fifty years. Because of the medium degree of patination, a more recent date is not likely. Site 31 consists of an incised horse head, a bull executed with three-dimensional perspective, and names and dates.

Site 32

This rock art site contains only a finely incised anthropomorph with a headdress, a geometric design, and a name and date.

Site 33

The images at this site are quite modern-looking. There are several incised horses with riders as well as an incised mask with horns.

Site 34

Similar to the sites mentioned above (sites 31, 32, and 33), the figures here are all incised and probably carved recently. There are incised horses (one with a saddle), names, dates, initials, a mask with horns, a plant figure, serpents, and geometric designs.

Notes

Chapter 1

1. The Zunis attribute value not only to their immediate environment but to all of the lands that they used in the past and continue to use in the present. These lands extend well beyond the bounds of the contemporary reservation. *See* T. J. Ferguson and E. Richard Hart, *A Zuni Atlas*, especially pp. 35–58.

2. Barbara Tedlock, "The Beautiful and the Dangerous: Zuni Ritual and Cosmology as an Aesthetic System," pp. 246–65.

3. For a general introduction to the ecology of the Zuni-Cibola region *see* C. Gregory Crampton, *The Zunis of Cibola*, pp. 1–9, and Ferguson and Hart, pp. 3–19.

4. This trip and the later one are described in the section entitled "Zuñi Comes East," in *Zuñi: Selected Writings of Frank Hamilton Cushing*, ed., Jesse Green, pp. 407–25.

5. *See* Frederick W. Hodge, "Hawikuh Bonework," pp. 69–70.

6. *The Zunis: Experiences and Descriptions*, p. 20.

7. In archaeology of the American Southwest the term "prehistoric" refers, in general, to the time prior to the existence of written records or historical accounts, that is, pre-A.D. 1540 (prior to contact with the Spanish). The term "historic" refers to the time from which there began to be a written record. In the American Southwest the historic period begins with the Spanish Conquest in A.D. 1540 and continues to A.D. 1900. The period from A.D. 1900 to the present is

referred to as the modern or contemporary period—a time when Native American tribes in the Southwest underwent radical cultural change.

8. Ferguson and Hart, p. 25.

9. The general chronological descriptions and sequences in this chapter are drawn almost directly from Ferguson and Hart, pp. 25–27. *See also* Keith Kintigh, *Settlement, Subsistence, and Society in Late Zuni Prehistory,* pp. 1–5. For a more general discussion of southwestern chronology, *see* William D. Lipe, "The Southwest," pp. 327–401.

10. Richard I. Ford, "Gardening and Farming Before A.D. 1000: Patterns of Prehistoric Cultivation North of Mexico," pp. 6–27.

11. *See* Frank H. H. Roberts, Jr., "The Village of the Great Kivas on the Zuñi Reservation, New Mexico," pp. 156–57.

12. John B. Rinaldo, "Notes on the Origins of Historic Zuni Culture," pp. 86–89; Richard B. Woodbury, "Zuni Prehistory and History to 1850," pp. 467–72.

13. For a brief overview of Anasazi building alignments in relationship to astronomical practice, *see* Ray A. Williamson, "North America: A Multiplicity of Astronomies," pp. 65–75.

14. For a description of the Rio Grande style and its rapid spread to the Little Colorado River drainage, *see especially* Polly Schaafsma, *Indian Rock Art of the Southwest,* pp. 252–60. For a discussion of the spread of the kachina cult from the south *see* Polly Schaafsma and Curtis F. Schaafsma, "Evidence for the Origins of the Pueblo Katchina Cult as Suggested by Southwestern Rock Art," pp. 535–45.

15. *See* Richard B. Woodbury, "The Antecedents of Zuni Culture," pp. 557–63; Patty J. Watson, Steven A. LeBlanc, and Charles L. Redman, "Aspects of Zuni Prehistory: Preliminary Report on Excavation and Survey in the El Morro Valley of New Mexico," pp. 201–18.

16. Cited in Crampton, p. 18. *See also* pp. 13–30, for further information on early Spanish explorers in the Southwest.

17. The term "Refuge Period" was first used by Leslie Spier in describing eighteenth-century sites at Zuni. *See* Leslie Spier, "An Outline for a Chronology of Zuñi Ruins," p. 276. This term was later adopted by members of the Zuni Archaeology Program. *See especially* the discussion of this term as applied to the Kyaki:ma site in T. J. Ferguson, William A. Dodge, and Barbara J. Mills, "Archaeological Investigations at Kyaki:ma."

18. Crampton, p. 40. *See also* J. Manuel Espinosa, ed. and trans.,

First Expedition of Vargas into New Mexico, 1692.

19. Woodbury, "Zuni Prehistory and History to 1850," p. 472.

20. Fred Eggan and Triloki N. Pandey, "Zuni History, 1850–1970," p. 476.

21. Crampton, p. 2.

22. Alvina Quam, trans., *The Zunis: Self-Portrayals by the Zuni People,* p. 180.

23. *See, for example,* Ruth Benedict, *Zuni Mythology;* Ruth L. Bunzel, *The Pueblo Potter: A Study of Creative Imagination in Primitive Art,* "Introduction to Zuñi Ceremonialism," "Zuñi Origin Myths," "Zuñi Ritual Poetry," "Zuñi Katcinas: An Analytical Study"; Frank H. Cushing, "The Zuñi Social, Mythic and Religious Systems," "Zuñi Fetiches," "Outlines of Zuñi Creation Myths," "Zuñi Breadstuff"; J. Walter Fewkes, "A Few Summer Ceremonials at Zuñi Pueblo"; Elsie C. Parsons, "Notes on Zuñi," "The Origin Myth of Zuñi," *Pueblo Indian Religion;* Matilda C. Stevenson, "The Religious Life of the Zuñi Child," "Zuñi Ancestral Gods and Masks," "The Zuñi Indians: Their Mythology, Esoteric Fraternities, and Ceremonies"; Dennis Tedlock, "Zuni Religion and World View."

24. An excellent bibliographic essay by Barbara and Dennis Tedlock (included in Woodbury, "Zuni Prehistory and History to 1850," pp. 472–73) delineates the most important works on Zuni ceremonialism, household activities, legal system, kinship, attitudes toward witchcraft, verbal art, and the graphic arts.

25. Edmund Ladd, "Zuni Social and Political Organization," p. 482.

26. Ibid.

27. Fred Eggan, *Social Organization of the Western Pueblos,* p. 62.

28. Ladd, "Zuni Social and Political Organization," p. 487, provides a list of contemporary Zuni clans.

29. Eggan, p. 62.

30. Ladd, "Zuni Social and Political Organization," p. 487.

31. Cushing, "Outlines of Zuñi Creation Myths," p. 369. Although Cushing is sometimes accused of overinterpretation, Eggan seems to agree with him. *See* Eggan, p. 300. I will discuss the wide-ranging association of many aspects of Zuni life with directionalism in more detail in Chapter 3.

32. Edmund J. Ladd, "Zuni Economy," p. 494.

33. Ibid.

34. It might be more appropriate to regard the members of the Kachina Society as actors in sacred theater rather than impersonators. I use the term "impersonator" because it is the most widely used in the ethnographic literature and also because it lends itself to the idea of taking on the personality of the god. The kachina impersonators do more than act out a part; in the context of ritual activity, they become the god. The Zunis believe that the impersonator who dons the kachina mask becomes infused with the spirit of that kachina. The power of the mask, particularly as it relates to rock art representations of masks, is discussed further in Chapter 5.

35. *See* M. Stevenson, "The Zuñi Indians," pp. 407–608, for a complete description of these fraternities. *See also* Dennis Tedlock, "Zuni Religion and World View," pp. 502–7, for a summary description of these societies.

36. The Zuni hierarchy of powerful beings, including the Beast Gods, Twin War Gods, and predators and game animals, will be discussed in Chapter 4.

37. D. Tedlock, "Zuni Religion and World View," p. 506; Ladd, "Zuni Social and Political Organization," p. 485.

38. Green, pp. 10–11.

39. D. Tedlock, "Zuni Religion and World View," p. 507.

40. Ladd, "Zuni Social and Political Organization," pp. 488–91; Eggan and Pandey, pp. 477–79.

41. The Zuni Public School District is the first state district with boundaries that conform to an Indian Reservation. It is thus Zuni controlled, but nevertheless not entirely independent since it is under the ultimate authority of the State of New Mexico. T. J. Ferguson, personal communication.

42. Quam, p. 38.

43. Ladd, "Zuni Economy," p. 498.

44. M. Jane Young, "We Were Going to Have a Barbeque, But the Cow Ran Away: Production, Form, and Function of the Zuni Tribal Fair," p. 46.

Chapter 2

1. Richard B. Woodbury and Natalie F. Woodbury, "Zuni Prehistory and El Morro National Monument," p. 56.

2. Polly Schaafsma and M. Jane Young, "Early Masks and Faces in Southwest Rock Art," pp. 23–26.

3. The various rock art sites in the Zuni locale that have been documented and for which a tentative temporal framework has been established are described in M. Jane Young, "Images of Power, Images of Beauty: Contemporary Zuni Perceptions of Rock Art," pp. 31–92. *See also* the Appendix to this book.

4. I mention here not those who have questioned the application of the term "art" to studies of rock art, but rather those who have incorporated in their works an implicit response to such questions. *See especially* Campbell Grant, *Rock Art of the American Indian,* pp. 18–27; Travis Hudson and Georgia Lee, "Function and Symbolism in Chumash Rock Art"; W. W. Newcomb, Jr., and Forrest Kirkland, *The Rock Art of the Texas Indians,* pp. 14–18; Polly Schaafsma, *Indian Rock Art of the Southwest,* pp. 1–32. For an excellent discussion of the similarities and differences between rock art and urban graffiti *see* Klaus F. Wellmann, "Just Like Graffiti?: A Comparative Analysis of North American Indian Rock Drawings and Modern Urban Graffiti."

5. I use the designation "Zuni-Cibola region" to describe the area that includes the reservation as well as archaeological and rock art sites for which a clear relationship to Zuni has been demonstrated.

6. *See* Barbara J. Mills, "Zuni Rock Art Survey: A Review of Archaeological Site Records, Dating, and Bibliographic References"; Frank H. H. Roberts, Jr., "The Village of the Great Kivas on the Zuñi Reservation, New Mexico"; Woodbury and Woodbury, pp. 56–60.

7. Polly Schaafsma, personal communication.

8. Frank H. Cushing, *My Adventures in Zuñi,* p. 40.

9. Zuni morning prayers to the sun are described by Ruth L. Bunzel, "Introduction to Zuñi Ceremonialism," p. 499; Cushing, *My Adventures in Zuñi,* p. 26; Matilda C. Stevenson, "The Zuñi Indians: Their Mythology, Esoteric Fraternities, and Ceremonies," p. 109. For a discussion of the east-west orientation of altars *see* M. Stevenson, "The Zuñi Indians," pp. 345, 536.

10. The Zuni verbs for these two states are *ya:,* "finished" or "made," and *k'abi,* "unfinished" or "raw." Lévi-Strauss suggests that such terms are almost universals among indigenous peoples. *See* Claude Lévi-Strauss, *The Raw and the Cooked: Introduction to the Science of Mythology: 1.* The categories "raw" and "finished," as they pertain to Zuni cultural symbolism, will be discussed further in Chapters 3 and 4.

11. For a detailed discussion of the terms "finished beings" (that

is, human beings) and "raw beings" (that is, nonhuman, powerful beings) see Chapter 4. There are varying degrees of "rawness," but basically newborn babies are considered to be "raw beings" (just as the people were when they lived in the fourth underworld, before they reached the surface of this earth and were dazzled by the light of the sun) until the day they are presented to the sun, upon which they become human or "finished." When people die, they return to the status of "raw beings" and often become kachinas. For a discussion of the role played by the sun in the origin myth and the presentation of a newborn child as a reenactment of this event, see Matilda C. Stevenson, "The Religious Life of the Zuñi Child," p. 546; Dennis Tedlock, "An American Indian View of Death," p. 265.

12. Schaafsma, Indian Rock Art of the Southwest, p. 177.

13. La Van Martineau, The Rocks Begin to Speak, suggests that rock art constitutes a pan-Indian system of writing akin to language. For an evaluation and criticism of Martineau's approach, see Schaafsma, Indian Rock Art of the Southwest, p. 13. Her major argument is that Martineau's hypothesis is invalid because it does not take into account the cultural affiliations of the creators of rock art or the time periods within which the pictographs and petroglyphs were produced.

14. The use of features of style, content, and technique as aids in establishing a temporal framework for rock art is outlined by Campbell Grant, Canyon de Chelly: Its People and Rock Art; Polly Schaafsma, Rock Art in the Navajo Reservoir District; Schaafsma, Indian Rock Art of the Southwest; Christy G. Turner, II, Petroglyphs of the Glen Canyon Region. For an excellent summary of such methods of dating rock art see Klaus F. Wellmann, A Survey of North American Indian Rock Art, pp. 20–24. The use of pottery in dating rock art is discussed by Schaafsma, Indian Rock Art of the Southwest. E. Wesley Jernigan provides comparative data for another art form in Jewelry of the Prehistoric Southwest. Comparisons between imagery in rock art and kiva murals are outlined by Grant, Canyon de Chelly, and Schaafsma, Indian Rock Art of the Southwest.

15. See Meyer Schapiro, "Style," pp. 287–312, and Schaafsma, Indian Rock Art of the Southwest, p. 8. For discussions of the significance of style in determining chronological sequences, see Hudson and Lee, "Function and Symbolism in Chumash Rock Art," pp. 7–17, and Morton H. Levine, "Prehistoric Art and Ideology," pp. 949–64.

16. The most comprehensive work that outlines style and chronological ordering of the rock art of areas surrounding the Zuni-Cibola region is Schaafsma, *Indian Rock Art of the Southwest*. My own discussion of style and relative dating is based largely on a view of the Zuni area rock art as part of the overall southwestern framework established by Schaafsma. *See especially* chapters 3 and 5 of her book.

17. Schaafsma and Young, "Early Masks and Faces in Southwest Rock Art," pp. 23–26.

18. Schaafsma, *Indian Rock Art of the Southwest*, pp. 72–74, 109.

19. Polly Schaafsma, *Rock Art in New Mexico*, p. 3.

20. Schaafsma, *Indian Rock Art of the Southwest*, p. 136.

21. For further discussion of the Rio Grande style complex in the Southwest in general, *see* Schaafsma, *Indian Rock Art of the Southwest*, pp. 160–61.

22. The deeply gouged shields also occur at Tovakwa in the Jemez during A.D. 1300–1620; the elaborate rectangular designs occur in the Hopi area. Polly Schaafsma, personal communication.

23. Although horned serpents belonging to the Rio Grande style complex appear throughout the Pueblo area, there are figures in Zuni rock art (especially pictographs) that represent Kolowisi specifically and are similar in coloration, form, and style to representations of Kolowisi in Zuni pottery and kiva murals. For example, the Kolowisi figures at site 14 that I was not permitted to photograph are very much like those in Figures 49, 50, and 51. Of the other images mentioned here, deer with heart lines are the most distinctively Zuni. This type of figure was probably introduced after the sixteenth century by the Athabaskans. *See* Schaafsma, *Rock Art in the Navajo Reservoir District*, pp. 57, 59.

24. For a detailed discussion of the archaeology of the Zuni-Cibola region, including the various interactional spheres of prehistoric and historic groups, *see* Fred Eggan and Triloki N. Pandey, "Zuni History, 1850–1970"; T. J. Ferguson and E. Richard Hart, *A Zuni Atlas*, pp. 25–35; Keith Kintigh, *Settlement, Subsistence, and Society in Late Zuni Prehistory*, pp. 1–6; John B. Rinaldo, "Notes on the Origins of Historic Zuni Culture"; and Richard B. Woodbury, "Zuni Prehistory and History to 1850."

25. Sally Cole has pointed out a similarity between mask- or head-like figures in Basketmaker II rock art of the central San Juan region and a "trophy" head found with a Basketmaker burial. *See* "Analysis

of a San Juan (Basketmaker) Style Painted Mask in Grand Gulch, Utah," pp. 1–6.

26. "Panel" as used here and throughout this book refers to an expanse of image-bearing rock treated as a unit; generally, a single rock face.

27. For a discussion of fluteplayers in rock art of the Southwest, their guise as rain priests, and their possible association with the Hopi kachina Kokopelli, *see especially* Schaafsma, *Indian Rock Art of the Southwest*, pp. 122, 125, 136–41.

28. As will be discussed further in Chapter 5, I believe that some of the rock art depictions of deer, bear, bison, and mountain sheep were shot at to insure successful hunting rather than as an act of vandalism.

29. According to Polly Schaafsma, personal communication, in Canyon de Chelly there is a Navajo pictograph depicting humanlike heads on corn plants.

30. Schaafsma, *Indian Rock Art of the Southwest*, pp. 105–62, 243–89, discusses these styles and their spheres of influence in rock art of the American Southwest.

31. *See* Barton Wright, *Pueblo Shields*, p. 1. Polly Schaafsma, personal communication.

32. For one of the rock art depictions and a discussion of shields in rock art *see* Schaafsma, *Rock Art in New Mexico*, pp. 157–60, Figure 137. For the other rock art depiction, *see* Schaafsma, *Indian Rock Art of the Southwest*, p. 258, Figure 200. For the kiva mural depiction, *see* Frank C. Hibben, *Kiva Art of the Anasazi at Pottery Mound*, pp. 132–33, Figures 103–4. These three figures are very similar to Figure 36 of this book. Polly Schaafsma (personal communication) has recently suggested that the shields at Zuni Rock Art Survey site 3 (Figure 36) as well as the masks/shields at site 2 (Figure 14) are quite similar to rock art figures located at a Jemez (one of the Rio Grande Pueblo groups) habitation site dating from A.D. 1300–1620. This would fit with my relative dating of these Zuni figures as well.

33. Frank H. Cushing, "A Study of Pueblo Pottery as Illustrative of Zuñi Culture Growth," p. 515.

34. For a discussion of the being of the zenith as both eagle and "Knife-Wing," *see* Bunzel, "Introduction to Zuñi Ceremonialism," p. 528.

35. The earliest date, A.D. 400, is suggested for some elements at

site 17. *See* Schaafsma and Young, "Early Masks and Faces in Southwest Rock Art," pp. 23–26.

36. The Zuni commentary referenced in this book, except where otherwise noted, is from fieldwork conducted at the Pueblo of Zuni during the summers of 1979–1981 and 1983–1984.

37. A computer-assisted distributional analysis of the data derived from these sortings will be the subject of a separate forthcoming article: M. Jane Young and John M. Roberts, "Local Rock Art Motifs: A Contemporary Zuni View." *See also* Young, "Images of Power, Images of Beauty."

38. Ruth L. Bunzel, *The Pueblo Potter: A Study of Creative Imagination in Primitive Art*, p. 70.

39. Ibid., p. 87.

40. Ibid., p. 54.

41. The term "organization of diversity" is based on Anthony Wallace's discussion in *Culture and Personality*, pp. 23–24, 128–29. I am grateful to Dell Hymes for suggesting its applicability to this particular situation.

42. *See* J. David Lewis-Williams, *Believing and Seeing: Symbolic Meanings in Southern San Rock Paintings*, p. 36, for a somewhat similar situation. Lewis-Williams showed photographs of animal and human figures to his South African informants and found that they identified animal images "with ease" but had difficulty with human figures.

Chapter 3

1. Claire Farrer, "Play and Inter-Ethnic Communication: A Practical Ethnography of the Mescalero Apache"; Claire Farrer, "Singing for Life: The Mescalero Apache Girls' Puberty Ceremony," pp. 125–59; Claire Farrer and Bernard Second, "Living the Sky: Aspects of Mescalero Apache Ethnoastronomy," pp. 137–50; Nancy D. Munn, *Walbiri Iconography: Graphic Representation and Cultural Symbolism in a Central Australian Society*; Barbara Tedlock, "Songs of the Zuni Kachina Society: Composition, Rehearsal, and Performance," pp. 7–35; Barbara Tedlock, "The Beautiful and the Dangerous: Zuni Ritual and Cosmology as an Aesthetic System," pp. 246–65.

2. Munn, pp. 171–73.

3. B. Tedlock, "The Beautiful and the Dangerous," p. 265.

4. Much of Barbara Tedlock's recent research involves an investigation of the Zuni cosmological outlook as well, but our approaches are still somewhat different. She posits an underlying aesthetic framework that informs cosmology, whereas I posit an underlying cosmological principle that informs aesthetics. Although Tedlock and I are approaching Zuni cultural symbolism from different perspectives our research is complementary, however, and contributes to the same holistic view of the culture.

5. Von Del Chamberlain, *When Stars Came Down to Earth: Cosmology of the Skidi Pawnee Indians of North America*, and Gary Urton, *At the Crossroads of the Earth and the Sky: An Andean Cosmology*.

6. Although there is no longer a sun priest at Zuni, this duty has been taken over by another official.

7. Elsie C. Parsons, "Notes on Zuñi," pp. 296–99.

8. Frank H. Cushing, *My Adventures in Zuñi*, p. 41. Michael Zeilik, personal communication, has found similar references in the unpublished diaries of J. G. Bourke.

9. It is noteworthy that the number four is the sacred or pattern number of many, although by no means all, Native American peoples. Thus, the importance of the number four for the Zunis is not peculiar to them but part of a broader context. For the importance of the number four in Zuni mythology, *see* Ruth Benedict, "Zuñi Mythology," pp. 1–276; Ruth L. Bunzel, "Zuñi Origin Myths," pp. 547–609; Frank H. Cushing, "Outlines of Zuñi Creation Myths," pp. 321–447; Elsie C. Parsons, "The Origin Myth of Zuñi," pp. 135–62; Matilda C. Stevenson, "The Zuñi Indians: Their Mythology, Esoteric Fraternities, and Ceremonies," pp. 20–61; Dennis Tedlock, trans., *Finding the Center: Narrative Poetry of the Zuni Indians*, pp. 225–98. In addition to these versions of the Zuni origin myth, all of which emphasize the ceremonial importance of the number four, Dell Hymes, "Particle, Pause and Pattern in American Indian Verse," pp. 7–51, demonstrates that the number four is also central in the repetition and patterning of Zuni narrative verse.

10. Dennis Tedlock, "Zuni Religion and World View," p. 508.

11. Ruth L. Bunzel, *The Pueblo Potter: A Study of Creative Imagination in Primitive Art*, p. 23.

12. This description of the semicardinal directions as the ritual directions and counterclockwise as the ritual order is a generalization. I am grateful to Barbara and Dennis Tedlock for pointing out

to me that at Zuni the use of cardinal versus semicardinal directions, as well as the use of clockwise versus counterclockwise, depends on the particular ceremonial context. In his unpublished notes, J. P. Harrington gives "archaic Zuni words" used for the directions in Zuni ceremonies. He translates these directional words as the semicardinal directions, that is, "northeast, northwest, southwest, southeast," and states that they refer to the solstice extremes. *See* J. P. Harrington, "Unpublished manuscripts and papers pertaining to fieldwork at the Zuni Indian Reservation."

13. Bunzel, "Zuñi Origin Myths," pp. 601–2; Cushing, "Outlines of Zuñi Creation Myths," pp. 428–29; M. Stevenson, "The Zuñi Indians," p. 46; D. Tedlock, *Finding the Center*, pp. 278–80. In various versions of the Zuni origin myth (those contained in the ethnographic record as well as those I heard during my fieldwork), the terms "heart" and "navel" were both used in referring to this particular event. Sometimes one or the other is used, sometimes both together. Both terms, however, refer to a conceptual center that is the critical factor in this myth event.

14. Ruth L. Bunzel, "Introduction to Zuñi Ceremonialism," p. 514; M. Stevenson, "The Zuñi Indians," p. 46.

15. D. Tedlock, "Zuni Religion and World View," p. 499.

16. Ibid.

17. M. Stevenson, "The Zuñi Indians," p. 22; Matilda C. Stevenson, "Ethnobotany of the Zuñi Indians," p. 89; D. Tedlock, "Zuni Religion and World View," pp. 499–500.

18. Bunzel, "Zuñi Ritual Poetry," p. 784; D. Tedlock, "Zuni Religion and World View," p. 500. When cardinal rather than semicardinal directions are employed as the directional model, the following associations are made: yellow mountain lion/north, blue bear/west, red badger/south, and white wolf/east. *See* Frank H. Cushing, "Zuñi Fetiches," pp. 16–18, 24–25. Each of the species of prey animals is again divided into six varieties, according to color. Thus, for example, although the mountain lion is primarily associated with the north and the color yellow, there is a mountain lion representative for each of the other directions/colors as well.

19. Frank H. Cushing, "Discussion and Remarks on Shamanism," p. 7.

20. There is a Zuni symbol used in certain contexts to stand for the six-part directional scheme, the *hepakinne*, that has been described as a sunflower as well as corn and squash blossoms. See

Bunzel, *The Pueblo Potter*, pp. 92, 95; M. Stevenson, "The Zuñi Indians," p. 134. Painted on Zuni water jars and on the masks of the Salimobia and Shitsukia kachinas, the *hepakinne* is a hexagonal design inside a circle, generally with each division painted in one of the colors associated with the six directions. Among other meanings, Zunis say that it represents the "differently colored lightning" associated with those directions (Ruth L. Bunzel, "Zuñi Katcinas: An Analytical Study," p. 923). Nevertheless, my point is that, although it may be used occasionally, the four- or six-part design is not so much a prevalent symbol in Zuni graphic art as a prevalent pattern of arrangement and association.

21. Such multivalent or multireferential symbols have been described by Victor Turner as nuclear or condensed symbols. *See especially* his *The Forest of Symbols*, pp. 295, 298. *See also* Farrer, "Play and Inter-Ethnic Communication"; Farrer, "Singing for Life"; Farrer and Second, "Living the Sky"; and Munn, *Walbiri Iconography*, pp. 171–73.

22. Turner, *The Forest of Symbols*, p. 298, discusses the power of conflation inherent in a nuclear symbol.

23. B. Tedlock, "The Beautiful and the Dangerous."

24. I first heard the term "aesthetic of accumulation" in an informal colloquium on the home altars of Mexican American women presented by Kay Turner, a graduate student in the Folklore Program at the University of Texas at Austin. In subsequent discussion we agreed that the same sort of principle of elaborate redundancy seemed to operate at Zuni. Although she does not specifically use the term "aesthetic of accumulation" in her writings, Turner's scholarly works offer an excellent portrait of the principle of elaboration in Mexican American folk art. *See especially* Kay Turner, "Mexican American Home Altars: Towards Their Interpretation," pp. 309–26 and Kay Turner, "Mexican American Women's Home Altars: The Art of Relationship."

25. Hymes, "Particle, Pause and Pattern in American Indian Verse," pp. 7–51; Bunzel, *The Pueblo Potter*, p. 23.

26. For excellent examples of the recent attention given to ethnopoetics, *see* Dell Hymes, *"In Vain I Tried to Tell You": Essays in Native American Ethnopoetics*; D. Tedlock, trans., *Finding the Center: Narrative Poetry of the Zuni Indians*; Dennis Tedlock, *The Spoken Word and the Work of Interpretation*; and Barre Toelken and Tacheeni Scott, "Poetic Retranslation and the 'Pretty Languages' of Yellowman," pp. 65–116.

27. This is from my retranslation of Bunzel, "Zuñi Ritual Poetry," pp. 710–56.

28. For the entire translation *see* M. Jane Young, "Translation and Analysis of Zuni Ritual Poetry."

29. M. Jane Young and Ray A. Williamson, "Ethnoastronomy: The Zuni Case," pp. 183–91.

30. For a more general discussion of Native American attitudes towards the U.S. space program *see* M. Jane Young, "'Pity the Indians of Outer Space': Native American Views of the Space Program."

31. Although I describe only one such performance, during her fieldwork at Zuni, Barbara Tedlock heard stories of a whole series of clown performances enacted to mimic aspects of the U.S. moon shots. *See* Barbara Tedlock, "Boundaries of Belief," pp. 70–77.

32. Not only are kivas commonly subterranean, but, according to Zuni ritual practice specifically and Puebloan symbolism more generally, they frequently contain a hole called the *sipapu* that represents the hole through which the people climbed after traveling through the four underworlds to reach the surface of this earth. For a description of the location and symbolism of the *sipapu, see* Frank H. H. Roberts, Jr., "Shabik'eshchee Village, A Late Basket Maker Site in The Chaco Canyon, New Mexico," p. 12.

33. Another example of Zuni humorous imitations of Anglo-Americans is described by M. Stevenson, "The Zuñi Indians," p. 209. Such clown performances among the Hopi are described by Alfonso Ortiz, "Ritual Drama and the Pueblo World View," pp. 158–61. For examples of other Native American humorous yet critical portrayals of members of "mainstream" society, *see* Keith H. Basso, *Portraits of "The Whiteman": Linguistic Play and Cultural Symbols Among the Western Apache;* and Frank G. Speck and Leonard Broom, *Cherokee Dance and Drama*, pp. 36–37.

34. For similar Zuni descriptions of the end of the world, *see* Alvina Quam, trans., *The Zunis: Self-Portrayals by the Zuni People,* p. 1; and Dennis Tedlock, "An American Indian View of Death," p. 270.

35. *See* Prewitt Edelman, "Working Back: The New Physics and Pueblo Mythology," p. 305.

36. I am grateful to Dell Hymes for his comments and suggestions that have served as catalysts in the formation of this discussion of the dialectic interaction between the myth time and the "here and now."

Chapter 4

1. In general, this division into such time periods in the card-sorting experiment is my own synthesis, based on my establishment of a temporal framework for the rock art of this area, and was not a distinction made by my Zuni colleagues, with the exception of two individuals who divided images into groups of "old" and "contemporary."

2. For similar accounts of what the people in the fourth underworld looked like, *see* Ruth Benedict, *Zuni Mythology*, pp. 3–5; Ruth L. Bunzel, "Zuñi Origin Myths," pp. 584–91; Frank H. Cushing, "Outlines of Zuñi Creation Myths," pp. 383–84; Matilda C. Stevenson, "The Zuñi Indians: Their Mythology, Esoteric Fraternities, and Ceremonies," p. 28; Dennis Tedlock, trans., *Finding the Center: Narrative Poetry of the Zuni Indians*, p. 264; and Dennis Tedlock, "An American Indian View of Death," p. 268.

3. Matilda Stevenson, "The Zuñi Indians," p. 42, Plate VII.

4. Frank H. Cushing, "Zuñi Fetiches," pp. 9–11; D. Tedlock, "An American Indian View of Death," pp. 264–70; Dennis Tedlock, "Zuni Religion and World View," pp. 499–508. The terminology I use here, although similar to that used by other scholars, is from my own translations of Zuni materials, especially M. Jane Young, "Translation and Analysis of Zuni Ritual Poetry." For subsequent discussion of the finished/raw contrast, I rely most heavily on my own translations and on Zuni commentary about these terms that I recorded during my fieldwork.

5. Ruth L. Bunzel, *The Pueblo Potter: A Study of Creative Imagination in Primitive Art*, pp. 23–24, 69–71; Ruth L. Bunzel, "Introduction to Zuñi Ceremonialism," pp. 491–93. *See* M. Stevenson, "The Zuñi Indians," Plate XXXVI, for a depiction of "the sacred frog" as well as Kolowisi in a kiva mural (the same as my Figure 51); Plates III, XLIII, LXX, and LXXV in Stevenson depict frogs, tadpoles, and dragonflies on the backs of kachina masks.

6. Because of its use to describe images to which magical powers are attributed by primitive societies, the word "fetish" has negative connotations for members of Western society, but I use it here because it is the word the Zunis themselves use for these images.

7. According to Cushing, "Zuñi Fetiches," pp. 20–30, the Prey God fetishes used in hunting are the same animals as the Beast Gods with these exceptions: the coyote replaces the bear of the west; the

wild cat replaces the badger of the south; and the red-tailed hawk is added to the eagle of the zenith.

8. Cushing, "Zuñi Fetiches," pp. 20–30; D. Tedlock, "Zuni Religion and World View," pp. 500–01.

9. In the *Pueblo Potter*, Plate IX, page 26, Bunzel shows two Zuni pottery drums that contain depictions of the Beast Gods. One of these drums portrays a mountain lion chasing a deer.

10. Although some Zunis identified these animals as "Beast Gods," most used the term *wema:we*. Because I have some knowledge of the Zuni language, I was able to follow and translate such terms. Often, particularly for the "animal" category, my Zuni colleagues gave only the Zuni name, in accord with one man who repeatedly said, "I don't know what it is in English." *See* Ruth F. Kirk, "Introduction to Zuni Fetishism," p. 235, for the description of a similar situation, i.e., "In Zuni it would be easy to explain, but hard to tell it in English."

11. Cushing, "Zuñi Fetiches," pp. 14–15.

12. M. Stevenson, "The Zuñi Indians," p. 49.

13. Ibid., p. 453 and Plate CVIII.

14. Bunzel, *The Pueblo Potter*, p. 93, Figure 2; M. Stevenson, "The Zuñi Indians," p. 94, Plate XIII.

15. Although a Zuni man who went with me to this site described these as "the Kolowisi of the six directions," references in the ethnographic literature usually mention Kolowisi only in relation to the four directions; *see* D. Tedlock, "Zuni Religion and World View," p. 499. For a discussion of Kolowisi as both individual and multiple in Zuni thought, *see* Bunzel, "Introduction to Zuñi Ceremonialism," pp. 515–16.

16. The quotation is from a tape recording made at Zuni by Von Del Chamberlain in 1978. Mr. Chamberlain very graciously permitted me to listen to and transcribe the tape. This comment is from a well-educated and very articulate Zuni man—hence, his rather formal style of explication. Note in this quotation the reference to the marks of the flood as an "explanation" of the banded sandstone comprising the mesa of Corn Mountain. For the association of Kolowisi with the flood, *see* Benedict, *Zuni Mythology*, pp. 10–11; Bunzel, "Introduction to Zuñi Ceremonialism," p. 516; and M. Stevenson, "The Zuñi Indians," p. 84, note f. Kirk, p. 237, gives a rendition of this story similar to the one Chamberlain taped, including the description of the resultant two stone pillars as related to fertility

shrines. She does not mention Kolowisi in relation to the flood story, however.

17. J. Walter Fewkes, "A Few Tusayan Pictographs," p. 20; J. Walter Fewkes, "Ancient Pueblo and Mexican Water Symbol," pp. 535–38.

18. Interestingly, according to Cushing, Zunis regard a "concretion exhibiting spiral or concentric lines . . . as a symbol of the Midmost itself." He suggests that this is because spiral lines resemble the marks made by the whirlwind, "the midmost of all the winds of the world." See Frank H. Cushing, "Discussion and Remarks on Shamanism," p. 11.

19. Florence H. Ellis and Laurens Hammack, "The Inner Sanctum of Feather Cave, A Mogollon Sun and Earth Shrine Linking Mexico and the Southwest," p. 35; Florence H. Ellis, "A Thousand Years of the Pueblo Sun-Moon-Star Calendar," pp. 74–75.

20. John Peabody Harrington, "Unpublished Manuscripts and Papers Pertaining to Field Work at Zuni"; Frederick W. Hodge and Frank H. Cushing, "Unpublished Manuscripts and Papers Pertaining to Field Work at Zuni"; Frank McNitt, ed., *Navaho Expedition: Journal of a Military Reconnaissance from Santa Fe, New Mexico, to the Navaho Country Made in 1849 by Lieutenant James H. Simpson*, pp. 120–42. The terms "hieroglyphs" and "designs" were often used by Zunis to describe rock art, especially geometric figures. This may relate to the present-day idea that rock art constitutes a "message" from the ancestors, although it is in no way a suggestion that each image literally represents a Zuni word.

21. Elsie C. Parsons, *Pueblo Indian Religion*, p. 448, discusses the ejection of fluid as an omen in such ritual contexts.

22. Elsie C. Parsons, "Notes on Zuñi," p. 167; Elsie C. Parsons and Ralph L. Beals, "The Sacred Clowns of the Pueblo and Mayo-Yaqui Indians," Table 1. Although my Zuni colleagues described the projections on the heads of the Newekwe as "squash blossoms," they are referred to in the ethnographic literature as "knobs of corn husk." See Parsons, "Notes on Zuñi," p. 233, and M. Stevenson, "The Zuñi Indians," p. 436.

23. Both Bunzel, "Zuñi Origin Myths," p. 592, and Dennis Tedlock, *The Spoken Word and the Work of Interpretation*, p. 244, cite instances of a narration of the origin myth during which the narrator recites that the people journeyed for four days. The narrator then adds (either as an aside or as part of the narration) that it was four years. Tedlock suggests that this is due to the special way that time

is perceived in this context.

24. M. Stevenson, "The Zuñi Indians," p. 40.

25. This is from the same tape recording as that discussed in note 16. This story was repeated twice during Chamberlain's tape recorded discussion with this Zuni man. The first time was an elaborated version that is transcribed here and broken into lines on the basis of breath pauses. The second time, the narrator repeated these remarks in an abbreviated version that I included in an earlier article. *See* M. Jane Young, "Images of Power and the Power of Images: The Significance of Rock Art for Contemporary Zunis," p. 14. The elaborated version was elicited by Chamberlain's use of the word "story" and was performed from beginning to end in one monologue—a monologue that has obvious poetic patterning and constitutes a "breakthrough into performance." *See* Dell Hymes, "Breakthrough into Performance."

26. Robert J. Smith, *The Art of the Festival*, p. 98.

27. Travis Hudson and Georgia Lee, "Function and Symbolism in Chumash Rock Art," p. 25.

28. Sally McLendon, "Cultural Presuppositions and Discourse Analysis: Patterns of Presupposition and Assertion of Information in Eastern Pomo and Russian Narrative," pp. 161–62. For an excellent discussion of the linking of specific places in the landscape with narratives by the Western Apache, *see* Keith H. Basso, "'Stalking with Stories': Names, Places, and Moral Narratives among the Western Apache," pp. 19–55.

29. McLendon, p. 163.

30. I am grateful to Richard Bauman for suggesting that I pursue this idea.

31. For the association of Zuni fetishes with the myth time *see* Kirk, pp. 154–55.

32. Smith, *The Art of the Festival*, p. 99. Kay Turner describes similar evocative power for Catholic icons. *See* "The Cultural Semiotics of Religious Icons: La Virgen de San Juan de los Lagos," p. 318.

33. Robert Plant Armstrong, *The Powers of Presence: Consciousness, Myth and Affecting Presence*, pp. 14–15. I use Armstrong's term, "affecting presence," throughout this book to refer to evocative, emotionally charged, and, hence, powerful symbols.

34. Robert Plant Armstrong, *The Affecting Presence: An Essay in Humanistic Anthropology*, p. 4. My use, both implicit and explicit,

of the concepts "power of evocation" and "power of invocation" is also based on Armstrong. *See especially* Armstrong, *The Powers of Presence*, pp. 3–20.

35. Nancy Munn describes a similar utilization of graphic images for the Walbiri. *See* Nancy Munn, *Walbiri Iconography: Graphic Representation and Cultural Symbolism in a Central Australian Society*, p. 5.

Chapter 5

1. Ruth L. Bunzel, "Introduction to Zuñi Ceremonialism," pp. 489–92.

2. For a further discussion of such iconic power, *see* Kay Turner, "The Cultural Semiotics of Religious Icons: La Virgen de San Juan de los Lagos," pp. 317–61.

3. Ruth L. Bunzel, *The Pueblo Potter: A Study of Creative Imagination in Primitive Art*, pp. 23–24, 69–71. Bunzel points out that the water-related designs are painted not on pottery water jars, but on the bowls that are used to hold sacred cornmeal. This emphasizes the connection between sufficient water and the growth of plants, especially life-giving corn.

4. Frank H. Cushing, "Zuñi Fetiches," pp. 11–12.

5. Bunzel, *The Pueblo Potter*, pp. 94–95.

6. Matilda C. Stevenson, "The Zuñi Indians: Their Mythology, Esoteric Fraternities, and Ceremonies," p. 439.

7. Occupied during the early part of the eleventh century, this area contains the ruins of a large, multiroomed living complex that included two large and several smaller circular kivas. For a discussion of the rock art here, *see* M. Jane Young, "Images of Power, Images of Beauty: Contemporary Zuni Perceptions of Rock Art," p. 66, and the description of site 1 in the Appendix of this book. Frank H. H. Roberts, Jr., "The Village of the Great Kivas on the Zuñi Reservation, New Mexico," describes the archaeological work conducted at this site.

8. Zunis made these and the following identifications as well as those listed in the captions for Figures 69, 70, 74–76.

9. Bunzel, "Introduction to Zuñi Ceremonialism," p. 506; M. Stevenson, "The Zuñi Indians," pp. 97, 141, 146, 564.

10. Barbara Tedlock, "Kachina Dance Songs in Zuni Society: The Role of Esthetics in Social Integration," pp. 90–92.

11. Ibid.

12. Ruth L. Bunzel, "Zuñi Ritual Poetry," pp. 615–20; M. Jane Young, "Translation and Analysis of Zuni Ritual Poetry."

13. Bunzel, "Introduction to Zuñi Ceremonialism," pp. 492, 505–6, 522; Elsie C. Parsons, "Notes on Zuñi," pp. 238–41; M. Stevenson, "The Zuñi Indians," pp. 166, 252.

14. M. Stevenson, "The Zuñi Indians," p. 166.

15. B. Tedlock, "Kachina Dance Songs in Zuni Society," pp. 69–70.

16. Ruth L. Bunzel, "Zuñi Katcinas," pp. 873–74.

17. Bunzel, "Zuñi Ritual Poetry," p. 619; Young, "Translation and Analysis of Zuni Ritual Poetry."

18. *See, for example,* J. Walter Fewkes, "A Few Summer Ceremonials at Zuñi Pueblo," pp. 9–10; M. Stevenson, "The Zuñi Indians," pp. 40, 43, 294.

19. Bunzel, "Zuñi Ritual Poetry," p. 717; Young, "Translation and Analysis of Zuni Ritual Poetry."

20. Frank H. Cushing, "Outlines of Zuñi Creation Myths," p. 381; Frank H. Cushing, *Zuñi Folk Tales,* pp. 378–79; M. Stevenson, "The Zuñi Indians," p. 24.

21. Fewkes, pp. 9–10; Ruth F. Kirk, "Introduction to Zuni Fetishism," p. 237; Matilda C. Stevenson, "The Religious Life of the Zuñi Child," pp. 539–40; M. Stevenson, "The Zuñi Indians," pp. 294–95.

22. Fewkes, pp. 9–10; M. Stevenson, "The Religious Life of the Zuñi Child," pp. 539–40; M. Stevenson, "The Zuñi Indians," pp. 294–95.

23. M. Stevenson, "The Religious Life of the Zuñi Child," p. 540.

24. M. Stevenson, "The Zuñi Indians," Plate XII.

25. The Zunis with whom I worked never called themselves "shepherds," but used the term "sheepherders" instead.

26. Polly Schaafsma, *Indian Rock Art of the Southwest,* p. 119.

27. Florence H. Ellis and Laurens Hammack, "The Inner Sanctum of Feather Cave, A Mogollon Sun and Earth Shrine Linking Mexico and the Southwest," p. 35.

28. For more information on this individual site *see* Young, "Images of Power, Images of Beauty," pp. 68–69, as well as the descriptions of site 5 in the Appendix to this book.

29. M. Stevenson, "The Zuñi Indians," pp. 15–16, 349–50.

30. Both Polly Schaafsma and I have seen small painted footprints in southwestern rock art that look like the imprints of babies' feet.

Schaafsma (personal communication) has suggested that getting a stamped footprint from a baby may have been an easier way of obtaining a "signature" than getting the baby to open its hand, but nevertheless, served the same function.

31. Parsons, "Notes on Zuñi," p. 167.

32. For a discussion of the symbolism of roadrunner tracks in southwestern art in general, see Polly Schaafsma, "Supper or Symbol: The Roadrunner Track in Southwest Art and Ritual."

33. See Edmund J. Ladd, "Zuni Social and Political Organization," p. 487, Table 2, for a list of current Zuni clans.

34. Elsie C. Parsons, Pueblo Indian Religion, p. 359; M. Stevenson, "The Zuñi Indians," pp. 40–42. Frank H. Cushing states explicitly that the Zuni farmer set boundary stones, sometimes "sculptured with his tokens," at the corners of his fields. See "Zuñi Breadstuff," p. 153.

35. For a description of clan symbols painted on the backs of runners in ceremonial foot races, see M. Stevenson, "The Zuñi Indians," p. 322.

36. Helen Michaelis, "Willowsprings: A Hopi Petroglyph Site," p. 9. See also Leo W. Simmons, ed., Sun Chief, p. 234; Mischa Titiev, "A Hopi Salt Expedition," pp. 244–58; Klaus F. Wellman, "Just Like Graffiti?: A Comparative Analysis of North American Indian Rock Drawings and Modern Urban Graffiti," p. 6.

37. Bunzel, "Introduction to Zuñi Ceremonialism," pp. 520n, 538; Parsons, Pueblo Indian Religion, p. 478; M. Stevenson, "The Zuñi Indians," pp. 153–62.

38. Wellmann, "Just Like Graffiti," pp. 9–10; C. Daryll Forde, "Hopi Agriculture and Land Ownership," pp. 367–68; Henry R. Voth, Traditions of the Hopi, p. 23.

39. Forde, pp. 367–68.

40. Polly Schaafsma and M. Jane Young, "Early Masks and Faces in Southwest Rock Art," pp. 23–26.

41. See Bunzel, "Zuñi Katcinas," pp. 941–46, 969–75; M. Stevenson, "The Zuñi Indians," pp. 33, 227–41; and Barton Wright, Kachinas of the Zuni, pp. 30–46, for a description of this group of kachinas and their role in Zuni ritual life.

42. There are six pairs of Salimobia, one pair for each of the six directions. Their masks are painted in the particular colors that symbolize the respective directions with which they are associated.

43. Members of the Hunters' Society are involved in ceremonial

hunts and are called upon to dance in the mixed kachina dance in which animals are impersonated. Kirk, pp. 195–98, suggests that the deer and mountain sheep impersonators who participate in this dance are particularly important because they represent the other wild animals this dance will bring to the Zuni hunters. Similarly, Bunzel states that the mixed dance, *wotemlha,* is performed to draw game animals to the hunters of the pueblo. *See* Bunzel, "Zuñi Katcinas," pp. 906–7, 1025–26, 1030–31, and Wright, *Kachinas of the Zuni,* pp. 93–103, for a description of this dance, including a list of animals that are impersonated. M. Stevenson, "The Zuñi Indians," pp. 438–41, notes that the Zuni Hunters' Fraternity is made up of huntsmen who, on special occasions, imitate the game they wish to kill.

44. Matilda C. Stevenson, "Zuñi Ancestral Gods and Masks," p. 36.

45. Bunzel, "Zuñi Katcinas," pp. 844, 862, 902; M. Stevenson, "The Zuñi Indians," pp. 88, 252.

46. Bunzel, "Zuñi Katcinas," p. 845.

47. Dennis Tedlock, "An American Indian View of Death," pp. 253–60.

48. Bunzel, "Introduction to Zuñi Ceremonialism," pp. 519, 862.

Chapter 6

1. I am grateful to Margaret Hardin for suggesting that I entertain the children by giving them paper and crayons. When she stayed at Zuni she did this herself and also found that a number of the children drew either kachinas or scenes from the landscape around the pueblo.

2. Florence H. Ellis and Laurens Hammack, "The Inner Sanctum of Feather Cave, A Mogollon Sun and Earth Shrine Linking Mexico and the Southwest," p. 35; Florence H. Ellis, "A Thousand Years of the Pueblo Sun-Moon-Star Calendar," pp. 74–75.

3. Because of this dynamic style and also because it depicts a specific Zuni kachina, I date this image as post-A.D. 1325 despite the fact that the technique of execution is pecking.

4. For more information about the initiation of Zuni boys into the Kachina Society *see* Ruth L. Bunzel, "Zuñi Katcinas: An Analytical Study," pp. 975–1002, and Barton Wright, *Kachinas of the Zuni,* pp. 50–66.

5. David Ley and Roman Cybriwsky, "Urban Graffiti as Territorial Markers," pp. 491–505.

6. Chalking on top of or creating rubbings of images on soft sandstone wears away the stone and thus distorts the figure. For an overview of rock art recording techniques, see David R. Stuart, "Recording Southwestern Rock Art Sites," pp. 183–99.

7. Ruth L. Bunzel, *The Pueblo Potter: A Study of Creative Imagination in Primitive Art*; H. P. Mera, *Pueblo Designs: 176 Illustrations of the "Rain Bird."*

8. Frank H. H. Roberts, Jr., "The Village of the Great Kivas on the Zuñi Reservation," pp. 149–52. The following quotes in this paragraph are from Roberts, but the contemporary interpretations made by this Zuni man were almost exactly the same.

9. Roberts, ibid, p. 151; M. Jane Young, fieldnotes, 1979–1981. This quote is from my Zuni colleague. Roberts's version is much longer and more elaborate.

10. John C. Brandt and Ray A. Williamson, "The 1054 Supernova and Native American Rock Art," p. 33.

11. This site has generated a great deal of interest in the past five years. *See especially* Kendrick Frazier, "The Anasazi Sun Dagger," pp. 56–67, and Anna Sofaer, Volker Zinser, and Rolf Sinclair, "A Unique Solar Marking Construct," pp. 283–91. Both articles point out that the "dagger" of light falling on the spiral petroglyphs is produced by the rays of sunlight falling on a special configuration of boulders. This "dagger" changes appearance throughout the year as a consequence of the apparent motion of the sun.

12. I am grateful to Dell H. Hymes for his suggestion that I make this point.

13. *See* M. Jane Young, "We Were Going to Have a Barbeque, But the Cow Ran Away: Production, Form, and Function of the Zuni Tribal Fair," pp. 42–48.

14. Matilda C. Stevenson, "The Zuñi Indians: Their Mythology, Esoteric Fraternities, and Ceremonies," pp. 34–35, 40.

Appendix

1. Graffiti are not necessarily regarded as cases of vandalism. Tribal members were most disturbed when names, dates, initials, and other graffiti were executed on top of other, older elements. This constituted a kind of vandalism—the defacement of older images. In Chapters 5 and 6, I discuss the various attitudes of the Zunis toward vandalism.

2. *See* M. Jane Young, "Images of Power, Images of Beauty: Contemporary Zuni Perceptions of Rock Art," pp. 257–61, for sample maps, contact sheet overlays, and report forms for individual rock art panels and entire sites.

3. For suggestions concerning the technical aspects of rock art recording, *see* Colonel James G. Bain, "Techniques and Procedures for Rock Art Recording"; David Stuart, "Recording Southwestern Rock Art Sites," pp. 183–99; Solveig A. Turpin, Richard P. Watson, Sarah Dennett, and Hans Muessig, "Stereophotogrammetric Documentation of Exposed Archaeological Features," pp. 329–37.

4. Linda Robertson, personal communication, 1981. Both Robertson's archaeological records and my own rock art records for this site are on file at the Zuni Archaeology Program and the Laboratory of Anthropology of the Museum of New Mexico.

Bibliography

Adair, John J. *The Navajo and Pueblo Silversmiths*. Norman: University of Oklahoma Press, 1944.

Adair, John J., and Evon Z. Vogt. "Navaho and Zuni Veterans: A Study of Contrasting Modes of Culture Change." *American Anthropologist* 51 (1949): 547–61.

Anderson, Frank G. "The Pueblo Kachina Cult: A Historical Reconstruction." *Southwestern Journal of Anthropology* 11 (1955): 404–19.

Anderson, Keith M. "Ethnographic Analogy and Archeological Interpretation." *Science* 163 (1969): 133–38.

Armstrong, Robert Plant. *The Affecting Presence: An Essay in Humanistic Anthropology*. Urbana: University of Illinois Press, 1971.

———. *Wellspring: On the Myth and Source of Culture*. Berkeley: University of California Press, 1975.

———. *The Powers of Presence: Consciousness, Myth and Affecting Presence*. Philadelphia: University of Pennsylvania Press, 1981.

Ascher, Robert. "Analogy in Archaeological Interpretation." *Southwestern Journal of Anthropology* 17 (1961): 317–25.

Babcock, Barbara, ed. *The Reversible World: Symbolic Inversion in Art and Society*. Ithaca and London: Cornell University Press, 1978.

———. "Arrange Me into Disorder: Fragments and Reflections on Ritual Clowning." In *Rite, Drama, Festival, Spectacle*. Edited by John J. MacAloon. Pp. 102–28. Philadelphia: ISHI, 1984.

Bahr, Donald. "On the Complexity of Southwest Indian Emergence Myths." *Journal of Anthropological Research* 33 (1977): 317–49.

Bain, Colonel James G. "Techniques and Procedures for Rock Art Recording." *Center of Anthropological Study Monograph* 3, 1975.

Bandelier, Adolph F. A. "An Outline of the Documentary History of the Zuñi Tribe." *Journal of American Ethnology and Archaeology* 3 (1892): 1–115.

Basso, Keith H. *Portraits of "The Whiteman": Linguistic Play and Cultural Symbols Among the Western Apache.* Cambridge: Cambridge University Press, 1979.

———. "'Stalking with Stories': Names, Places, and Moral Narratives among the Western Apache." In *Text, Play, and Story: The Construction and Reconstruction of Self and Society.* Edited by Edward M. Bruner. Pp. 19–55. Washington, D.C.: The American Ethnological Society, 1984.

Bateson, Gregory. "Style, Grace and Information in Primitive Art." In *Steps to an Ecology of Mind*, pp. 128–52. New York: Ballantine Books, 1972.

Beeson, William H. "Archaeological Survey Near St. John's, Arizona: A Methodological Study." Ph.D. diss., University of Arizona, 1966.

Benedict, Ruth. *Zuni Mythology.* 2 vols. Columbia University Contributions to Anthropology, no. 21. New York: Columbia University Press, 1935.

Brandt, John C., and Ray A. Williamson. "The 1054 Supernova and Native American Rock Art." *Archaeoastronomy*, Supplement to *Journal for the History of Astronomy* 1 (1979): 1–38.

Breuil, Abbé Henri. *Four Hundred Centuries of Cave Art.* Translated by Mary E. Boyle. Paris: Centre d'Etudes et de Documentation Préhistoriques, 1952.

Bunzel, Ruth L. *The Pueblo Potter: A Study of Creative Imagination in Primitive Art.* 1929. Reprint. New York: Dover Publications, 1972.

———. "Introduction to Zuñi Ceremonialism," "Zuñi Origin Myths," "Zuñi Ritual Poetry," "Zuñi Katcinas: An Analytical Study." In *Forty-Seventh Annual Report of the Bureau of American Ethnology for the Years 1929–1930.* Pp. 467–1086. Washington, D.C. Government Printing Office, 1932.

———. *Zuni Texts.* Publications of the American Ethnological Society, 15. New York: G.E. Stechert & Co., 1933.

Chamberlain, Von Del. Field tape. Pueblo of Zuni. August, 1978.

————. *When Stars Came Down to Earth: Cosmology of the Skidi Pawnee Indians of North America.* Los Altos, Calif., and College Park, Md.: Ballena Press and Center for Archaeoastronomy, 1982.

Clark, E. Culpepper, Michael J. Hyde, and Eva M. McMahan. "Communication in the Oral History Interview: Investigating Problems of Interpreting Oral Data." *International Journal of Oral History* 1 (1980): 28–40.

Cole, Sally. "Analysis of a San Juan (Basketmaker) Style Painted Mask in Grand Gulch, Utah." *Southwestern Lore* 50 (1984): 1–6.

Crampton, C. Gregory. *The Zunis of Cibola.* Salt Lake City: University of Utah Press, 1977.

Culin, Stewart. "The Road to Beauty." *Brooklyn Museum Quarterly* 14 (1927): 41–50.

Cushing, Frank H. "The Zuñi Social, Mythic and Religious Systems." *Popular Science Monthly* 21 (1882): 186–92.

————. "Zuñi Fetiches." In *Second Annual Report of the Bureau of American Ethnology for the Years 1880–1881.* Pp. 3–45. Washington, D.C.: Government Printing Office, 1883.

————. "A Study of Pueblo Pottery as Illustrative of Zuñi Culture Growth." In *Fourth Annual Report of the Bureau of American Ethnology for the Years 1882–1883.* Pp. 467–521. Washington, D.C.: Government Printing Office, 1886.

————. "Outlines of Zuñi Creation Myths." In *Thirteenth Annual Report of the Bureau of American Ethnology for the Years 1891–1892.* Pp. 321–447. Washington, D.C.: Government Printing Office, 1896.

————. "Discussion and Remarks on Shamanism." *Proceedings of the American Philosophical Society* 36 (1897): 1–14.

————. *Zuñi Folk Tales.* New York: G.P. Putnam's Sons, 1901.

————. *My Adventures in Zuñi.* 1882. Reprint. Palmer Lake, Colo.: Filter Press, 1967.

————. "Zuñi Breadstuff." *Indian Notes and Monographs* 8. 1920. Reprint. New York: Museum of the American Indian, 1974.

Danto, Arthur. *The Transfiguration of the Commonplace.* Cambridge: Harvard University Press, 1981.

Davenhauer, B. P. "Some Aspects of Language and Time in Ritual Worship." *International Journal for Philosophy of Religion* 6 (1975): 54–62.

Dutton, Bertha P. *Sun Father's Way: The Kiva Murals of Kuaua.*

Albuquerque: University of New Mexico Press, 1963.

Edelman, Prewitt. "Working Back: The New Physics and Pueblo Mythology." *Southwest Review* 58 (1973): 302–6.

Eggan, Fred. *Social Organization of the Western Pueblos.* Chicago and London: The University of Chicago Press, 1950.

Eggan, Fred, and Triloki N. Pandey. "Zuni History, 1850–1970." In *Handbook of North American Indians, Southwest,* Vol. 9. Edited by Alfonso Ortiz. Pp. 474–81. Washington, D.C.: Government Printing Office, 1979.

Ellis, Florence Hawley. "A Thousand Years of the Pueblo Sun-Moon-Star Calendar." In *Archaeoastronomy in Pre-Columbian America.* Edited by Anthony F. Aveni. Pp. 59–87. Austin and London: University of Texas Press, 1975.

Ellis, Florence Hawley, and Laurens Hammack. "The Inner Sanctum of Feather Cave, A Mogollon Sun and Earth Shrine Linking Mexico and the Southwest." *American Antiquity* 33 (1968): 25–44.

Espinosa, J. Manuel, ed. and trans. *First Expedition of Vargas into New Mexico, 1692.* Albuquerque: University of New Mexico Press, 1940.

Farrer, Claire. "Play and Inter-Ethnic Communication: A Practical Ethnography of the Mescalero Apache." Ph.D. diss., University of Texas at Austin, 1977.

———. "'Singing for Life': The Mescalero Apache Girls' Puberty Ceremony." In *Southwestern Indian Ritual Drama.* Edited by Charlotte J. Frisbie. Pp. 125–59. Albuquerque: University of New Mexico Press, 1980.

Farrer, Claire, and Bernard Second. "Living the Sky: Aspects of Mescalero Apache Ethnoastronomy." In *Archaeoastronomy in the Americas.* Edited by Ray A. Williamson. Pp. 137–50. Los Altos, Calif., and College Park, Md.: Ballena Press and Center for Archaeoastronomy, 1981.

Ferg, Alan. "Petroglyphs of the Silver Creek/Five Mile Draw Confluence, Snowflake, Arizona." Unpublished manuscript, University of Arizona, Tucson, 1974.

Ferguson, T. J., William A. Dodge, and Barbara J. Mills. "Archaeological Investigations at Kyaki:ma." Zuni Indian Reservation, McKinley County, New Mexico. Unpublished manuscript, Pueblo of Zuni, 1977.

Ferguson, T. J., and E. Richard Hart. *A Zuni Atlas.* Norman and London: University of Oklahoma Press, 1985.

Fewkes, J. Walter. "A Few Summer Ceremonials at Zuñi Pueblo." *Journal of American Ethnology and Archaeology* 1 (1891): 1–62.

———. "Reconnaissance of Ruins in or near the Zuñi Reservation." *Journal of American Ethnology and Archaeology* 1 (1891): 95–133.

———. "A Few Tusayan Pictographs." *American Anthropologist*, old ser., 5 (1892): 9–26.

———. "Ancient Pueblo and Mexican Water Symbol." *American Anthropologist*, new ser., 6 (1904): 535–38.

Firth, Raymond. *Symbols: Public and Private.* Ithaca: Cornell University Press, 1973.

Ford, Richard I. "Gardening and Farming before A.D. 1000: Patterns of Prehistoric Cultivation North of Mexico." *Journal of Ethnobiology* 1 (1981): 6–27.

Forde, C. Daryll. "Hopi Agriculture and Land Ownership." *Journal of the Royal Anthropological Institute* 61 (1931): 357–405.

Frazier, Kendrick. "The Anasazi Sun Dagger." *Science 80* 1:1 (1979): 57–67.

Glassie, Henry. "Structure and Function, Folklore and the Artifact." *Semiotica* 7 (1973): 313–51.

———. "Archaeology and Folklore: Common Anxieties, Common Hopes." In *Historical Archaeology and the Importance of Material Things.* Edited by Leland Ferguson. Pp. 13–35. Special Publication 2. Columbia: Society for Historical Archaeology, 1977.

———. "Meaningful Things and Appropriate Myths: The Artifact's Place in American Studies." *Prospects* 3 (1977): 1–49.

Grant, Campbell. *Rock Art of the American Indian.* New York: Thomas Y. Crowell, 1967.

———. *Canyon de Chelly: Its People and Rock Art.* Tucson: The University of Arizona Press, 1978.

Green, Jesse, ed. *Zuñi: Selected Writings of Frank Hamilton Cushing.* Lincoln and London: University of Nebraska Press, 1979.

Hallowell, Irving A. *Culture and Experience.* Philadelphia: University of Pennsylvania Press, 1955.

Handy, E. L. "Zuñi Tales." *Journal of American Folk-Lore* 31 (1918): 451–71.

Hardin, Margaret Ann. *Gifts of Mother Earth: Ceramics in the Zuni Tradition.* Phoenix: The Heard Museum, 1983.

Harlow, Francis H. *Modern Pueblo Pottery, 1880–1960.* Flagstaff: Northland Press, 1977.

Harrington, John P. Unpublished manuscripts and papers pertaining to fieldwork at Zuni. National Anthropological Archives, Smithsonian Institution, n.d.

Hawley, Florence. "Kokopelli, of the Prehistoric Southwestern Pueblo Pantheon." *American Anthropologist* 39 (1937): 644–46.

Heizer, Robert F., and Martin A. Baumhoff. "Great Basin Petroglyphs and Prehistoric Game Trails." *Science* 129 (1959): 904–5.

———. *Prehistoric Rock Art of Nevada and Eastern California.* Berkeley: University of California Press, 1962.

Heizer, Robert F., and C. W. Clewlow, Jr. *Prehistoric Rock Art of California.* 2 vols. Ramona, Calif.: Ballena Press, 1973.

Hibben, Frank C. *Kiva Art of the Anasazi at Pottery Mound.* Las Vegas, Nev.: KC Publications, 1975.

Hodge, Frederick W. "Hawikuh Bonework." *Indian Notes and Monographs* 3 (1920): 63–151.

———. "Circular Kivas Near Hawikuh." *Contributions from the Museum of the American Indian, Heye Foundation* 7 (1923): 1–37.

Hodge, Frederick W., and Frank H. Cushing. Unpublished manuscripts and papers pertaining to fieldwork at Zuni. Southwest Museum, Los Angeles, n.d.

Hudson, Travis, and Georgia Lee. "Function and Symbolism in Chumash Rock Art." Paper presented at the Annual Meetings of the Southwestern Anthropological Association, Santa Barbara, March, 1981, and the Society for American Archaeology, San Diego, April, 1981.

Hudson, Travis, and Ernest Underhay. *Crystals in the Sky: An Intellectual Odyssey Involving Chumash Astronomy, Cosmology and Rock Art.* Socorro, N.M.: Ballena Press, 1978.

Hymes, Dell. "Breakthrough into Performance." In *Folklore: Performance and Communication.* Edited by Dan Ben-Amos and Kenneth S. Goldstein. Pp. 11–74. The Hague: Mouton, 1975.

———. "Discovering Oral Performance and Measured Verse in American Indian Narrative." *New Literary History* 8 (1977): 431–58.

———. "Particle, Pause and Pattern in American Indian Verse." *American Indian Culture and Research Journal* 4:4 (1980): 7–51.

———. *"In Vain I Tried to Tell You": Essays in Native American Ethnopoetics.* Studies in Native American Literature, 1. Philadelphia: University of Pennsylvania Press, 1981.

Jernigan, E. Wesley. *Jewelry of the Prehistoric Southwest.* School of American Research Southwest Indian Art Series. Albuquerque: University of New Mexico Press, 1978.

Jones, Michael Owen. "The Concept of 'Aesthetics' in the Traditional Arts." *Western Folklore* 30 (1971): 77–104.

Jopling, Carol F., ed. *Art and Aesthetics in Primitive Societies.* New York: E. P. Dutton, 1971.

Kintigh, Keith. *Settlement, Subsistence, and Society in Late Zuni Prehistory.* Anthropological Papers of the University of Arizona, Number 44. Tucson, Arizona: The University of Arizona Press, 1985.

Kirk, Ruth F. "Introduction to Zuni Fetishism." *El Palacio* 50:6–10 (1943): 117–29, 146–59, 183–98, 206–19, 235–45.

Kroeber, Alfred L. "Thoughts on Zuñi Religion." In *Holmes Anniversary Volume: Anthropological Essays Presented to William Henry Holmes in Honor of His Seventieth Birthday, December 1916.* Pp. 269–77. Washington, D.C.: James William Bryan Press, 1916.

————. "Zuñi Kin and Clan." *Anthropological Papers of the American Museum of Natural History* 18 (1919): 39–204.

Kroeber, Karl, ed. *Traditional American Indian Literatures: Texts and Interpretations.* Lincoln: University of Nebraska Press, 1981.

Ladd, Edmund J. "Zuni Social and Political Organization." In *Handbook of North American Indians, Southwest,* Vol. 9. Edited by Alfonso Ortiz. Pp. 482–91. Washington, D.C.: Government Printing Office, 1979.

————. "Zuni Economy." In *Handbook of North American Indians, Southwest,* Vol. 9. Edited by Alfonso Ortiz. Pp. 492–98. Washington, D.C.: Government Printing Office, 1979.

Layton, Robert. *The Anthropology of Art.* New York: Columbia University Press, 1981.

————. "The Cultural Context of Hunter-Gatherer Rock Art." *Man* 20 (1985): 434–53.

Leach, Edmund. *Culture and Communication: The Logic by Which Symbols are Connected.* Cambridge: Cambridge University Press, 1976.

Lee, Georgia. *The Portable Cosmos: Effigies, Ornaments, and Incised Stone from the Chumash Area.* Socorro, N.M.: Ballena Press, 1981.

Leighton, Dorothea C., and John Adair. *People of the Middle Place:*

A Study of the Zuni Indians. Behavior Science Monographs. New Haven, Conn.: Human Relations Area Files Press, 1966.

Levine, Morton H. "Prehistoric Art and Ideology." *American Anthropologist* 59 (1957): 949–64.

Lévi-Strauss, Claude. *The Raw and the Cooked: Introduction to the Science of Mythology: 1.* Translated by John and Doreen Weightman. New York: Harper and Row, 1969.

———. "The Structural Study of Myth." In *Myth: A Symposium.* Edited by Thomas A. Sebeok. Pp. 81–106. 1955. Reprint. Bloomington: Indiana University Press, 1972.

———. *From Honey to Ashes: Introduction to the Science of Mythology: 2.* Translated by John and Doreen Weightman. New York: Harper & Row, 1973.

Lewis-Williams, J. David. *Believing and Seeing: Symbolic Meanings in Southern San Rock Paintings.* New York: Academic Press, 1981.

Ley, David, and Roman Cybriwsky. "Urban Graffiti as Territorial Markers." *Annals of the Association of American Geographers* 64 (1974): 491–505.

Lipe, William D. "The Southwest." In *Ancient Native Americans.* Edited by J. D. Jennings. Pp. 327–401. San Francisco: W. H. Freeman and Company, 1978.

Longacre, William A., ed. *Reconstructing Prehistoric Pueblo Societies.* School of American Research Advanced Seminar Series. Albuquerque: University of New Mexico Press, 1970.

Lummis, Trevor. "Structure and Validity in Oral Evidence." *International Journal of Oral History* 2 (1981): 109–20.

Martineau, La Van. *The Rocks Begin to Speak.* Las Vegas, Nev.: KC Publications, 1973.

Matejka, Ladislav, and Irwin R. Titunik, eds. *Semiotics of Art.* Cambridge and London: The MIT Press, 1976.

McLendon, Sally. "Cultural Presuppositions and Discourse Analysis: Patterns of Presupposition and Assertion of Information in Eastern Pomo and Russian Narrative." In *Linguistics and Anthropology.* Edited by Muriel Saville-Troike. Pp. 153–89. Washington, D.C.: Georgetown University Press, 1977.

McNitt, Frank, ed. *Navaho Expedition: Journal of a Military Reconnaissance from Santa Fe, New Mexico, to the Navaho Country Made in 1849 by Lieutenant James H. Simpson.* Norman: University of Oklahoma Press, 1964.

Mead, George R. *Rock Art North of the Mexican-American Border:*

An Annotated Bibliography. Colorado State College Museum Occasional Publications in Anthropology, Archaeology Series, No. 5. Greely, Colorado, 1968.

Mera, H. P. *Pueblo Designs: 176 Illustrations of the "Rain Bird."* 1938. Reprint. New York: Dover Publications, 1970.

Michaelis, Helen. "Willowsprings: A Hopi Petroglyph Site. *Journal of New World Archaeology* 4:2 (1981): 2–23.

Mills, Barbara J. "Zuni Rock Art Survey: A Review of Archaeological Site Records, Dating, and Bibliographic References." Zuni Indian Reservation, McKinley County, New Mexico. Unpublished manuscript, Pueblo of Zuni, 1980.

Moore, David R. "Australian Aboriginal Rock Art: Its Relevance to the European Palaeolithic." *Bolletino del Centro Camuno di Studi Preistorici* 7 (1971).

Munn, Nancy. *Walbiri Iconography: Graphic Representation and Cultural Symbolism in a Central Australian Society.* Ithaca and London: Cornell University Press, 1973.

Newcomb, W. W., Jr., and Forrest Kirkland. *The Rock Art of Texas Indians.* Austin: University of Texas Press, 1967.

Newman, Stanley. "Vocabulary Levels: Zuñi Sacred and Slang Usage." *Southwestern Journal of Anthropology* 11 (1955): 345–54.

———. *Zuni Dictionary.* Indiana University Research Center in Anthropology, Folklore and Linguistics, Publication 6. Bloomington, 1958.

———. *Zuni Grammar.* University of New Mexico Publications in Anthropology 14. Albuquerque, 1965.

Ortiz, Alfonso. *The Tewa World: Space, Time, Being, and Becoming in a Pueblo Society.* Chicago and London: University of Chicago Press, 1969.

———. "Ritual Drama and the Pueblo World View." In *New Perspectives on the Pueblos.* Edited by Alfonso Ortiz. Pp. 135–61. Albuquerque: University of New Mexico Press, 1972.

Parsons, Elsie C. "The Zuñi A'doshlě and Suukě." *American Anthropologist* 18 (1916): 338–47.

———. "The Zuñi Mo'lawia." *Journal of American Folk-Lore* 29 (1916): 392–99.

———. "Notes on Zuñi." *Memoirs of the American Anthropological Association* 4:3–4 (1917): 151–327.

———. "Increase by Magic: A Zuñi Pattern." *American Anthropologist* 21 (1919): 279–86.

———. "Winter and Summer Dance Series in Zuñi in 1918." *Uni-*

versity of California Publications in American Archaeology and Ethnology 17 (1922): 171–216.

———. "The Origin Myth of Zuñi." Journal of American Folk-Lore 36 (1923): 135–62.

———. "Zuñi Tales." Journal of American Folk-Lore 43 (1930): 1–58.

———. "The Humpbacked Flute Player of the Southwest." American Anthropologist 40 (1938): 337–38.

———. Pueblo Indian Religion. 2 vols. Chicago: University of Chicago Press, 1939.

Parsons, Elsie C., and Ralph L. Beals. "The Sacred Clowns of the Pueblo and Mayo-Yaqui Indians." American Anthropologist 39:4 (1934): 491–514.

Pilles, Peter J., Jr. "Petroglyphs of the Little Colorado River Valley, Arizona." In American Indian Rock Art, Vol. 1. Edited by Shari T. Grove. Pp. 1–26. Farmington, N.M.: San Juan County Museum Association, 1975.

Pueblo of Zuni. The Zunis: Experiences and Descriptions. Salt Lake City: [The Pueblo of Zuni], 1973.

Quam, Alvina, trans. The Zunis: Self-Portrayals by the Zuni People. Albuquerque: University of New Mexico Press, 1971.

Reed, Erik K. "Eastern-Central Arizona Archaeology in Relation to the Western Pueblos." Southwestern Journal of Anthropology 6 (1950): 120–38.

———. "Painted Pottery and Zuñi History." Southwestern Journal of Anthropology 11 (1955): 178–93.

Renaud, Etienne B. Petroglyphs of North Central New Mexico. University of Denver Archaeological Survey, 11th report. Denver, 1938.

———. "Kokopelli: A Study in Pueblo Mythology." Southwestern Lore 14 (1948): 25–40.

Rinaldo, John B. "Notes on the Origins of Historic Zuni Culture." The Kiva 29 (1964): 86–98.

Roberts, Frank H. H., Jr. "Shabik'eshchee Village, A Late Basket Maker Site in the Chaco Canyon, New Mexico." Bureau of American Ethnology Bulletin 92. Washington, D.C.: Government Printing Office, 1929.

———. "The Village of the Great Kivas on the Zuñi Reservation, New Mexico," Bureau of American Ethnology Bulletin 111. Washington, D.C.: Government Printing Office, 1932.

Roberts, John M. *Zuni Daily Life*. 1956. Reprint. New Haven, Conn.: Human Relations Area Files Press, 1965.

———. "The Zuni." In *Variations in Value Orientations*. Edited by F. R. Kluckhohn and F. L. Strodtbeck. Pp. 285–316. Evanston, Ill., and Elmsford, N.Y.: Row, Peterson, 1961.

Roberts, John M., and Chong Pil Choe. "Korean Animal Entities with Supernatural Attributes: A Study in Expressive Belief." *Arctic Anthropology* 21 (1984): 109–21.

Rohn, Arthur H. "American Southwest." In *Chronologies in New World Archaeology*. Edited by R. E. Taylor and Clement W. Meighan. Pp. 201–22. New York: Academic Press, 1978.

Schaafsma, Polly. *Rock Art in the Navajo Reservoir District*. Papers in Anthropology, No. 7. Santa Fe: Museum of New Mexico, 1963.

———. *Early Navaho Rock Paintings and Carvings*. Santa Fe: Museum of Navaho Ceremonial Art, 1966.

———. "The Los Lunas Petroglyphs." *El Palacio* 75 (1968): 13–24.

———. *The Rock Art of Utah*. Papers of the Peabody Museum of Archaeology and Ethnology, Vol. 65. Cambridge: Peabody Museum, 1971.

———. *Rock Art in New Mexico*. Santa Fe: State Planning Office, 1972.

———. *Rock Art in the Cochiti Reservoir District*. Papers in Anthropology, No. 16. Santa Fe: Museum of New Mexico, 1975.

———. "Rock Art and Ideology of the Mimbres and Jornada Mogollon." *The Artifact* 13 (1975): 2–14.

———. *Indian Rock Art of the Southwest*. School of American Research Southwest Indian Arts Series. Albuquerque: University of New Mexico Press, 1980.

———. "Supper or Symbol: The Roadrunner Track in Southwest Art and Ritual." In *Animals in Art*. Edited by Howard Morphy. London: Allen and Unwin, forthcoming.

———. "Form, Content, and Function: Theory and Method in North American Rock Art Studies." In *Advances in Archaeological Method and Theory*, Vol. 8. Edited by Michael Schiffer. Pp. 237–77. New York: Academic Press, 1985.

Schaafsma, Polly, and Curtis F. Schaafsma. "Evidence for the Origins of the Pueblo Katchina Cult as Suggested by Southwestern Rock Art." *American Antiquity* 39 (1974): 535–45.

Schaafsma, Polly, and M. Jane Young. "Early Masks and Faces in Southwestern Rock Art." In *Papers in Honor of Charlie Steen*.

Edited by Nancy Fox. Pp. 11–33. Santa Fe: Archaeological Society of New Mexico, 1983.

Schapiro, Meyer. "Style." In *Anthropology Today.* Edited by A. L. Kroeber. Pp. 287–312. Chicago: University of Chicago Press, 1953.

Simmons, Leo W., ed. *Sun Chief.* New Haven: Yale University Press, 1942.

Sims, Agnes C. "Migration Story in Stone." *El Palacio* 56 (1949): 67–76.

———. *San Cristobal Petroglyphs.* Santa Fe: Southwestern Editions, 1950.

———. "Rock Carvings, A Record of Folk History." In *Sun Father's Way.* By Bertha P. Dutton. Pp. 214–20. Albuquerque: University of New Mexico Press, 1963.

Smith, Robert J. *The Art of the Festival.* University of Kansas Publications in Anthropology Number 6. Lawrence: University of Kansas Libraries, 1975.

Smith, Watson. *Kiva Mural Decorations at Awatovi and Kawaika-a, with a Survey of other Wall Paintings in the Pueblo Southwest.* Papers of the Peabody Museum of American Archaeology and Ethnology, Vol. 37. Cambridge, Mass.: Peabody Museum, 1952.

Smith, Watson, and John M. Roberts. *Zuni Law: A Field of Values.* Papers of the Peabody Museum of American Archaeology and Ethnology, Vol. 43. Cambridge, Mass.: Peabody Museum, 1954.

Smith, Watson, Richard B. Woodbury, and Natalie F. S. Woodbury, eds. *The Excavation of Hawikuh by Frederick Webb Hodge.* Contributions from the Museum of the American Indian, Vol. 20. New York: Museum of the American Indian, 1966.

Sofaer, Anna, Volker Zinser, and Rolf Sinclair. "A Unique Solar Marking Construct." *Science* 206 (1979): 283–91.

Speck, Frank G., and Leonard Broom. *Cherokee Dance and Drama.* 1951. Reprint. Norman: University of Oklahoma Press, 1983.

Spicer, Edward H. *Cycles of Conquest: The Impact of Spain, Mexico, and the United States on the Indians of the Southwest, 1533–1960.* Tucson: University of Arizona Press, 1962.

Spier, Leslie. "An Outline for a Chronology of Zuñi Ruins." *Anthropological Papers of the American Museum of Natural History* 18 (1917): 207–331.

————. "Zuñi Chronology." *Proceedings of the National Academy of Sciences* 3 (1917): 280–83.

Stevenson, James. "Illustrated Catalogue of the Collections Obtained from the Indians of New Mexico and Arizona in 1879." In *Second Annual Report of the Bureau of American Ethnology for the Years 1880–1881.* Pp. 307–465. Washington, D.C.: Government Printing Office, 1883.

————. "Illustrated Catalogue of the Collections Obtained from the Pueblos of Zuñi, New Mexico, and Walpi, Arizona, in 1881." In *Third Annual Report of the Bureau of American Ethnology for the Years 1881–1882.* Pp. 511–94. Washington, D.C.: Government Printing Office, 1884.

Stevenson, Matilda C. "The Religious Life of the Zuñi Child." In *Fifth Annual Report of the Bureau of American Ethnology for the Years 1883–1884.* Pp. 533–55. Washington, D.C.: Government Printing Office, 1887.

————. "Zuñi Ancestral Gods and Masks." *American Anthropologist* 11:2 (1898): 33–40.

————. "The Zuñi Indians: Their Mythology, Esoteric Fraternities, and Ceremonies." In *Twenty-Third Annual Report of the Bureau of American Ethnology for the Years 1901–1902.* Pp. 3–634. Washington, D.C.: Government Printing Office, 1904.

————. "Ethnobotany of the Zuñi Indians." In *Thirtieth Annual Report of the Bureau of American Ethnology for the Years 1908–1909.* Pp. 31–102. Washington, D.C.: Government Printing Office, 1915.

Stuart, David R. "Recording Southwestern Rock Art Sites." *The Kiva* 43 (1978): 183–99.

Tanner, Clara Lee. *Southwest Indian Craft Arts.* Tucson: University of Arizona Press, 1968.

————. *Southwest Indian Painting: A Changing Art.* 2nd edition. Tucson: University of Arizona Press, 1973.

————. *Prehistoric Southwestern Craft Arts.* Tucson: University of Arizona Press, 1976.

Tanner, Clara Lee, and Florence Connolly. "Petroglyphs in the Southwest." *The Kiva* 3 (1938): 13–16.

Tedlock, Barbara. "Kachina Dance Songs in Zuni Society: The Role of Esthetics in Social Integration." Master's thesis, Wesleyan University, 1973.

——. "Boundaries of Belief." *Parabola* 4 (1979): 70–77.

——. "Songs of the Zuni Kachina Society: Composition, Rehearsal, and Performance." In *Southwestern Indian Ritual Drama*. Edited by Charlotte J. Frisbie. Pp. 7–35. Albuquerque: University of New Mexico Press, 1980.

——. "Zuni Sacred Theater." *American Indian Quarterly* 7 (1983): 93–110.

——. "The Beautiful and the Dangerous: Zuni Ritual and Cosmology as an Aesthetic System." *Conjunctions: Bi-annual Volumes of New Writing* 6 (1984): 246–65.

Tedlock, Dennis. "The Ethnography of Tale-Telling at Zuni." Ph.D. diss., Tulane University, 1968.

——. trans. *Finding the Center: Narrative Poetry of the Zuni Indians*, by Andrew Peynetsa and Walter Sanchez. New York: Dial Press, 1972.

——. "An American Indian View of Death." In *Teachings from the American Earth*. Edited by Dennis Tedlock and Barbara Tedlock. Pp. 248–71. New York: Liveright, 1975.

——. "From Prayer to Reprimand." In *Language in Religious Practice*. Edited by William J. Samarin. Pp. 72–83. Rowley, Mass.: Newbury House Publishers, 1976.

——. "The Analogical Tradition and the Emergence of a Dialogical Anthropology." *Journal of Anthropological Research* 35 (1979): 387–400.

——. "Zuni Religion and World View." In *Handbook of North American Indians, Southwest*, Vol. 9. Edited by Alfonso Ortiz. Pp. 499–508. Washington, D.C.: Government Printing Office, 1979.

——. *The Spoken Word and the Work of Interpretation*. Philadelphia: University of Pennsylvania Press, 1983.

Titiev, Mischa. "A Hopi Salt Expedition." *American Anthropologist* 39 (1937): 244–58.

Toelken, Barre, and Tacheeni Scott. "Poetic Retranslation and the 'Pretty Languages' of Yellowman." In *Traditional American Indian Literatures: Texts and Interpretations*. Edited by Karl Kroeber. Pp. 65–116. Lincoln and London: University of Nebraska Press, 1981.

Turner, Christy G., II. *Petroglyphs of the Glen Canyon Region*. Bulletin no. 38, Glen Canyon Series, No. 4. Flagstaff: Museum of Northern Arizona, 1963.

Turner, Kay. "Mexican American Home Altars: Towards Their Interpretation." *Aztlán—International Journal of Chicano Studies Research* 13 (1982): 309–26.

———. "The Cultural Semiotics of Religious Icons: La Virgen de San Juan de los Lagos." *Semiotica* 47 (1983): 317–61.

———. "Mexican American Women's Home Altars: The Art of Relationship." Ph.D. diss., University of Texas at Austin, 1988.

Turner, Victor. *The Forest of Symbols.* Ithaca and London: Cornell University Press, 1967.

———. *Dramas, Fields, and Metaphors: Symbolic Action in Human Society.* Ithaca and London: Cornell University Press, 1974.

Turpin, Solveig A., Richard P. Watson, Sarah Dennett, and Hans Muessig. "Stereophotogrammetric Documentation of Exposed Archaeological Features." *Journal of Field Archaeology* 6 (1979): 329–37.

Ucko, Peter J., ed. *Form in Indigenous Art: Schematisation in the Art of Aboriginal Australia and Prehistoric Europe.* Prehistory and Material Culture Series, No. 13, Australian Institute of Aboriginal Studies, Canberra. Atlantic Highlands, New Jersey: Humanities Press, 1977.

Ucko, Peter J., and Andrée Rosenfeld. *Paleolithic Cave Art.* New York: McGraw-Hill Book Co., 1967.

Urton, Gary. *At the Crossroads of the Earth and the Sky: An Andean Cosmology.* Austin: University of Texas Press, 1981.

Vansina, Jan. *Oral Tradition: A Study in Historical Methodology.* Translated by H. M. Wright. 1961. Reprint. Middlesex, England: Penguin University Books, 1973.

Vastokas, Joan M., and Romas K. Vastokas. *Sacred Art of the Algonkians: A Study of the Peterborough Petroglyphs.* Peterborough, Ontario: Mansard Press, 1973.

Vogt, Evon Z., and Ethel M. Albert, eds. *People of Rimrock: A Study of Values in Five Cultures.* Cambridge: Harvard University Press, 1966.

Voth, Henry R. *Traditions of the Hopi.* Field Museum of Natural History Publication 96. Anthropological Series 8. Chicago, 1905.

Wallace, Anthony. *Culture and Personality.* 2nd edition, 1970. New York: Random House, 1961.

Watson, Patty J., Steven A. LeBlanc, and Charles L. Redman. "Aspects of Zuni Prehistory: Preliminary Report on Excavations and Survey in the El Morro Valley of New Mexico." *Journal of Field Archaeology* 7:2 (1980): 201–18.

Wellmann, Klaus F. *A Survey of North American Indian Rock Art.*

Graz, Austria: Akademische Druck- und Verlagsanstalt, 1979.

———. "Just Like Graffiti?: A Comparative Analysis of North American Indian Rock Drawings and Modern Urban Graffiti." Paper presented at the Anthropology Colloquium, Department of Anthropology, University of Arkansas, Fayetteville, 1979.

Williamson, Ray A. "North America: A Multiplicity of Astronomies." In *Archaeoastronomy in the Americas*. Edited by Ray A. Williamson. Pp. 61–80. Los Altos, Calif., and College Park, Md.: Ballena Press and Center for Archaeoastronomy, 1981.

———. *Living the Sky: The Cosmos of the American Indian*. Boston: Houghton Mifflin Company, 1984.

Witherspoon, Gary. *Language and Art in the Navajo Universe*. Ann Arbor: The University of Michigan Press, 1977.

Woodbury, Richard B. "The Antecedents of Zuni Culture." *Transactions of the New York Academy of Sciences* series 2, 18 (1956): 557–63.

———. "Zuni Prehistory and History to 1850." In *Handbook of North American Indians, Southwest*, vol. 9. Edited by Alfonso Ortiz. Pp. 467–73. Washington, D.C.: Government Printing Office, 1979.

Woodbury, Richard B., and Natalie F. S. Woodbury, "Zuni Prehistory and El Morro National Monument." *Southwestern Lore* 21 (1956): 56–60.

Wormington, H. M. *Prehistoric Indians of the Southwest*. Denver, Colo.: The Denver Museum of Natural History, 1947.

Wright, Barton. *Pueblo Shields*. Flagstaff: Northland Press, 1976.

———. *Kachinas of the Zuni*. Flagstaff: Northland Press, 1985.

Young, M. Jane. "Translation and Analysis of Zuni Ritual Poetry." Master's thesis, University of Pennsylvania, 1978.

———. "We Were Going to Have a Barbeque, But the Cow Ran Away: Production, Form, and Function of the Zuni Tribal Fair." *Southwest Folklore* 5:4 (1982): 42–48.

———. "Images of Power, Images of Beauty: Contemporary Zuni Perceptions of Rock Art." Ph.D. diss., University of Pennsylvania, 1982.

———. "Images of Power and the Power of Images: The Significance of Rock Art for Contemporary Zunis." *Journal of American Folklore* 98 (1985): 3–48.

———. "Humor and Anti-Humor in Western Puebloan Puppetry Performances." In *Humor and Comedy in Puppeting*. Edited by Dina Sherzer and Joel Sherzer. Pp. 127–50. Bowling Green, Ohio: The Popular Press, 1987.

———. "'Pity the Indians of Outer Space': Native American Views of the Space Program." *Western Folklore,* 46: 4 (1987): 269–79.

———. "Astronomy in Pueblo and Navajo World Views." In *Ethnoastronomy: Indigenous Astronomical and Cosmological Traditions of the World.* Edited by Von Del Chamberlain, M. Jane Young, and John B. Carlson. Los Altos, Calif., and Thousand Oaks, Calif.: Ballena Press and Slo'w Press, forthcoming.

Young, M. Jane, and Nancy L. Bartman. *Rock Art of the Zuni-Cibola Region.* Philadelphia: [Pueblo of Zuni], 1981.

Young, M. Jane, and John M. Roberts. "Local Rock Art Motifs: A Contemporary Zuni View." n.d. Unpublished paper.

Young, M. Jane, and Ray A. Williamson. "Ethnoastronomy: The Zuni Case." In *Archaeoastronomy in the Americas.* Edited by Ray A. Williamson. Pp. 183–91. Los Altos, Calif., and College Park, Md.: Ballena Press and Center for Archaeoastronomy, 1981.

Index